RAF
TOP GUN

ETERNITY

He who binds to himself a joy
Does the winged life destroy;
But he who kisses the joy as it flies
Lives in eternity's sunrise.

W. Blake

RAF
Top Gun

*The Story of Battle of Britain Ace and
World Air Speed Record Holder
Air Cdre E. M. 'Teddy' Donaldson
CB, CBE, DSO, AFC*, LoM (USA)*

Nick Thomas

Pen & Sword
AVIATION

First published in Great Britain in 2008 by
Pen & Sword Aviation
an imprint of
Pen & Sword Books Ltd
47 Church Street
Barnsley
South Yorkshire
S70 2AS

ISBN 978 1 84415 685 6

A CIP catalogue record for this book is
available from the British Library.

Typeset in Palatino by
Phoenix Typesetting, Auldgirth, Dumfriesshire

Printed and bound in England by
CPI UK

Pen & Sword Books Ltd incorporates the imprints of Pen & Sword Aviation,
Pen & Sword Maritime, Pen & Sword Military, Wharncliffe Local History,
Pen & Sword Select, Pen & Sword Military Classics and Leo Cooper.

For a complete list of Pen & Sword titles please contact
PEN & SWORD BOOKS LIMITED
47 Church Street, Barnsley, South Yorkshire, S70 2AS, England
E-mail: enquiries@pen-and-sword.co.uk
Website: www.pen-and-sword.co.uk

Contents

Foreword

Air Commodore P. M. Brothers
CBE DSO DFC and BAR

Chairman of the Battle of Britain Fighter Association

It was a Sunday in early 1937 and I was Duty Officer at Biggin Hill for the weekend, so my girlfriend, later to be my wife, came for afternoon tea in the Ladies Room. To our surprise the door burst open and in bounced a small, fair-haired officer accompanied by his friend, a Biggin Hill officer named Shand. I may have nodded a greeting, but under the circumstances they were not the most popular visitors. For the first time I had met Teddy Donaldson and I was not impressed by this laughing, chattering Cavalier who had chosen to invade our privacy depsite the availability of the rest of the Officers' Mess!

War came and went and we did not meet again until 1968 when I was Director of Public Relations in the Ministry of Defence and Teddy was Air Correspondent for *The Daily Telegraph*. We met at Press Briefings and air shows and became firm friends, both being Battle of Britain pilots.

This biography of Air Commodore Edward Mortlock Donaldson CB, CBE, DSO, AFC and Bar, better know as Teddy, paints a comprehensive picture of a man devoted to the Royal Air Force, into which he was commissioned in 1931, and it tells of his family background, his Service career and World War II in great detail. Here was a man who appeared on the surface to be a laughing, happy irrepressible officer when in fact he was a thoughtful dedicated person who tackled any task he was given with energy and determination after thoroughly evaluating the problem confronting him.

His efforts in America to help the USAAF at first were not well received, his deep study of the possibilities of disaster when considering the attack on the world air speed record in a Meteor, and his courage in flying the aircraft and gaining the record speak for themselves. The laughing Cavalier was not the man I first thought but a man who was a credit to the Service and himself, whose name and fame were legendary throughout the Royal Air Force and in aviation circles generally.

I could continue by picking out particular details of his outstanding career but it is preferable to let you, the reader, do it yourself. I commend this biography; you will find it both well detailed and well worth study.

Pete Brothers
January 2008

Introduction

As Britain was still recovering from the ravages of nearly six years of war, the first indication that she would continue to have a stake in high speed flying came in an announcement from the Air Ministry on 12 July 1946. A High Speed Flight was to be formed at Tangmere, a Royal Air Force Station in Fighter Command, with the task of endeavouring to increase the performance of aircraft and to make an attempt on the world air speed record. Its commanding officer was to be fighter ace and former Battle of Britain squadron commander Group Captain Edward Mortlock 'Teddy' Donaldson DSO, AFC.

Donaldson, already a household name from his pre-war flying days as the RAF's aerobatics team leader, was appointed to deal with the complicated logistics, technical challenges and, most significantly, the as yet unknown compressibility difficulties of the record attempt. His mission was simple – to push the 'Star', a specially adapted Meteor IV, to the limits of controllability and establish a new world air speed record. This could only be achieved under certain climatic conditions; ideally, an air temperature of 30 degrees Celsius was required in what cruelly turned out to be the coldest summer on record. To succeed, Group Captain Donaldson would have to fly at sea level where a fraction of a degree out from true and level flight could prove fatal.

No one understood more than Teddy that his team's task would be an extremely dangerous one as the Meteor airframe was not designed to withstand the increased stress levels caused by compressibility. Donaldson could have enjoyed reflected glory without taking any of the risks, but this was not his way. He flew with courage and tenacity, flying the Star almost to the point of destruction, finally clinching the record as well as being the first man to break the historic 1,000 Kmph barrier.

Teddy Donaldson was one of three aviator brothers who joined the Royal Air Force in the 1930s, each of whom won the DSO as wartime squadron commanders. His elder brother lost his life, tragically, at the end of the Norway Campaign of 1940; his younger brother reached high rank having served with distinction during the defence of Malta and earning a string of gallantry awards. Indeed, all three brothers were highly decorated fighter pilots resulting in their proud mother attending an unprecedented eleven investiture ceremonies at Buckingham Palace. 'I don't breed milksops!' was her blunt reply to journalists eager to extract the secret of her rearing such gallant offspring.

Born in 1912, the son of a colonial judge, Donaldson might have been expected to have had a life of great privilege. However, the premature death of his father meant that he was brought up by his mother, a former Norland Nurse and family employee, who fought to keep her children from the clutches of over-bearing grandparents and their middle-class world. Having opted out of the last year of his agricultural degree course in Canada, Teddy had already gained a reputation of being a raconteur. He had known personal hardships too. A combination of bad luck and hot-headedness led to Donaldson being forced to undertake a number of menial jobs before being escorted, penniless, by a 'Mounty' onto a ship bound for England, his passage paid for by his aging grandmother.

Teddy's first experience of flying was at the age of 16 as a passenger in one of the many privately owned aircraft that did the pleasure circuits during the inter-war years. Most of the flight was spent head-down in the cockpit, feeling very ill. Years later and despite his air-sickness, Teddy obtained a short-service commission in the RAF to train as a pilot. Never throwing off his frailty as a passenger, Donaldson never-the-less quickly became one of the leading exponents of aerobatics and a crack-shot, twice winning the RAF's air to air gunnery trophy.

As the RAF's aerobatic team leader, Donaldson was presented to the 'Three Kings' in 1935 (George V and his sons, The Prince of Wales (Edward VIII) and The Duke of York (George VI)) when they made the first royal visit to the annual RAF Air Show; he was then only four years into his commission. Two years later Donaldson's team thrilled the crowds at the International Air Show in Zurich, overshadowing the Germans and Italians. Teddy travelled to Zurich with a second, more important, mission – to gather data on the new German Messerschmitt Bf 109 and, just as importantly, the pilots' training programme.

When war was declared, Donaldson was commanding No 151 (F) Squadron flying Hawker Hurricanes out of North Weald. He was Mentioned-in-Dispatches and awarded the Distinguished Service Order for his outstanding leadership during their first engagements with the enemy in early 1940, being personally credited with destroying two aircraft and damaging two more.

Flying throughout the Battle of France, the evacuation from Dunkirk and the early phases of the Battle of Britain, Teddy's eventual 'tally' stood at 10½ enemy aircraft destroyed and another ten damaged or probably destroyed; in truth, Donaldson's log book modestly recorded that he shot at many more without a 'claim' being made. Despite his high number of confirmed 'kills', no further combat awards were to follow, possibly due to the tragic death of his wingman, Jack Hamar, during impromptu aerobatics over their own aerodrome – an act which was banned by the Air Ministry but which Teddy and his wingman had performed on something of a regular basis throughout the early summer of 1940.

No 151 Squadron's reputation for being a reliable bomber escort and not leaving their charge to go 'hunting' enemy aircraft led to Teddy's men being chosen for more than their fair share of escort operations, something for which the legendary Basil Embry and Keith Park were full of praise. However, Teddy was as keen as any to get in amongst the enemy when on patrol, often noting in his log book his disappointment when the Germans failed to engage, preferring to look for easier prey.

Donaldson epitomized Winston Churchill's bulldog spirit. During his time commanding No. 151 (F) Squadron Donaldson had led tirelessly from the front, frequently pushing himself and his men to the limits. Thanks to his example and leadership they were always a happy and keen bunch who would follow their commander into the jaws of hell and back. Teddy had shared their dangers and their hardships too, always selecting himself for the most dangerous sorties, sleeping alongside his wingman in a slit trench at North Weald during the Battle of Britain. All knew him as a supreme tactician and a fearless leader, and for many he remained a life-long friend.

Following his tour of combat, Donaldson spent a year as a flying instructor in the UK where once again his whole-hearted commitment earned him the admiration of all concerned. For the outstanding effectiveness of his training of ab initio pilots, many of whom had to be thrown into battle whilst still in their teens, Donaldson was later awarded the Air Force Cross.

Donaldson's next posting involved braving the ever-present threat of the German U-boats and crossing the Atlantic for a lengthy secondment as a gunnery instructor in the USA, training American Gunnery Instructors, setting up new gunnery schools and re-writing both the courses and instruction manuals. Initially resented as a 'Limey' trying to teach the USAAF how to shoot straight, Teddy found his posting a thankless task. However, in his inimitable style, his arrival at each course was proceeded by the most daring display of aerobatics any of the Americans had ever seen, before landing and asking for the whereabouts of the Officers' Mess – Teddy had no time to gain the pilots' respect, he had to command it the second he landed if he was to have their undivided attention and teach them all they needed to know in order to save their lives in combat.

The measure of the man was such that his bravery and skill in the air became a legend across the USA, whether it was at official air shows or doing impromptu aerobatics. Despite his hero status, Teddy always remained approachable to all ranks. He knew how to communicate on all levels and was always quick with his infectious smile and self effacing humour.

For his energy and innovation Teddy was awarded the American Legion of Merit by the President, also being made a Command Pilot in the USAAF, only the second British pilot to be presented with the silver wings.

Back in Britain, Donaldson converted onto the new jet aircraft. He later commanded Colerne when it became the first all-jet airbase. It was this experience, and a blagged flight in one of the early American proto-type jets, that led to Teddy's selection to lead the reformed High Speed Flight.

Teddy understood that the RAF had one chance to set the new record with the Meteor IV airframe, otherwise the Americans would take the record beyond the limits of anything the RAF could then muster – this was seen as an opportunity to demonstrate that post-war Britain was still a world leader and its industry world-beaters.

Over two million holiday-makers watched the build-up to the record attempt. Finally, on 7 September 1946, and with only days to spare, Teddy snatched the record. Despite stealing the title from under the noses of the Americans, they heralded Teddy's achievement, christening Donaldson 'Mr Mercury' and inviting him to attend prestigious aeronautical events in the USA. In England he enjoyed a lower profile after the excitement of the record died down, although the Royal Aeronautical Society presented him with the Britannia Trophy in 1947 while the RAF recognised his bravery in the air with the award of a Bar to his wartime AFC.

A brilliant and courageous pilot, tactician, and crack-shot, Donaldson was, like so many other heroes, also a flawed, stubborn character. This genial and boisterous man's man lived for the day. Some might say he could be reckless in both his military and private life, almost to the point of self destruction. Although Teddy tried hard at being a devoted family man, three failed marriages are a testimony of the price he paid for his uncompromising focus on his personal interests as well as his chosen profession, perhaps typical of a single-seat aviator and a sports car driver who would always go as fast as he could in both. His ego knew no bounds. Sadly, his greatest asset was at odds with domestic bliss.

Teddy, short and stocky with bright blue eyes and fine fair hair, thinning from his mid-twenties, had a warm infectious smile. He craved attention and whatever the circumstance he always took centre-stage with his piercing laugh. There can scarcely be an image of Teddy which doesn't show him in his chosen role, even during the stressful days of the summer of 1940 when he risked his life on a daily basis. Then sporting a blonde handle-bar moustache he may be found the morning after being plucked out of the English Channel, joking with his Station Commander, Victor Beamish and his fellow pilots in front of his new 'ship'.

Teddy's post war commands took him to Germany, Aden and finally, to the RAF Flying College at Manby from where he took early retirement from the Service, having been offered the position as Air Correspondent with *The Daily Telegraph*, a role which Teddy held between 1961–78.

After his retirement from the Royal Air Force, Teddy was able to spend more time pursuing his passion for sailing, while he was always a regular in the RAF Club where he would hold court as an accomplished raconteur.

Teddy died at the Royal Naval Hospital, Haslar on June 2nd 1992 and was buried at his beloved Tangmere from where he had flown the 'Star' Meteor IV into the record books some forty-six years earlier.

Teddy was fearless in life, relentless in combat and skilful in the air. He was a man of his age and whose bravery was apparently limitless. Yet he often felt pigeon-holed as merely a stunt-pilot and perhaps some-times overlooked when it came to promotion. Donaldson was also denied the additional gallantry awards his combat record surely demanded, having to do with a Mentioned-in-Dispatches to account for the additional 8½ enemy aircraft he destroyed and 8 'probables' accrued after the award of his DSO – other 'aces' might have expected a DFC for his hard-earned victories in the air and perhaps a Bar to his DSO for his courage and leadership during the difficult early phases of the Battle of Britain.

But for Teddy it wasn't about medals, it was about getting his men through to the other side and getting the job done. The Germans were the enemy but they were also pilots, and Donaldson evidently didn't encourage the emblazoning of aircraft with Swastikas to gloat at the demise of a fellow aviator.

Above all, Donaldson was a quintessential 'top gun' fighter pilot, an airman's airman, and perhaps because he achieved so much of many a boy's dream he never really grew up. In adversity, however, there wasn't a man under his charge who he wouldn't help nor expect to come to his aid be it in the air or on the ground. In essence, Teddy Donaldson was a man who lived life to the full; he lived as he flew – at full throttle.

Nick Thomas
5 Nov 2007

Acknowledgements

I am very much indebted to Teddy Donaldson's relatives who have taken a great interest in his achievements, many attending the sixtieth anniversary event held at the Tangmere Aviation Museum in September 2006.

Thanks are due to Teddy's niece, Mrs Sally Rudman, and his granddaughter, Mrs Kate Gregory, both of whom gave much support and encouragement, also kindly supplying a number of original family photographs which have been used within these pages. Jane Donaldson, Arthur Donaldson's third wife, kindly supplied corrections to the first chapter, for which I am most grateful.

Mr Donald Donaldson, Teddy's oldest brother, was able to assist greatly with information relating to the family's early days in the Malayan Peninsula and Selsey, as well as adding much background information. Thanks are also due to Donald's son, Mark, who was able to help with a number of facts, as well as kindly relaying many of his father's recollections via the Internet.

The *Grimsby Telegraph* kindly gave permission for a number of photographs, including one of Teddy on his retirement day, to be included.

Such has been the generosity of Teddy's family that few photographs have had to be sourced from elsewhere.

Thanks are due also to the Right Honourable Iain Duncan Smith MP for kind permission to quote from his late father's book *Spitfire into Battle* (John Murray 1981).

Reference has been made to an unpublished manuscript by Neil Potter. Despite being heavily annotated by Teddy himself, this document nevertheless included a large number of inaccuracies, while omitting anything but the barest mention of his combat years. Here much emphasis has been placed on Teddy's own log book and that of David Blomeley, while the Squadron Record and Combat Reports held at Kew have been used to fill the many gaps. However, many of the early details in the Potter manuscript have been corroborated by Donald Donaldson.

I should particularly like to thank Teddy Donaldson's stepson, Wing Commander Julian Stapleton MBE, who kindly loaned a number of original photographs, and whose unique insight into Teddy's later years proved invaluable. Wing Commander Stapleton not only proof-read the entire text but also contributed towards a number of chapters.

Over the years a number of members of the Battle of Britain Fighter Association have generously given their time to assist me with this work. These pages have benefited from correspondence with Air Commodore John Ellacombe CB DFC and Bar, Wing Commander Anthony Forster DFC, and Squadron Leader David Blomeley DFC AFC. The latter had close associations with Stafford and it was through David's wartime experiences that Teddy's story first came to my attention.

My thanks go to them all, and to the many Battle of Britain pilots and aircrew who have helped me to build up a lasting archive which has and will be used to perpetuate the memory of the 'Few'.

Finally, my sincere thanks go to Air Commodore Peter Brothers CBE DSO DFC and Bar, Chairman of the Battle of Britain Fighter Association. Air Commodore Brothers, who has worked tirelessly to promote the ideals of the Association, very kindly agreed to write the Foreword to this work, for which I am truly grateful. His standing in the military and aviation communities lends great weight to the efforts of one who was not there.

CHAPTER ONE

Early Tribulations

Generations of Teddy Donaldson's family were members of the 'professional' classes, his father and grandfather having been members of the legal profession. It was perhaps then through his mother's influences that Teddy and two of his brothers joined one of the armed services rather than the bar.

Teddy's paternal grandfather, Alexander Leathes Donaldson, a solicitor, had raised his family in Malaya and Singapore, his sons boarding at Haileybury public school in Hertfordshire before progressing to University.

During his time out on the Malayan Peninsula Alexander had purchased interests in both the rubber and the tin industries. While these were the boom years for the rubber plantation owners (records reveal that production in Malaya soared from 200 tons per annum in 1900 to millions of tons by 1920), Teddy recalled that the family fortune was made through his grandfather's mining investments.

While still out in the Far East, Alexander purchased Hatton Hall, an imposing mansion in Windlesham, Surrey. It was here that the Donaldson family came during their frequent visits back to England and where they settled when Alexander finally left the Malayan circuit. The village, a traditional farming community based around several manors and an ancient church, was an ideal location for a quiet and respectable retirement.

His years out in Malaya and Singapore were rewarded by the Crown with the offer of a knighthood. However, as Teddy explained, his grandfather looked to the future and not the past: 'Grandfather traded his knighthood for an entrance into the Malayan Civil Service for his son, and in those pre-war days that was easy enough to do. So my father became a judge.'

This shrewd move was to be the making of the young Charles Egerton Donaldson, who would follow a well-trodden path of service for King and Empire. His first posting was to Kuala Lumpur. Here the cost of living was such that even a fairly junior civil servant could live in relative luxury. Charles, on his chief magistrate's salary, was able to afford a semi-palatial residence and surrounded himself with an army of servants.

Aged thirty-six and still a bachelor, Charles was on one of his frequent visits to his parents' home in Surrey. Here his mother had been busy match-making, finding him the ideal, quietly supportive, rank-enhancing partner. They were mortified when, instead of courting their chosen bride-to-be, he fell hopelessly in love with Gwendoline Mary Macdonald, only daughter of Donald Macdonald and his wife Edith Amy (née Dixon), then a 21-year-old Norland Nurse working for the Donaldson family at Hatton Hall.

The whirlwind romance saw the couple married on 19 April 1909 within five months of their first meeting, much to the outrage of the Donaldsons, who considered that the judge had committed social suicide in marrying beneath not only *his* 'station' but also, embarrass-ingly, that of the family. Gwendoline was blamed for 'turning Charles's head'. She would be his undoing. Even in later life, when she had proved herself worthy of the Donaldson name, she was never accepted as 'family' by her elders in the Donaldson Clan.

And so it was that Charles and his new bride left these shores under a storm cloud. Charles reassured his young bride that 10,000 miles from England no one would be scandalized by either the details of their engagement or the inequalities of their rank, and that it did not matter. They loved each other and that was sufficient. His parents probably secretly hoped that the young girl would prove them right and crumble, unable to cope with the pressures of living out in the colonies, thousands of miles from home. But the 21-year-old was made of sterner stuff.

Despite the family's reservations over class and age differences, Teddy's parents were very well suited. Certainly his early childhood memories were of a perfect family life: a doting mother and a caring father who never missed the opportunity to escape from work to be at home with Gwendoline and the children. The couple had four boys in quick succession, Donald was the eldest, born at Kuala Lumpur on 25 August 1909, then John William, known as 'Jack', born two years later, then Edward Mortlock or 'Teddy' (born on 22 February 1912 at Seremban, Neger, Sembilan, Malaya) and finally Arthur Hay who was born at Weymouth on 9 January 1915. Donald later recalled how Arthur was presented to his siblings by their father, who pretended to produce him from the fireplace, claiming that he had been left by a stork.

Charles, like his father, was a crack shot, but unlike Alexander, he only hunted as a necessity. Alexander enjoyed the thrill of the hunt and his grandsons recalled how he would proudly show them his many trophies. He also donated a number of live beasts to London Zoo.

By contrast Charles hated shooting any healthy animal. However, injured or older tigers, which could no longer catch their usual game, often turned to prowling for human flesh. Man-eaters had to be shot and Gwendoline would accompany Charles on his all-night vigils. The pair would wait on a purpose-made platform set on stilts, peering down through loopholes at the scene below, where a bleating goat stood as bait. Donald later recalled that during one hunt, Gwendoline showed her hot-headed side by storming off into the night after a row with Charles, with no regard for the dangers posed by the lurking tiger.

The houses of rich Europeans were susceptible to robbers and the Donaldson home was no exception. Having already lost silver plate to burglars, Charles kept a loaded revolver under his pillow at night. His first line of defence, however, was a taut wire netting surrounding the veranda. This was designed to make an audible twang if cut through. Meanwhile a shotgun loaded with salt-filled cartridges was close to hand to ward off any trespassers prowling in the grounds.

Charles once confided to his eldest son that he hated having to don the 'black cap' in order to pronounce a capital sentence. He considered every life to be precious but felt his duty to King and Empire to be paramount. Donald recalled his father saying that he had on one occasion been thanked by a defendant he had just sentenced to death for having given him a fair trial.

Charles's position as His Majesty's senior representative in Kuala Lumpur, meant that the Donaldson household was always in demand and the family was regularly invited to attend dinners and balls. Their father insisted on always dressing for dinner, despite the extreme heat and humidity. Teddy recalled many house-guests passing through the doors, while Charles made a number of personal friends, including the Sultan of Johore.

Their father owned a Model T Ford and held the first driver's licence ever issued on the Malayan Peninsula (an iron disc with a '1' on it). Teddy and his brothers delighted in emptying the rainwater out of the roof by jumping up from their seats and pushing against the fabric – bucketloads of water would whoosh off, much to Charles's annoyance.

Another of the boys' lasting memories of the drive from Kuala Lumpur to their home was of a huge tiger jumping in front of the car, caught by its headlights as it glided through the rain-saturated air.

Naturally Teddy and his brothers were often the centre of attention, and it was probably during these early years that the confident Teddy first developed the art of being the showman. The boys were used to travel too, journeying to and from England, spending time at Hatton Hall.

The idyllic life came to an abrupt and tragic end at Christmas 1918. Teddy's father, who had always been very mechanically minded and might have been an engineer had he not studied law, enjoyed sharing this interest with his boys. He was a skilled craftsman and had once made a long-case clock from scratch, including the mechanism and the hardwood case. This Teddy later inherited and wound-up religiously. He was very proud of his father's clock, which he swore always kept perfect time.

Charles built a train set for the children on the veranda. He ordered a new train kit from Europe and was busy showing them how to cast a flywheel. This involved pouring molten lead from an earthenware crucible into a closed mould. Naturally, Teddy and his brothers were intrigued by the whole process and looked on with excitement as their father made their toy. When he stepped out of the room momentarily, Teddy's older brother Jack began spitting into the red-hot lead making it hiss violently. The others laughed at his game without understanding the dangers.

Suddenly and without warning the crucible erupted with an ear-piercing bang, splashing molten lead around the room. Jack took the main force of the blast, his face and eyes receiving burns, while his brothers reeled with hand, leg and facial injuries.

Hearing the explosion their father raced to their aid. Fearing Jack had lost his sight and that the others would be scarred for life, he immediately attended to the brothers' injuries. Shocked by their distress and with the knowledge that he was partly to blame for the whole sorry incident, Charles collapsed clutching his chest. He lay there, semi-paralysed, his skin pale and clammy, his pulse fast and erratic. He had been left with a weak heart as a result of rheumatic fever, and was diagnosed as having had a heart attack. He died the following day.

Teddy, still two months short of his seventh birthday, was too young initially to understand the finality of his father's passing. Donald, as the eldest brother, was anxious to protect their mother by trying to explain the concept of death in order to save her from having to break their hearts. His first attempt, 'Daddy's gone to Heaven', seemed to Teddy a quite excellent arrangement and nothing to be sad about.

Donald could tell from their expressions that his brothers just did not get the message. He skipped the middle ground and put it more bluntly. 'Daddy,' he announced, 'is dead and we will never see him again.' At this revelation the three little faces drained of all colour. They probably did not need Donald's next instruction: 'Now all of you cry to show Mummy how sorry we are.' Perhaps he should have further clarified this by saying; 'how sorry we are that he is dead', as his statement left the door open to the thought that it was *they* who had killed their father.

Gwendoline valiantly tried to do what she could to make something of Christmas for the sake of her children but the image of his father's face, eyes staring in disbelief as he grasped at his chest, was to remain with Teddy for the rest of his life.

Only Donald was considered old enough to go to their father's funeral, which was attended by many of his friends as well as an impressive procession of government officials and local dignitaries. Charles had been a high-ranking Freemason and Donald later recalled the Masonic overtones to the proceedings. A pair of white gloves was placed on the casket, while shots were fired at the head and feet of the coffin before his father was laid to rest.

Early the following year, Gwendoline decided that Malaya was no place to raise her family alone; they would return to England where she could find work and provide them with the best education.

The passage, via Canada and America, was a great adventure for the young boys who, without the guidance of their father, became over-excited. They had to be warned by their mother to be on their 'best behaviour' on a number of occasions. One incident showed the daredevil nature, and no little head for heights, of the four when they collectively walked the ledges around the upper floors of their Canadian hotel. The tricksters played havoc too with fellow passengers on the long Atlantic crossing, earning a further reprimand from Gwendoline which was endorsed by the ship's captain for good measure.

Once back in England, Teddy's mother was eager to give the family a sense of stability. She struggled to pay their school fees but was adamant that all four of her boys would attend King's School, Rochester. She was, however, eventually forced to swallow her pride and accept financial assistance from the Freemasons and the Black and White Club.

The boys, aware of the sacrifices their mother was making to put them through school, worked hard at their classes, although their mischievous nature often got the better of them. Donald recalled how they once emptied the house across the road from the school by throwing a stink-bomb into the kitchen.

Gwendoline's determination paid off; the boys rewarded her faith in them, each in turn passing the entrance examination for Christ's Hospital School, near Horsham in Sussex, also known as the Bluecoat School.

On the train journey to school at the beginning of term, Donald would have all the brothers empty out their pockets so that they could share their resources out fairly. All four were allergic to bullies and had no compunction about tackling bigger boys whom they would give a sound thrashing.

Teddy, although never particularly frail, had been plagued by illness during his youth. While in Vancouver he contracted scarlet fever and later, back in England, he suffered with rheumatic fever. Despite the size of his grandparents' mansion, his grandmother, with whom the family stayed during the school holidays, said she 'could not live with an invalid'. Consequently, his mother took him away from the austere surroundings of Hatton Hall, with its menagerie of taxidermy specimens, the most memorable of which for the boys was a snakeskin that dangled down the stairs, to settle in Selsey where she later purchased the new family home which was called Crookhaven and lay on the seafront.

Between school terms Gwendoline provided accommodation for the children of colonial civil servants, earning enough both to support the family and to cover the mortgage. The boarders were generally a few years older than Teddy but he would waste little time in striking up a rapport, putting each at their ease and introducing them to the delights of the sand, shingle and gravel beaches and the local countryside. It was here, on Selsey Bill, that he developed his greatest pleasure – sailing. The waters around the Bill could, however, be quite treacherous, with sand-bars and tidal currents catching out the uninitiated but Teddy soon mastered them and spent many a long day sailing up and down the coast.

With so many children in the house Teddy, already showing an apti-tude for leadership, would organize games and expeditions for their 'guests'. Together the children formed their own cricket eleven, with Mrs Donaldson arranging their fixtures.

The Donaldson brothers were the scourge of the neighbourhood. Their high-spirited antics included some sharp-shooting with an air rifle by Jack, who lodged a pellet in the ample rump of a rather stern female doctor while she tended her garden. On another occasion he killed a seagull. Their mother warning him that he 'would end up in a watery grave'. Tragically these words would come back to haunt Gwendoline in the summer of 1940. Teddy, meanwhile, demonstrated an early love for speed and danger, receiving a fine from the local bobby for riding his bicycle in a 'reckless manner'.

Teddy was not alone in his love of cycling. In fact the whole family regularly took to the roads around Selsey, and it was not unknown for them to cover 20–30 miles a day. Their mother would pack a picnic or they would stop and pick blackberries at the roadside, eat a few home-made sandwiches and guzzle a bottle of fizzy lemonade from the big wicker basket suspended from the front of their mother's bicycle.

Their days in rural Windlesham had instilled a love of nature in all the family and while at Christ's Hospital Donald had been particularly proud of his vegetable garden, so it came as no surprise when Donald announced that he wanted to become a farmer. Soon both he and Jack had begun to focus on agriculture at school, and Teddy was soon to follow.

Donald was coming up to the end of his schooling at Christ's Hospital. Gwendoline, in consultation with the school's headmaster, Sir William Hamilton Fyfe, decided that he should go to New Zealand on the Prince of Wales's Scheme. This was a scheme designed to place public school boys onto farms in New Zealand, as cadets, with favourable terms for financing a farming property at the end of the cadetship. The idea was that eventually the whole family would join him as his siblings progressed through the education system.

Following a spell as a farm cadet on the Duke of Richmond's estate at Goodwood, Donald set sail on the SS *Rangitoto* with a letter of introduction, travelling in steerage. As they approached Wellington, Donald hatched a plan to make a Jolly Roger out of a sheet and so the SS *Rangitoto* sailed into the harbour under the flag of piracy much to the annoyance of her captain.

Donald was only sixteen when he left these shores, and remained in New Zealand for the rest of his life, apart from a three-year spell in England in the early 1960s when he caught up with his two surviving brothers whilst renting a flat in London and taking a part-time job at Harrods.

Not long after going to New Zealand, Donald was visited by one of the Donaldson Clan still bitter towards their mother for 'throwing herself' at their father all those years earlier. Donald had been a premature baby and they told him that his mother had had an affair and that he was conceived out of wedlock. This had a terrible effect on the young Donald, half a world away from his family, and struggling to make a new beginning for them.

As the oldest son, he felt his responsibilities keenly. When he reached New Zealand, he and the other former public school boys found that the government did not recognize their status. This meant that when their cadetships ended the promised assistance in setting up on their own farm was not forthcoming. Donald wrote to New Zealand's Prime Minister, Gordon Coates, who replied that as there was no Prince of Wales's Scheme in New Zealand, New Zealanders came first. There was going to be no farm and no new beginning.

Isolated from his family, apart from letters from Jack and their mother, and without anything to show for all his endeavours, apart from a crippling foot injury caused by an axe blow while clearing tree roots, he cast himself as the 'black sheep' of the family. Regrettably the family's old unity and its dreams of farming together were gone forever.

Back in England, unaware of the pain and anguish Donald was going through, their mother was faced by a disaster of her own when the family's home on the Selsey seafront was washed away as a result of sea erosion. The insurance company denied her claim stating that the loss was an 'act of God'. Undaunted, their mother started again from nothing, taking on several jobs and eventually earning enough money to put down a deposit on what was to be their new home in Selsey. Standing on the corner of Grafton Road and Seal Road, Utopia is believed to have been built using some of the reclaimed stones from the Donaldson's lost home.

Encouraging all of her sons equally, Teddy's mother ensured that he was able to follow his dream, even if this meant splitting the family. He passed an entrance exam to study at McGill University in Canada, and so she saved hard for his fare.

It was 1928 and the sixteen-year-old Teddy was enjoying his last school holiday before the tight family unit was broken up further when he had to sail out to Canada.

The inter-war years was the era of the flying circus, when First World War aces flew around the country staging air shows, often to crowds in their tens of thousands. The pilots took on movie-star status and even to say that you had flown in an aircraft was to attain a certain kudos. Today, many of the barnstorming pilots' names have slipped into history, but in the 1920s and 1930s they were on every young boy's lips.

During the summer months pilots would tour holiday resorts or visit racecourses giving flights to the paying public, and this is how Teddy, like many other Battle of Britain pilots, gained his first flying experience.

It was an Avro 504K, or as Teddy put it, a 'sticks and string' biplane that came to Selsey providing joyrides at 5 shillings a go. The Avro dated from the Great War, when more than 8,000 were built by AV Roe and subcontractors such as Grahame-White Aviation at Hendon. It has been rated as the greatest trainer ever produced and, with its 110 hp Le Rhone rotary piston engine, it had a maximum speed of 95 mph.

Clad in a borrowed First World War flying helmet, motor-cycling goggles and a thick winter coat, Teddy approached the oil-spattered biplane ready to soar with the birds and maybe buzz his house and the outskirts of the town. Ever the daredevil, he handed his savings over and climbed into the passenger's cockpit, relishing the thought of his first flying experience.

Strapped into the tiny cockpit, he looked out at his admirers gathered at the edge of the landing ground. He gave a wave, acknowledging the shouts of encouragement from his brothers, friends and curious onlookers. Suddenly the engine coughed into action. Teddy felt the vibration through his body with the building revs. Exhaust smoke filled his nostrils as the aircraft rolled forward, building up speed, slowly at first.

As the flimsy Avro bounced and accelerated across the open grassland, struggling to get into the crisp early morning air, Teddy began to question his judgement in parting with his hard cash. Suddenly they were up, free from terra firma and he looked over the edge of the cockpit to see the ground fall away. This was his first mistake. He began to feel a little queasy and rather scared. As the flight progressed, the adverse effects increased, and so it was that Teddy spent nearly all of his flight with his head down in the cockpit looking at his knees, the cold air rushing past his head, roaring in his ears as the tired old machine was buffeted by the wind.

It was only a wide circuit and bump but it was more than enough for Teddy. He hastily undid the straps and baled out of the cockpit, stumbling off the wing unceremoniously onto the ground, nauseous, disorientated and miserable. Biggles he was not and, he must have thought, he never would be. Far from the intended source of admiration from his peers, the episode was one he wanted to forget as soon as possible.

As holidays drew to a close, Teddy's thoughts focused not on the warm fields of Selsey but on the forests and plains of Quebec, where he was to spend the next three years receiving a higher education. But what should have been the making of the young Donaldson nearly became his undoing.

CHAPTER TWO

Canadian Escapade

It was with trepidation that the young Teddy Donaldson stepped aboard the ship bound for the icy shores of Canada. He could not help remembering the day his eldest brother had left home and the sadness in his mother's eyes as she kissed him goodbye. Together they had been such a tight-unit and now it seemed that, one by one, they were being dispersed to the four points of the compass. Would they ever be a family again? He now knew how Donald had felt all those years before. He cut a sad figure as he dragged his luggage down the steep steps leading to the cabin that would be his home for the next few weeks.

The journey was a long but uneventful one and saw Teddy make the reverse voyage to the one the recently bereaved Mrs Donaldson and her boys had made ten years earlier. Halfway into it Teddy's thoughts began to turn from the sadness of leaving the halcyon days of Selsey to his immediate future. He had earned a place on a three-year agriculture degree course at MacDonald College, McGill University. The course would include both academic study and hands-on farming, both within the 2 square miles of the college grounds and managing a smallholding out in the wilds.

Founded by Sir William MacDonald in 1907, MacDonald College was located at St Anne de Belle Vue in south-western Quebec. It had its own accommodation, gymnasium and café. However, there were few ready distractions like cinemas or off-campus dance halls for several miles, while the campus itself was intended to be well regimented.

MacDonald's was a mixed-sex college, with male students being outnumbered nine to one, and Teddy's eyes were opened to a whole new world. The boys' introduction to college life came in their walk from the male dormitories down to the dining area in the women's hall of residence. Lining the freshmen's route were hundreds of beautiful young ladies who, following a time-honoured tradition were leaning out of their windows and making rather suggestive comments to all in the procession. Many a young man earned a cruel nickname which stuck for their entire college life. Teddy, however, was not short of self-confidence. He used his ready charm and quick wit to fend off any unwelcome remarks, and did what he could to win over the anonymous hecklers. As he drew closer to the halls, catching the glances of the young women, for which he exchanged a warm smile, it suddenly dawned on him that being a young devil-may-care man, thousands of miles away from home, might have its advantages after all.

At the best of times Teddy looked upon rules as mere helpful suggestions for the uninitiated. He noted the 'guidance' to freshmen not to date girls during their first six months at college and considered that technically this did not extend to teachers; a young lady of French extraction had already caught his eye.

The affair was steamy but brief. Almost inevitably fellow students, jealous of his relationship and generally extravagant living, broke the students' code and informed on the lovers. Teddy was sentenced to have his head shaved as a ritual humiliation for having brought the college into disrepute. This punishment, carried out by fellow students, was intended as a deterrent. It actually had the reverse effect with all the young women feeling sorry for Teddy. His bald head became a status symbol, bringing him even more dates and an enviable reputation.

Teddy recalled with dismay the brutality shown towards the freshmen by the more senior boys, the master apparently turning a blind eye to the beatings. The 'tribal' initiations began a few days into their first term. The freshmen stripped naked before being forced to undertake various tasks. These included climbing over the dormatories or crawling under the carpets with seniors lashing out at the moving forms. Others were made to eat all sorts of unpalatable and indigestible 'food'. The 'finale' involved launching the poor youths off a balcony over a concrete patio and into a pool. There were injuries when freshman slipped out of the hands of their tormentors and landed short on the concrete slabs, yet the practice continued beyond Teddy's days.

Anyone who backed out of a challenge was turned on ruthlessly under this form of licensed anarchy. Teddy recalled that one boy, having failed a particular task, was sentenced to be tortured with a red-hot iron. The poor unfortunate was blindfolded and prepared for the iron. To complete the scene a fire was lit, the intention being for the victim to smell the smoke and feel the ambient temperature rising. Trembling with fear and pleading for his skin, the lad was held down and the 'branding' commenced. However, instead of burning the lad, his torturers used an icicle on his bare flesh. Things had got completely out of hand. The shock of the ordeal proved too much for the sixteen-year-old who, tragically, suffered a heart attack.

The students' first year was spent studying and working on the college's model farm. Placements on a real farm took up the whole of the second year. With his reputation established, Teddy's social life helped the first year go very quickly. Out-of-term time was spent away from campus, Teddy making a beeline for the local bars and ski slopes, always in the company of the fairer sex.

His second year, however, could not have been more different. Nothing short of hard labour on a nineteenth-century convict plantation could have prepared him for this experience. He was sent to a 120-acre farm some 150 miles south-west of Montreal. The farmer took students every year. He cared nothing for his charges; to him they were little short of slave labour. Despite his own predicament, Teddy felt sorry for the man's wife and fourteen-year-old daughter. There was always an 'atmosphere' between the farmer and his wife. Their relationship was one of financial dependence and neither talked directly to the other; instead, the farmer spoke to his wife through Teddy. It was a grim, dour world, with no laughter; in fact, there was little else but hard work and still more hard work.

So much for learning how to run a farm from 'hands-on' experience. For Teddy, work meant shovelling manure. Autumn and winter were spent just shovelling manure. Sleeping, waking, shovelling, punctuated only by three meagre meals, which were eaten in silence for fear of giving the farmer a topic on which to rant endlessly.

Spring brought the first changes, with Teddy being allowed to milk the farm's herd of nineteen cows, which he did by hand before moving on to mucking out and grooming six horses as well as harnessing a team up to a cart. Then, after the horses were sorted, it was back to the fine art of shovelling manure until dusk when the cows needed a second milking.

The cows were brought in from the fields by a collie called Roger. A very gentle dog, Roger loved to be in Teddy's company. It was easy to see why as whenever the poor thing got within range of the farmer he would let out a curse and give the dog a sound kicking in the ribs.

That the farmer had a temper was beyond doubt. On one occasion, having completed his daily tasks, Teddy was enjoying a good soak in the tub, daydreaming of his days back at the college. A shout came up the stairs; the farmer wanted him to come down and help him 'to sort the apples.' Teddy called back down saying he was in the bath. The next thing he heard was the heavy stamp of the farmer's feet on the staircase, quickly followed by a crash, as the farmer's fist came through the door. Dragged backwards out of the room and launched down the stairs, Teddy arrived at their foot in a crumpled heap. He 'sorted the apples' naked, bruised and dripping wet.

On another occasion Teddy accompanied the farmer on his horse and cart. Next thing the young lad knew he was picking himself off the track and walking back, dusty and bloodied, a mile or so to the farm. He had been knocked out and simply left in the middle of the road.

During the summer the farmer would frequently disappear for long weekends of drinking and debauchery. His wife and daughter took the opportunity to escape to spend time with their friends on nearby farms, leaving Teddy to run the farm on his own from Friday to Tuesday.

Having taught himself how to handle the plough rig, Teddy was able to add ploughing into his extended daily routine. The next big thing was to bring the crops in during July. The farmer was already set to go on another of his drinking binges, while the women had their own plans. With the farm deserted, Teddy was left with the farmer's words ringing in his head: 'When you have finished your chores, Edward, get cracking in the 20-acre field, cut and rake it and get in as much as you can.'

With his daily tasks just about in hand, he hitched up the farmer's pride and joy, a brand new hay-cart and headed down to the field, where he set up the hay cutter. It was a long and lonely day cutting the crop. His only entertainment was watching Roger wagging his tail as he darted in and out of the crop, chasing rats and birds. The team were playing Teddy up. They could sense his inexperience with the cutter, and he had to use the whip and reins to try and keep them on a straight and steady course.

Then disaster struck. Teddy could see that Roger was chasing a bird along the line between the crop and stubble. He tried to halt the team but they trod on relentlessly. In desperation Teddy threw the mechanism to raise the cutters above danger height. All was in vain and Roger ran straight into the revolving blades. There was an ear-piercing shriek and a whimper, and then silence. Teddy stared at the horrific scene. The collie looked up at him pitifully as he endeavoured to stand. Teddy raced back to the farm to retrieve the farmer's gun. The breathless youth sprinted back to find poor Roger had dragged himself off towards a stream. Here Teddy briefly comforted the bloody collie as best he could before putting him out of his misery.

Wracked with guilt, Teddy could do nothing more than finish the cut and bring the crop in. Throughout the rest of the day, the image of the dying collie passed through his mind; he replayed the scene and its different conclusions. The day was not done and the horses continued to play up, causing Teddy to clip the farmer's brand new cart, resulting in some minor damage.

Disasters always come in threes and the third came in the form of a replacement dog. Teddy had loved that little collie but, to the farmer, Roger was simply a tool for a job, and Teddy hoped that at least if he bought a new dog he would stay the farmer's anger. While the next-door farmer had no love for Teddy's boss, there was an age-old tradition of coming to one's neighbours' aid in times of crisis. It was with this thought in mind that Teddy journeyed the 4 miles to his farm, where he explained his predicament. Sure enough the farmer had a collie. He even refused to accept any payment for the dog and sent Teddy off with a hearty wave – little did Teddy then know why.

It was a grim-faced Teddy who greeted the farmer on his return. He explained the sad events of the previous few days as best he could, adding in mitigation that his chores and the harvesting had all been done to the farmer's specifications. He was more than half expecting a beating and was surprised when the farmer passed the incidents off as the tragic accidents they were. By then it was close to milking time and the farmer took his new collie off its leash, the three winding their way down to bring the cows in. Arriving at the field, some distance from the farmyard, Teddy was horrified when the new dog began barking and leaping at the cows. It lashed out and bit wildly at their heels and then began trying to pull animals down by their necks. Teddy had already grabbed a stick and with the farmer tried to fend the dog off, but nothing would deter it from attacking the cattle. Leaving Teddy trying to fend the beast off with sticks and his bare hands, the farmer ran back to the farmhouse. Shotgun in hand he staggered back, emptying two barrels into the collie before it fell lifelessly to the ground covered in its own and the cow's blood. There then began the sad process of killing the more badly wounded cattle, the remainder of the herd looking on. It was only then that Teddy had the time to reflect on why his neighbour had refused to accept any money for the new collie.

This sorry episode stayed with Teddy for many years, the image of Roger's injuries haunted him. The poor collie had loved to play in his company and trusted him. The look in his eyes hurt Teddy more than anything else, more than all the backbreaking toil or the beatings from the farmer.

One of Teddy's last jobs on the farm was working in the maize silo. It was 100 degrees and Teddy had to work twelve hours a day stark naked, trampling down the maize as it emptied into the top of the silo. The dust was choking, while there was the ever-present danger of being buried alive in the maize should he falter. Thankfully, he survived the ordeal but vowed never to go into a silo ever again.

It was with a glad heart that Teddy packed his bag to leave the farmhouse. He said his goodbyes to the farmer's wife and their daughter. Not wanting to ruin any report the farmer might be asked to file regarding his competence as a farm-hand, Teddy was forced to make a more than civil exchange with the farmer before turning his back and leaving for good.

And so he returned to the campus to complete his degree. With the relief of escaping the farm, Teddy admitted he went off the rails. He was soon in trouble with the college authorities as a result of over-indulging, trying no doubt to catch up on lost time. Brought before the Dean, he was reprimanded and a letter sent to his mother.

Unsettled, Teddy decided it would be better if he left after sitting the second-year exam, earning himself a diploma rather than the three-year degree. It was a decision he later regretted, as from here he began on a steep downward spiral.

Short of money, he took a job as a wages clerk, earning the princely sum of $11.50 a week. Unfortunately with the depression hitting Canada and election fever in the air, there was a great deal of tension among the French Canadians. One day things got out of hand on the shop floor and one of the workers was struck with a mallet and died. The factory owners decided to close down for seven weeks until after the elections when they hoped that politics would once more be put aside. Although assured of his job when the factory reopened, Teddy set off looking for temporary work. He and an adventurous friend decided to set off on a 350-mile journey to join a lumber camp cutting timbers for telegraph poles.

The two young men hardly had a cent between them and could not afford the train fare. His friend had an idea. What money they could put together they spent on two pairs of goggles and some extra clothing – they were ready to 'ride the rails'.

This was a very risky business, one which resulted in a number of fatalities every year on the Canadian railways. It involved running alongside a slow-moving freight car and diving onto the 'rails' or bracing wires or rods that ran the length of the underside of the wagons. To a man who had, with his brothers, delighted in 'tight-rope walking' on the balustrades of their skyscraper hotel while the Donaldson family were first in Canada all those years before, the rails held no fears. Teddy later explained: 'It was even possible to get some sleep if you wedged your body face down and with your hands so they didn't fall to the ground.'

While the additional layers of clothing helped keep off the cold, the goggles were meant to stop the sparks and iron filings coming off the wheels from getting in their eyes.

'The art to climbing on-board,' Teddy recalled, 'lay in finding a hilly section of track where the train would move at a crawl, and to avoid the trains during daylight, as the guards were ever vigilant.' Teddy's friend taught him how to catch the guard's pickaxe handle should he try to dislodge them while on the move. 'A good yank and the guard was off and rolling down the embankment.' This was not as jolly as Teddy made it seem, however, as one slip might have proved fatal, with the young-sters falling from the rails under the wheels of the carts.

It took thirty hours of vigilant rail riding and several changes of train, each with its inherent dangers, before the pair reached the loggers camp, where they were both taken on. Teddy tried to talk his way into felling but was given the less profitable job of de-branching. The hours were long, the accommodation was primitive, lacking any beds, and with sixty men sleeping in a single hut. The bonus, however, was that the wages were good.

Teddy worked hard at the logging camp and was considering staying on rather than going back to the factory. In the end the decision was taken out of his hands. Like so many other calamities, it all started at the bar. Teddy was never a whisky drinker but took to a quick drink before settling down in the crowded hut; it helped to blank out all the noise and got him off to sleep.

Making his way to the bar one evening, Teddy was jostled by a massive French Canadian. 'Lay off!' he said.

The lumberjack spat tobacco straight into his eyes, stinging them. Reaching back Teddy struck him with all his strength, and just like the best comedy fist-fights, his hardest shot had absolutely no effect. The man just stood there and shrugged. Within seconds all hell let loose with the whole bar getting involved. There were bottles, glasses, tables and chairs hurtling through the air in every direction as bedlam ensued.

Dodging the first blow directed at him, Teddy dived for the deck. Then came a tactical retreat towards the door as the fight raged above him.

As the door was flung open, a startled Teddy sprang to his feet and ran for his life, hotly pursued by a handful of the mob and a vicious hound, which chased at his heel, leaping up and giving him a nasty bite to the rear and tearing his trousers. Fortunately the dog, confused at the general scene, then turned on the loggers who were gathering around him and began biting them indiscriminately.

Although Teddy now had money, there was no time to buy a rail ticket – he had to leave the camp quickly. Heading straight for the railroad, he hid and waited for the first slow-moving train. Breaking cover he ran alongside the wagon before diving through the wheels and grabbing for the rail. There had been no time to collect any extra clothing or even his old set of goggles, and so the journey was bitterly cold and he was forced to cover his eyes with one hand for most of it. However, the ride was just brief enough to save his neck. At the first station he alighted and purchased a ticket back to his old office job.

On his arrival, Teddy found that his post had already been filled. Now he had no job. Fortunately, he had at least still got his wages, which were hidden away in a body belt, the only way to keep anything on the tough lumber scene. Not thinking when or where his next pay would come from, Teddy spent his money in his usual carefree manner, enjoying drinking and the company of a few lady friends.

Soon his money started running out. Unable to get an office job, he had to settle for work on a chicken farm, where he was fired for stunning the chickens while he retrieved eggs caught up in the wire of their coops. The protective hens would viciously peck his hands raw as he tried to fish out the stray eggs and so Teddy had developed a technique of administering a tap on the head sufficient to daze the bird long enough for him to snatch the eggs. He was caught by the farmer, who had long wondered why production was falling through the floor. 'Evidently,' Teddy chuckled, 'chickens don't lay eggs if they think that they are going to get a knock on the head for their troubles!'

It was 1930 and times were hard. Despite his diploma, the best job that he could secure was laying paving slabs – actually something of an exaggeration, as his role was turning the handle on the cement mixer. It was nearly as bad as working on the farm. For eight hours a day Teddy would stand turning the handle. His wages stretched to a hamburger and a glass of milk three times a day. But even this job was sought after. There would be a couple of men standing nearby watching him almost every minute of the day, waiting in the hope that he would stop for a couple of seconds so that they could get him fired and take his job.

Teddy saved what he could, and three weeks into the job was able to pass on the handle to the next poor person in the queue. He headed for Montreal, where he admitted he was a frequent resident at the Salvation Army hostel, paying 25 cents for a bowl of soup and a piece of bread.

He reached his lowest ebb on Christmas Day 1930, lying in his bed for the night with a blanket over his head crying his eyes out. 'I didn't feel the brave, young tough-guy that day.'

Ever resourceful, however, Teddy bounced back and used part of his meagre savings to buy a shovel. There was deep snow everywhere and this meant there were drives and doorways to be cleared for a few cents. This new 'career' was short-lived. He woke one night to hear the sound of melting snow running down the pipes and gutters of his lodgings. The melt had arrived two whole months early and ruined any plans he might have had.

His next job was as a car park attendant at a cinema. He was essentially working for tips, the wages being virtually non-existent. Some of the customers annoyed him and it was not long before the young hothead lost his temper. One day 'a nasty little man' turned up in a fancy black car and in the company of an 'exotic' woman. He went out of his way to be rude to Teddy and belittle him in front of his girl. The impetuous Donaldson bent the blade of his pocket-knife giving the tyres a fine pressure adjustment. He later recalled that they exploded with a gratifying and 'quite splendid' bang.

Considering his appointment to be at an end, Teddy moved on although not into another job; these were still difficult to find, even with his qualifications and willingness to turn his hand to practically anything that was legal.

One day while out job-hunting, he actually fainted from lack of food. He found himself being picked up by the police, who gave him food and a drink at the police station. One of the officers sat him down and made him talk through his predicament and look at his options. Eventually, Teddy swallowed his pride and sent a telegram home.

Naturally, having heard nothing from him since he had left college, his mother was furious. The next step was to contact his grandmother, who cabled him the steamer fare home. Aware that the young Donaldson might get cold feet and blow the money on beer and women, the police escorted him to the dockside and walked him on board.

Teddy later joked, 'This tough youngster, though temporarily slightly less tough, was still too much for that young and virile country.'

As the Canadian coastline slipped below the riding-rails, Teddy said goodbye to his reckless college days. Back in England he was to find his feet and transform the rough hewn teenager into a man.

CHAPTER THREE

Dawn of a Career

It was clear that this tremendous youthful energy required channelling. His wildest years over, now Teddy needed to be reined in, develop a greater degree of self-discipline and once more become a team player.

He craved excitement and adventure, a change of scene. Easily bored, he needed constantly to be challenged, pushing himself to his limits. The answer lay in a flying career with the Royal Air Force.

Jack had already given up all thoughts of a career in agriculture and had been serving as a pilot in the RAF for two years. Teddy saw his brother's glamorous new lifestyle and decided that this was for him. Despite the ignominy of his terrible air-sickness during his first ever flight, Teddy decided he could conquer his symptoms and become a pilot.

At nineteen, he was unable to enter the RAF College at Cranwell. All was not lost, however, as he might yet be accepted for a short-service commission.

The RAF was still facing cut-backs, as it had done under successive governments, and the number of officers with a permanent commission was close to an all-time low as a result of the anti-war sentiment which then prevailed.

Disarmament, particularly the reduction in the world's air forces in general and bombers in particular, was already high on the Government's agenda. The disarmament conferences began in Geneva a few months later, on 2 February 1932. They continued through to late November 1934, despite the obvious signs coming from the greatest potential threat to peace in Europe – Germany. Her withdrawal from these talks and the League of Nations on 4 November 1933, some eight months after Adolf Hitler's rise to power, would start the clock ticking towards the outbreak of the Second World War.

It was with this knowledge that Teddy sat down to complete his application form, coached by Jack and his mother, considering carefully the answer to every question before committing himself to paper.

After many months of waiting, the day finally came for Teddy to go before a selection board. The interview went well and the panel seemed suitably impressed with his application form and background, both educational and family. Fortunately, there were no awkward questions about his opting for a diploma rather than completing his degree course, nor about the missing months between the end of his second year at McGill and his return to England.

Towards the end of the interview Teddy was asked an observation question: 'Can you tell me the serial number of the train that you travelled in to this interview?'

'SN 13452,' was the quick response.

'Goooooooood,' came the drawn out reply, as though each letter and figure was being carefully scrutinized.

The board seemed pleased with him and he was thanked for his attendance and asked if he had any questions. There were none.

As he was escorted from the room, the interviewing officer who had asked the train question caught him on his own and enquired: 'Errrr Donaldson, did you really remember the number of that train?'

'No sir!' he smiled. And with this curious exchange the two parted.

The interview was not that strange by RAF standards. Such were the vagaries of officer interviews that places were offered on the basis of anything from a shared love of cycling to knowing the legendary Sidney Barnes's test bowling averages.

With the interview safely under his belt, there were still, however, the rigours of a physical to be faced. Usually this consisted of little more than an eye examination, measurements of lung capacity and blood pressure, and a simple test of balance whereby the candidates were asked to stand on one leg with their eyes closed. But in Teddy's case, these would focus on the after-effects of his childhood rheumatic fever, which included, most disturbingly of all, a heart murmur. This had not troubled him during his long hours on the farm and at lumber camp but Teddy still had a niggling fear that he might be knocked back. In the event his fitness levels defied all reason and he sailed though with an A1 rating.

Having cleared the first hurdle, Teddy was granted a commission as a pilot officer (Probationary), dated 26 March 1931. He was sent for his initial training at RAF Uxbridge. Once again his days in Canada stood him in good stead, and he found it easy to keep pace with the physical training, or PT as it was called. What did cause him some difficulty was the lack of freedom to come and go from camp and the strict regulation of his working day, which at times could be eighteen hours long.

On 11 July Teddy was posted to No. 2 Flying Training School, Digby, where he was to undergo a tough twelve-month course, the initial step of which was to fly without feeling sick.

His first flight on the *ab initio* flying course was on 14 July, as a passenger in an Avro Lynx piloted by Flying Officer Cox. Having survived his 'air experience' and 'aerodrome familiarization' flight without showing any signs of the nausea that had dogged him on his first ever flight, Teddy was up in the air again later the same day. His log book records that the fifteen-minute flight focused on 'taxiing' and 'handling of the engine', all rudimentary stuff but nevertheless it had to be covered before moving on to the next stage.

Soon he was up in the air again throwing the dual instruction Avro Lynx about. After enjoying the pure exhilaration of 'spinning', completing 'action in the event of fire' and getting an 'elementary forced landing' under his belt, he reached the eleven-hour threshold. If the RAF was to spend money on training a pilot, then they had to be ready for their first solo flight after the requisite number of hours – there were no second chances, no special cases, so he had to fly solo or he was off the course and out of the Service.

It was a nervous trainee pilot officer who climbed on board the dual-control Avro Lynx trainer at 1430 hours on 24 July, ten days after his first flight. Accompanied by his test supervisor, Flight Lieutenant Power, Teddy put the biplane though its paces during his thirty-minute solo test. His nerves were well founded. While flying himself he had managed to keep feelings of airsickness at bay but his earlier frailty still occasionally reared its head with his instructor at the controls. In the event he need not have worried; his flight went without a hitch and Power gave him a 'pass'. He would be allowed to go solo, which he did after eleven hours and ten minutes of dual flying time.

Teddy's next flight was little different from any other in the previous few days' 'circuits and bumps' – other than there was no calm voice offering corrective instructions via the Gosport tube, while the cockpit in front of him was empty. He was in absolute control.

As he waited on the aerodrome for the signal to take off, all his pre-flight checks completed, Teddy listened to the final words of advice from his instructor. He was to take off, put the aircraft through a few of the basic manoeuvres and put her down on the aerodrome.

His solo safely completed, Teddy taxied in, shut down, undid the straps, hitched up his parachute, climbed out onto the wing and jumped down. He strode confidently over to be greeted by his fellow pilot cadets, where congratulations and thanks were exchanged, and then he stepped over to the adjutant's room to sign the authorization book. After all that was done, he was ready for the next phase of his training.

With fifty hours under their belts all pilots were expected to be able to perform aerobatics, cross-country, stalls and take–offs and landings.

But as well as flying training there was the little matter of RAF discipline too. Teddy and his fellow trainee pilots pounded the tarmac of the parade ground under the ever-watchful eye of the drill instructor. The pistol range found him in his element, showing the whole class how it was done – having had plenty of practice in his youth at Selsey where he and his brothers had been the scourge of the neighbourhood. He was a natural.

The course had to be passed as a whole; failure in a single element meant the end of any hopes of an RAF career. While he could handle mathematics and navigation, and even the 'suggestions' regarding the conduct of an officer as contained within King's Regulations, there was nevertheless a stumbling block. Teddy found that he simply could not get a grasp of Morse code and the use of the signalling lamp. Ever resourceful, he took measures to ensure a pass; he slipped the sergeant examiner a crispy 10 shilling note. But for the corruptibility of a senior NCO, the RAF would have been robbed of one of its most influential fighter aces and gunnery instructors of his generation and might have faced a very different fate in the summer of 1940.

The station commander threw a party in the mess for the newly qualified pilots, inviting the officers' wives and local dignitaries to attend. Spirits were high and the alcohol flowed freely. Teddy managed to cut his hand when a glass-panelled door he was about to push open was pushed from the other side. A piece of cloth served as a suitable bandage and he was able to party on. Partway through the evening, the fire alarm sounded, bringing out the station fire brigade, complete with fire hose. Drunk as they were, they proceeded to spray water over the assembled cadets, leaving the dance floor awash with water and party debris.

Just as the party broke up and the soaked revellers made for their bed, Teddy was confronted by an officer from the station's regular staff: 'Donaldson, you are under close arrest. Go to your quarters.'

'What have I done, sir?' asked a bewildered Teddy.

'You know damn well. Now get to your quarters,' the reply.

As he was marched away Teddy tried to get information out of his escort. Their reply was that they really didn't have the slightest idea. All Teddy knew was that he was one step away from a court martial and possible expulsion from the Service.

It was a sleepless night as he wracked his brains trying to think of his transgression. The only misdemeanour that came to mind surrounded his Morse exam. Maybe, he thought, the NCO had had cold feet and had reported him.

Early the following morning the officer appeared at his door, looking a little sheepish: 'I am sorry. There has been a mistake. You are entirely free.'

No longer under suspicion, Teddy pressed to find out the nature of the charge. It transpired that during the evening someone had smashed the glass panel of one of the emergency alarm points, triggering the station fire bells. Teddy's bleeding hand was taken as a sign of his guilt by the over-eager officer. It was only when the real perpetrator stepped forward that Teddy's innocence became apparent.

'But, sir,' Teddy said, having already sensed he could play this to his advantage, 'an apology is not good enough.'

'What do you mean, Donaldson?' came the astonished reply.

'Well, sir, this is the end of the course and reports will be made on all of us. I rather suspect that the fact that I was put under arrest in front of all those people will result in me not getting a favourable report.'

'Oh, come now. Nonsense.'

'Oh, no sir. All my friends believe that I was responsible for this action, and certainly all those guests will. This has damaged my reputation and if I fail the course because of a bad report, you will be to blame.'

'Now look here, I will see to it that you get a good report,' the officer assured him.

'Well, sir, I will take no further action so long as you guarantee that my report will be favourable. . . If it is not, I shall most certainly take further steps.' Teddy pressed home the advantage.

Needless to say Teddy passed out with a glowing report. His logbook recording him as being 'an above average pilot' but with a 'tendency to be over confident'.

Pilot Officer E. M. Donaldson was posted to No. 3 Squadron at Upavon on 20 June 1932, his commission dated as of 26 June. Armed with the Bristol Bulldog, No. 3 was one of the earliest squadrons, formed as a part of the Royal Flying Corps in 1912.

The Bristol Bulldog was a biplane armed with two Vickers Mark II .303 machine-guns, which fired through the propeller blades using an interrupter. It had a reputation of occasionally jamming or letting the guns run away, almost cutting through the propeller blades. Teddy, who later flew in jet fighters was often amazed that he survived flying some of the earliest types, many of which would not have seemed out of place flying over the First World War trenches. Yet they were durable machines and he quickly became adept at throwing them about in the air, performing spins and loops, antics which could get him into serious trouble but later singled him out for the squadron's display team.

While serving at Upavon, Teddy was asked to make up the station's boxing team as they were a man short in the lightweight division. Although he was not a fan of boxing Teddy was aware that sporting prowess got a man noticed and he needed to earn a permanent commission.

His high fitness levels, combined with his compact power and general alertness, enabled him to make the final of the RAF's Wakefield Cup. Runner up in 1932, he won the competition the following year and was selected for the officers' boxing team.

Winning his fights, Teddy was an automatic selection for the RAF team. With time, however, he felt that he could no longer maintain the pace over the full three rounds. The crunch came during a competition against Cambridge University. Looking at his opponent, a tough, youthful student with fast hands, he felt sure that his best tactic was to go for a first-round knockout.

Stepping into the ring, Teddy cast his mind back to the Canadian lumber camp. He would go in with his hardest punch and end it there and then. Sure enough, seconds into the first round, Teddy threw such a heavy punch that the young medical student disappeared out of the ring. Looking over the ropes Teddy could see his opponent struggling to get up of the floor. But, to his astonishment the referee was not even counting. In his head Teddy counted the student down and out, but the referee remained silent, as if fazed by the manner of the knockout.

With his opponent rising to his feet with the luxury of recovery time, Teddy saw red, leaped out of the ring and proceeded to land a punch on his opponent as he stood there catching his breath, aiming to finish the job properly to the referee's satisfaction. Naturally, the two were parted by the crowd and by their seconds. The audience was immediately on Teddy's back, booing and calling him names, while coins and other objects were hurled in his direction. For a minute it looked as though it might turn into a free-for-all.

Once the situation calmed, the student was offered the chance to have the bout awarded to him or to fight on. Sensing the reason for Teddy's tactic, he proceeded to give Donaldson the soundest thrashing he had ever suffered.

Out of the ring Teddy and his opponent spent much of the remainder of the evening at the bar; it marked the end of Teddy's boxing career. There was no animosity whatsoever between the two, only mutual respect for a fellow boxer. Teddy never liked the sport and was happy to be dropped from the team, his duty done.

The story, however, did not end there. One particular member of the audience had been more vocal than most, vowing to deal out his own form of justice on Teddy. They were to meet months later while Teddy was in the Sudan. 'Are you Teddy Donaldson?' asked the tall and overly muscular stranger, an Australian army officer.

Teddy said he was and was met with considerable abuse and threatened with physical violence. 'I saw you at Cambridge and I swore that night I would belt the hell out of you if I ever saw you again; that was the dirtiest thing I ever saw.'

Having unsuccessfully tried to calm the situation, Teddy suggested the matter ought to be settled outside rather than have two officers fighting in a public bar. Stripping off his mess jacket, Teddy said: 'Queensbury rules?'

'Donaldson, you wouldn't even know what Queensbury rules are!' came the reply.

Squaring up to his opponent, Teddy gave him one last chance to back out before proceeding to give him a lesson in manners and a demon-stration of many of the tricks he had seen at the lumber camp. Despite his opponent's size it was an uneven match. Teddy's friends had to pull him off before he went too far.

'If I ever see you again, I'll do the same!' was Teddy's warning as he was led away. It was inevitable that their paths would cross again and months later his friends were still going into bars ahead of him to warn the Aussie of his impending arrival.

Out on the desert airstrip Teddy flew whenever he could. He later recalled: 'In those days I flew through cloud by the grace of God. My instruments were a ship's compass that did not function when tilted, a spirit level, an air-speed indicator and a very unreliable altimeter.'

On 26 March 1933, two years into his short service commission, Teddy was promoted to the rank of flying officer. A sure shot on the firing range, he was selected as one of two pilots (the second being his Commanding Officer (CO), Squadron Leader C.A. Stevens MC) from No. 3 Squadron to go to Sutton Bridge, Lincolnshire for the RAF's Brooke-Popham Air Firing Trophy, named after Air Chief Marshal Sir Robert Brooke-Popham GCVO KCB CMG DSO AFC.

The competition lasted from 19 to 20 October and involved, for the first time, air-to-air firing against a towed target, along with simulated ground attacks.

To Teddy's amazement he won, scoring 295 point, his nearest rival recording 257 points. He had competed against the RAF's best and most experienced fighter pilots and had beaten the lot. His victory was no flash in the pan either as he proved by taking the trophy the following year, the competition being held on 18 and 19 October 1934. This set him up for a unique treble, but that was to elude him, first through an over-seas posting and later by losing to Harry Broadhurst.

Teddy was posted as an instructor to the Central Flying School, Upavon on 29 August 1934, but whether this was through an administrative error or not is unclear. Possibly the Air Ministry were unaware of his value to his squadron. The posting was immediately cancelled and he returned to No. 3 Squadron, being reassigned from his former C Flight to B Flight.

Teddy's ability to perform slick aerobatics had already come to his CO's notice and he was selected as a member of the squadron's display team. During practice he came up with the idea of using smoke canisters to give the spectators a better show. And so it was that he staged the first display with smoke at Hendon on Empire Day, 24 May 1935. The exhibition was made all the more exciting by the fact that the aircraft's path remained outlined in the air. The use of smoke became part of the regular squadron display.

During Teddy's second flight of the day, a mock dog-fight with five

Hawker Harts, his Bristol Bulldog ran out of fuel and he was forced to make an emergency landing. He sighted a large playing field at Kenton, not too far off, and headed for that. On drawing closer he discovered that there was a cricket tournament in progress, with five or six matches being played. He buzzed the pitch in the hope of dispersing the players so that he could land. This failed and so he aimed instead for a nearby building site. Having effected a landing, the Bulldog was refuelled. He then taxied along the access strip, where a local policeman stopped the traffic, and used the road to take off. The press, always looking to put a heroic spin on any story, ignored the fact that he had run out of fuel halfway through a prestigious air show, and instead praised him for avoiding the cricket players. Teddy secretly chuckled at the headlines – little did they know that he had done all he could to get them to clear a path but they were simply too slow!

The Empire Day display was so well received that Teddy was selected as a member of the four-man RAF display team to lead the Hendon Air Pageant later that year, on 29 June. Practice began on 8 June, with an average of thirty minutes of display practice per day leading up to the big show. It was a rare honour for Teddy to be selected and he gave the show all he had, producing a display that once more won critical acclaim.

The squadron later attended the first ever RAF Royal Review at Mildenhall on 6 July 1935, a few months after the announcement that the RAF would be trebled in size over the next two years. Teddy's No. 3 Squadron was the most senior squadron on show and were given the honour of leading the Fighter Group of the formation, which involved some 350 aircraft. On landing, the squadron was inspected by King George V in the company of his sons the Prince of Wales and the Duke of York – the future Kings Edward VIII and George VI.

Air Chief Marshal Sir Robert Brooke-Popham, No. 3 Squadron's first CO, commanded the review. Both he and the King spent some time talking to Teddy, congratulating him on his back-to-back victories in the Brooke-Popham Trophy and commiserating with him at not being able to defend his title due to the squadron's posting overseas. Later on, Teddy was convinced that this attention nearly cost him his career and his life.

With No. 3 Squadron posted to the Sudan in early October 1935, Teddy was unable to defend his title and make it three in a row, a feat which he would undoubtedly have achieved.

CHAPTER FOUR

Scrapes in the Sudan

Early in 1935 the media revealed the existence of Germany's secret air force, the *Luftwaffe*, which numbered some 20,000 men and 2,000 aircraft of all types. In May of that year the Air Ministry announced the expansion of the RAF from its mere 850 aircraft in response to the German threat.

During this period of rearmament it was clear that Britain was going to have to defend its own shores and those of the British Empire against either the Germans or the Italians, both of whom were looking towards expansion.

Since the Italian occupation of the Abyssinian port of Massawa on the Red Sea in 1885, relations between the two states had remained strained. Open war had broken out ten years later when the Italians were defeated by the tribesmen.

Abyssinia had been guaranteed its independence in 1906 through a treaty signed by Great Britain, France and Italy. Later antagonisms had been settled without bloodshed when both sides agreed to settle their differences through the newly formed League of Nations. Talks eventually broke down and, following a long period of heightened tension, war broke out in October 1935.

Teddy's squadron was posted to the Sudan to prevent British interests from falling under the influence of its neighbours. The journey out to the Sudan was to be made by sea on board the SS *Cameronia*, their disassembled Bristol Bulldogs travelling in the SS *Antilochus*. Teddy was put in charge of the convoy transporting spare parts and other supplies from Kenley to the Liverpool Docks. The low-loaders moved at 15 mph along the narrow roads, driven day and night by a rotation of drivers. Some of the 'erks' thought the journey was an excuse to slack off and so Teddy had his job cut out keeping them in order to hit their loading deadline. The only incident of any note was a tree that was damaged when one trailer ran out of control and ended up in a ditch.

After an uneventful eight-day passage the ship docked at Alexandria, taking on board provisions before sailing down the Suez Canal and the

Red Sea, eventually arriving at Port Sudan on 18 October, their aircraft arriving some two days later.

Teddy found himself up before Squadron Leader G. Martyn, who had taken over as No. 3 Squadron's CO in March 1934. Martyn was in a terrible mood. Apparently there had been something of a national crisis and it all revolved around Teddy. The tree that had been damaged in transit had reputedly been planted some 250 years earlier by Queen Elizabeth I and the locals were rather upset at its being flattened!

Teddy was in the middle of supervising the reassembly of the squadron's eighteen Bulldogs and so escaped any official punishment, although his card was marked for not informing his CO of the incident. This was not the only time Teddy would suffer the wrath of Martyn, who had been promoted through the ranks and seemed to hold a grudge against 'blue-blooded' officers who came virtually straight from university. Teddy considered that the attention the King and the Air Chief Marshal had paid him earlier exacerbated his grudge against him.

No sooner were the aircraft uncrated, reassembled and air tested than Martyn stepped up and told Teddy that as he still had no direct orders to deploy, it might be an idea to keep the men busy by stripping the aircraft down and going through the whole process again. Finally, the Bulldogs were ready to be flown off to their operating base at Khartoum.

Stationed in the Sudan in response to the Abyssinian War, No. 3 Squadron's role was to carry out routine patrols to ensure that the Italians did not breach Sudanese airspace. This was the limit of their orders and the Italian aircraft were able to bomb, gas and strafe the largely defence-less tribesmen with impunity. Any fear of Italy's further expansionism was halted by the additional deployment of No. 8 and No. 29 Squadrons' Hawker Demons, along with the bombers of No. 47 Squadron.

In truth, Teddy never even saw an aircraft of the Italian *Regia Aeronautica*, only mile after mile of countryside, so he concentrated his efforts on routine patrols and staging a number of flying displays, greatly impressing the local sheikhs and tribesmen.

The operational corridor was dotted with emergency airstrips, each equipped with a set of steps and a petrol dump of 4-gallon tins, which frequently attracted the attention of looters. Teddy was not the tallest of pilots and found it very difficult to refuel without the aid of the steps. As a precaution he had his own spare set mounted on the outside of his aircraft, along the fuselage. However, his modification was spotted by Squadron Leader Martyn who came down on him like the proverbial ton of bricks. 'What on earth is that thing?' he shouted. 'Has it done its spinning trials with that contraption fastened on?' Teddy looked straight ahead, defenceless. Martyn was absolutely livid. 'You have no business to do that. You go up now and do a spinning test in it.'

There was nothing to be done but to follow the order. Teddy climbed into the cockpit and took off, giving himself a good deal of height before going into a spin. No matter what he did, however, he could not stop the spin as the aircraft hurtled towards the ground. With the air rushing past his face, he nearly blacked-out. Hardly able to breathe he desperately struggled to master the controls but all seemed lost, and he prepared for the end. Suddenly, resigned to his fate, his efforts overcame the flawed aerodynamics and he pulled the Bulldog out of the spin only a few brief moments from impact. The flight had scared him senseless. It taught him a valuable lesson, and he never did anything to alter the aerodynamics of an aircraft ever again.

He felt however, that he had been singled out. This was to become more apparent a few days later when the officers were out for an evening on the town. Teddy was feeling rather the worse for wear and went to the toilet where he made himself sick to clear his head. His CO, who was in the bar, found out and Teddy was summoned to his office the following morning, and asked about his previous night's conduct.

'Were you sick last night Donaldson?'

'Yes, sir.'

'Right. You know that your request for a permanent commission is before me for my recommendations and I shall endorse it that you are an outstanding pilot?'

'Yes, sir. Thank you.'

Martyn picked up the recommendation and waved it in front of Teddy dramatically. Then, with more than a little measure of pure malice, he grasped the top corners of the document and tore it up. 'That,' he said, 'is what I think of you after your disgusting behaviour last night. Being sick is not the way an officer would behave. Now get out of my office.'

Teddy had to accept that he was months away from the end of his commission and his RAF career. There was little chance of a reprieve. There was, however, a certain liberation in having nothing left to lose.

Revenge could be served lukewarm as well as cold and it was not long before Teddy was presented with a golden opportunity. The squadron were sent on an air exercise. Martyn was to fly with his section and Teddy would make sure he was aware of his presence, and remind him just how outstanding a pilot he really was.

Flying in the RAF's traditional tight 'vic', Teddy placed his wingtip ever closer to his CO's leading edge. Looking over, he could see the petrified look on Martyn's face, the colour draining the closer they came to contact. When they landed, he came up to Teddy and said: 'If I didn't know you better, I would have thought you were trying to kill me.'

'But I was, sir,' Teddy laughed.

A decidedly pale CO stood with his mouth wide open before regaining something of his composure. 'Ah, a good joke Donaldson.'

One of Teddy's fellow officers had committed some misdemeanour or other and Teddy had been ordered to escort him to Cairo to receive a Commander-in-Chief's reprimand. He had been warned that he would never rise above the rank of Flying Officer. Just as the two left the CO's office they were met by a messenger. 'Mr Donaldson, Mr—, Your promotion has just come through from England.'

The two looked at each other in astonishment. Teddy had been advanced to the rank of Flight Lieutenant. His friend had Teddy's extra rank-bar up as soon as a length of the tape could be found, much to the chagrin of their CO. The two were ordered home and made a slow seaward passage back to the UK, taking the opportunity to enjoy the benefits of the bar and their 'glamorous' status as RAF pilots.

Teddy's posting, with effect of 1 May, was to RAF Depot Uxbridge, his log book recording in a little more detail the nature of his new role, which was as Officer Commanding (OC) No. 2 (T) Squadron.

Squadron Leader Martyn's last signature in Teddy's log-book was for the month of March 1936; the annual mandatory assessment his flying skills is recoded as 'exceptional'. The heading 'Any special faults in flying which must be watched' remained blank – Teddy had got away with it!

There was, however, a sad end to this story. Teddy's friend, he later recalled, was to die within months. He took off without authority and was last heard of flying over the North Sea.

CHAPTER FIVE

More Skills and New Thrills

On 2 July 1936 Teddy received news of a new posting, taking over from Flight Lieutenant Theodore McEvoy as OC of No. 1 Squadron's A Flight based at Tangmere, near Chichester. He arrived at the squadron the following day, taking his first flight in the squadron's new Hawker Fury Mk 1 in the early afternoon. Designed by Sydney Camm, the fighter had a top speed of 250 mph. It was a delight for pilots of all abilities to fly, being light on the controls and very responsive. It was armed with two Vickers machine-guns, mounted along the top of the fuselage to the front of the pilot and synchronized to fire through the propeller. The feed was under the cockpit cowling, allowing the pilot to deal with a jam should it occur.

Teddy found that the influence of his predecessor had been immense. McEvoy had, during his year in command of A Flight, passed on his considerable experience as a pilot to his charge and moulded them into a mature and responsible unit. Teddy always acknowledged that his pilots owed a great debt of gratitude to 'Mac' McEvoy for the groundwork he put in that enabled them to win their spurs in action in later years. Their mutual respect as professional airmen led Teddy and Mac to remain lifelong friends.

Mac's achievements were made all the more outstanding owing to the fact that he had suffered from the crippling disease spondylitis (curvature of the spine) which overtook him before he was thirty. Whilst it was developing it caused him intense pain, and it was small consolation that once his spine had set in its curvature it no longer hurt; he was never afterwards able to stand straight. He could sit in a cockpit comfortably enough but, when strapped in, he was unable to turn his head sufficiently to see what was going on behind. He therefore wore a small mirror strapped to each forearm to check on the activities of the aircraft he was leading. Whenever one of his arms was raised, the following formation was always immaculate! Amazingly, Mac played golf as a pastime and, after the war, enjoyed turning out in a foursome of which the other members were the legless Douglas Bader, the fingerless Arthur Donaldson (Teddy's brother) and the one-armed Gus Walker (Air Chief Marshal Sir Augustus Walker GCB CBE DSO DFC AFC).

Teddy's job now was to maintain and develop the coherent unit created by McEvoy and take them to the next level as a Flight but, despite his own proficiency, it was still a steep learning curve for the new flight commander: a forty-minute practice at formation flying with his new pilots the following day, and then his next flight was to Northolt on 7 July, where he led A Flight during an inspection by King Edward VIII.

The rest of July and August were largely taken up with air exercises and mock dog-fighting, with several days spent patrolling and attacking 'enemy spotters'. This period saw him as acting squadron CO, handing over to Squadron Leader Cedric Hill in late August. This was seen as essential preparation for combat as, apart from the CO and Donaldson, only Pilot Officer H. E. C. Boxer and some the NCO pilots had spent more than a year on an operational unit.

There was a brief respite at the end of July when Teddy married Winifred Louise Constant, daughter of Maurice Stewart Constant, an engineer, at Christ's Church, Sutton, Surrey on 31 July 1936.

With his eldest brother, Donald, still in New Zealand, John Donaldson was Teddy's best man, while Winifred's cousin, Katherine Skingley, was her bridesmaid. Katherine and Winifred had grown up as sisters.

John and some of the brothers' RAF pals dressed Teddy's car up as a giant bed, Teddy having to drive his new bride off on their honeymoon peering over the blankets.

September saw Teddy flying gun-camera exercises and using the Sutton Bridge Ranges to keep his gunnery skill up to scratch ready to compete again in the Brooke-Popham Air Firing Trophy. In this, his third crack at the trophy, he came a close second to No. 19 Squadron's Flight Lieutenant Harry Broadhurst (later to become Air Chief Marshal Sir Harry Broadhurst GCB KBE DSO and Bar DFC and Bar AFC) who went on to beat Teddy's record, winning the trophy three times in a row.

A spin-off from his competition triumphs was that he was later selected to give instructional courses to the RAF's and Fleet Air Arm's gunnery instructors in 1939. These courses continued up until the outbreak of the war and directly influenced the gunnery skills of many of the pilots who were to fight during the summer of 1940.

On 22 September 1936 Flight Lieutenant Donaldson was temporarily attached as CO of No. 151 Fighter Squadron, based at North Weald. Equipped with Gloster Gauntlets, this squadron had been re-formed just over a month previously under Squadron Leader W. V. Hyde. The posting only lasted a fortnight with their new CO taking over the

Squadron on 2 October. Little did Teddy know that he was later to be one of its most illustrious commanders.

Meanwhile the RAF's home defence was undergoing a major reorganization. On 14 July 1936, the air defence of Great Britain had been separated into five commands – Training, Maintenance, Coastal, Bomber and Fighter. Fighter Command was placed under the leadership of Air Chief Marshal Sir Hugh Dowding, who had formerly been Air Member for Research and Development (later Lord Dowding of Bentley Priory GCB GCVO CMG).

Headquarters of the newly formed Fighter Command was at Bentley Priory at Stanmore, North London. The command comprised four Groups: No. 10 Group, the West Country; No. 11 Group, covering the south-east of England; No. 12 Group, the Midlands and East Anglia; and No. 13 Group, the north of England and Scotland.

The Spitfire and Hurricane prototypes were seen in public for the first time at the Hendon Air Show on 27 June 1936 (Hurricane K5083 first flown by George Bulman on 6 November 1935), with the RAF placing initial orders for 310 Spitfires and 500 Hurricanes.

The Air Staff, however, remained convinced of the importance of bombers over fighters and Dowding would face a continual struggle for resources. Their policy was heavily influenced by the Chief of Air Staff, Air Chief Marshal Sir Cyril Newall and the Director of Plans, Group Captain Arthur Harris, both bomber men.

In August of the same year the Royal Air Force Volunteer Reserve (RAFVR) was created to help produce part-time fliers who could boost the country's defences, ready to face the possibility of war with Germany.

By the spring of 1937, the expansion of the RAF was well under way. As the new eight-gun monoplane fighters were not yet ready for service, new squadrons, formed to await them, were temporarily equipped with biplanes. At the beginning of March, it was learned that some of No. 1 Squadron's pilots were to be permanently detached to reactivate No. 72 Squadron, equipped with Gloster Gladiators, with Flight Lieutenant Donaldson as its Acting CO. This news was received with mixed feelings, for no one was keen to leave the old outfit, especially when rumour was rife that No. 1 Squadron was on the shortlist for re-equipment with Hawker Hurricanes. But pride was duly swallowed, and Teddy moved with his pilots to an adjacent hangar at Tangmere to await their new aircraft. The only concession was that he was to return to his old unit when No. 72 Squadron had found its feet and a new CO was posted in.

No. 1 Squadron's CO, Cedric Hill, was promoted in May and, to the delight of his old squadron, he was appointed Station Commander of Tangmere. His place at the head of No. 1 was taken by Squadron Leader F.R.D. Swain AFC, who, during the previous September, had established

a new world altitude record in the Bristol 138a monoplane. Dressed
in a pressure suit that made him look like a cross between Ned Kelly and
a deep-sea diver, he had reached 49,967 ft. He was afterwards heard to
remark that he would have made it to 50,000 had he forgone a second
slice of toast at breakfast!

No. 1 Squadron, with Teddy and many of its better pilots detached,
was again lacking in age and experience. Henry Boxer was promoted to
flying officer and became a flight commander in Teddy's absence. The
remaining pilots comprised seven pilot officers and six sergeants.
Among the new arrivals were Acting Pilot Officers C.G.H. Crusoe and
M.H. 'Hilly' Brown. The latter, a rugged little Canadian, had crossed the
Atlantic to join the RAF after reading an article on the growing strength
of the *Luftwaffe*.

Teddy returned from No. 72 Squadron in May 1937, and immediately
set about re-establishing his leadership role in fighter attack exercises
and aerobatics. He led his flight in a fighter affiliation exercise with
No. 501 (B) Squadron Auxiliary Air Force, receiving particular praise
from their pilots and their CO, who wrote to Squadron Leader Swain:

> This perfect liaison was achieved by the willingness and deter-
> mination of Flight Lieutenant Donaldson and the Officers and
> Airmen of his Flight, to do everything in their power to assist us,
> and to ensure that no opportunity was lost to obtain the very best
> results from both the exercises and the liaison between the
> Auxiliary and Regular officers and airmen.
>
> In conclusion, I need hardly say that all the members of this
> Squadron look forward to further visits by your Squadron, and in
> the meantime we shall watch with special interest the display at
> Hendon by Flight Lieutenant Donaldson and his Flight.

There was time to get in valuable display practice in readiness for Empire
Day, and Teddy was always eager to perform aerobatics, sanctioned or
otherwise. He had approached his new CO and requested that he be
allowed to put together a display team for the summer. Squadron Leader
Swain agreed in principle, and it was decided that the team should be
composed of four aircraft if suitable pilots could be found, with Teddy
taking the lead.

Having been given the go-ahead, and after a week of practice, Teddy
selected Flying Officer Boxer and Pilot Officers Walker and Hanks. These
four, destined to become the most celebrated pre-war team of all, flew
together exclusively for the next fortnight, with the aim of being selected
to fill the star billing at Hendon.

Henry Boxer, known as 'Top' in those days, was to be Teddy's deputy.
He had joined the squadron in July 1935 along with his pal Pilot

Officer Peter Townsend (later of Battle of Britain fame and, as Group Captain Peter Townsend CVO DSO DFC and Bar, linked romantically with Princess Margaret), who had just pipped him for the Sword of Honour at Cranwell.

For 'Johnnie' Walker and 'Prosser' Hanks, this was a special achievement. Neither had seen much more than a year's total service and neither had over 200 hours in his log-book. Hanks, it should be added, was still a teenager.

RAF display teams had for many years maintained a fixed tight formation throughout their flight, the aircraft being literally tied together to create a spectacle for the crowds on the ground. Teddy felt that this made the displays too rigid and decided to break the practice and opt for manoeuvrability, thus allowing his aircraft to merge into different display configurations and to peel off to perform solo or dual aerobatics and later re-form on the main group.

On 29 May Teddy led No. 1 Squadron's display team on the first demonstration of his new flying programme in front of a crowd of thousands at RAF Tangmere, their home station. His log book records that he was in the air no less than three times during the day, putting in well over an hour of breathtaking aerobatics.

During a magnificent exhibition of flying skills in their Hawker Furies the Squadron stole the show, beginning with a loop and ending with a full roll, all in close formation with only half a wing span between aircraft. Then, from a line astern loop, they came out immediately into flight formation once more. Then a thrill went through the record crowd as one Fury slipped out of the line abreast loop a few moments prior to the four machines completing the full arc only to regain the 'V' formation again. Gasps came from all round the spectators' enclosure, as it seemed as if two aircraft had touched. The formation then broke before anyone could catch their breath as Pilot Officer Hanks and Flight Lieutenant Donaldson went straight into their individual aerobatics display.

During the formation flying Teddy was talking to the ground via wireless. Suddenly he broke into the commentary to say: 'There is an aircraft on fire.' He had seen a lone Fury flying towards Tangmere when it suddenly broke its flight path and spun in from 600 ft. A few minutes later it was announced that there was a small fire in the car park and that no one was to be alarmed. It was only later, as visitors drove home along the main Portsmouth to Brighton road, that they saw the wreckage in which Sergeant Pilot J.J. Tanfield had died.

Described by the press as a brilliant young pilot, Tanfield had taken his aircraft up earlier in the day for a test flight but experienced engine trouble and landed early. With a repair made, he took the Fury up to check it out. It was about 4 p.m. and No. 1 Squadron's display team were halfway through their display when Teddy saw the tragedy unfold

¼ mile away from Tanfield's home station. Sadly, there were always tragedies of this nature and Tanfield's death was not an isolated incident – such was the uncertain nature of flying.

In 1937 King George VI was crowned, and the RAF display at the Hendon Air Pageant was to be graced for the first time by the presence of a reigning monarch. In early June, and with the coronation only a matter of weeks away, Teddy was informed that his team was to represent No. 1 Squadron at Hendon on the 26th to coincide with the coronation. A letter arrived a few days later informing him that he was to be presented to the King immediately before the set-piece event. As team leader, Teddy choreographed his team's programme using his new box-of-four formation as opposed to the old 'vic' of three.

The Hendon show programme included displays by Nos. 43 and 56 Squadrons as well as representatives from other commands. Among the demonstrations was a training flight simulated by two pilots from Training Command. Teddy's brother, Flight Lieutenant J. W. 'Jack' Donaldson flew a Hawker Hart, the other being piloted by Flight Lieutenant G. A. Bartlett. This was probably the only time Teddy flew alongside his elder brother who, despite his longer service, held the same rank as him.

The No. 1 Squadron team and their display were advertised in the event programme as:

Flight Lieutenant E. M. Donaldson

Flying Officer H. E. C. Boxer

Pilot Officer P. R. Walker

Pilot Officer P. P. Hanks

1) In Diamond Formation – Half-roll, dive out, rocket loop

2) In Diamond Formation – Loop, roll, loop

3) In Line Astern Formation – Loop, forming diamond formation on second loop

4) In Diamond Formation – Roll, half-roll, dive out, loop, roll off top of loop

5) In Abreast Formation – Loop, forming diamond formation on second loop

6) In Diamond Formation – Three-quarter loop, half downward roll, half upward roll, loop out

7) In Line Astern Formation – Loop forming diamond formation, stall turn.

The Air Pageant was a great success. Teddy's young team were the stars of the show and won a rare standing ovation from the crowd. For many of the public, this final Hendon display was to be the last opportunity of appraising the skill of the young men who were soon to stand between them and invasion. No. 1 Squadron was the first to mount a four-man aerobatic team, and the enthusiastic reception given by the crowd fully justified the long hours of practice.

Of an earlier demonstration of the new four-plane formation *The Daily Telegraph* wrote:

> The new programme item seen yesterday (7 June) was the 'Box' formation flying by four planes of No. 1 Fighter Squadron, a beautiful piece of work.
>
> The 'Box' is made up of the usual three aircraft with a fourth machine astern completing the Square.
>
> No more finished performance has been seen at any Air Force display. The four machines changed formation whilst in the act of performing difficult aerobatics.

Not surprisingly, as highly skilled pilots, each of Teddy's team members that day went on to have very distinguished careers of their own, becoming Air Commodore 'Rex' Boxer, CB, OBE, Group Captain 'Johnnie' Walker CBE DSO DFC and Group Captain 'Prosser' Hanks DSO DFC AFC. The four remained great friends and frequently reunited in the RAF Club during the post-war years, their last big get-together being for Teddy's retirement party, held at RAF Manby in 1961.

In early September, with a month of aerobatics and displays under their belt, Teddy was asked to put the team through its paces over Tangmere once more, this time for the filming of *Shadow of the Wing*, an RAF commission which was never completed. The remainder of the month was devoted to patrols and interceptions as a part of naval cooperation exercises. These inter-service cooperation exercises were to prove vital in the years ahead, particularly for Teddy leading No. 151 Squadron on convoy escorts during the early phases of the Battle of Britain.

Another precursor to Teddy's role in the great air battle came the same year when he led a flight of No. 1 Squadron in an interception exercise that was the first of a kind. He was vectored onto a formation of 'enemy' bombers by his controller who, in turn, was being fed information from Britain's first radar. It was, of course, the use of radar, combined with information from the network of men of the Observer Corps, that proved so vital during the summer of 1940.

There had been much speculation about the possibility of aircraft being destroyed by 'death-rays'. However, experiments in the location of flying objects using radio waves had been conducted by the RAF as early as February 1935. Dowding, who attended the trials, was among the few supporters of the programme. He was aware that radar could not be relied upon on its own and that a secondary method of tracking the enemy and confirming their numbers, height and direction was required. The Observer Corps was to fulfil this role and during the epic air battle no radar plot could be acted upon without their confirmation.

CHAPTER SIX

Triumph in Zurich

Following on from No. 1 Squadron's acclaimed performance at Hendon, the Air Council decided to send Teddy's display team to the International Aviation Meeting, held once every four years, at Zurich. Despite the RAF's long and illustrious history, this was the first time that the Air Ministry had authorized an RAF unit to represent Britain at a major international air show on the continent. It was accepted that they would not have a realistic chance of winning any of the timed races, so they would be guests for these rather than enter any of the formal speed competitions.

The significance of the Zurich meeting was that the European Powers were anxious to show off the calibre of their pilots and equipment to a worried world. It was plain that the Germans and Italians were going to be there in force, so a British success was highly desirable in terms of prestige. Teddy and his team therefore had, quite justifiably, huge ambitions to demonstrate, with their own aerobatic display, that the RAF were supreme in the art of pure flying and that Britain's pride would be upheld.

As well as 250 civil aircraft from fourteen European countries, a number of national teams attended the Zurich meeting, including military aircraft from France, Belgium and Czechoslovakia, as well as from Germany and Italy.

Germany had been banned from building up a military air force under the terms of The Treaty of Versailles. However, on 26 February 1935, Adolf Hitler had announced his defiance of the Treaty and begun open rearmament. Designs for the legendary Messerschmitt Bf 109, Dornier Do 17, Heinkel He 111, Junkers Ju 88 and Junkers Ju 87 were already in developed blueprint form, while the Junkers Ju 52 was in regular use with the German Airline Lufthansa. The *Luftwaffe* had secretly built up an air force of 1,888 powered aircraft (the terms of the treaty only allowing them to fly gliders) and 20,000 officers and men. At its head was the First World War ace and Blue Max holder, Hermann Goering, the former commander of the famous Richthofen *Geschwader*.

In Britain, the mood remained firmly against war with Germany. In

June 1935, the League of Nations Union had received eleven million signatures appealing for peace – such sentiment no doubt emboldened the land-hungry Chancellor, Adolf Hitler.

By 1937, the Germans were able to show just how advanced they were by dominating the proceedings in Zurich. They swept the board in the climbing and diving competitions, as well as in all the classes of the timed circuits around the Alps – the Messerschmitt Bf 109 had already set a new world speed record and was soon to see combat in Spain with the German Condor Legion.

The six Furies selected for Zurich included the four normally flown by the team members. All six were given a thorough overhaul during mid-July with help from the Rolls-Royce and Hawker representatives at Tangmere. Whilst the four prime display aircraft were receiving loving attention in the hangar, their four pilots flew in other machines several times each day to perfect their sequence. Teddy's insistence on constant practice, whatever the weather, was to pay huge dividends in Switzerland.

All was eventually ready. The ground crew and spares set off for Zurich in a Bristol Bombay, followed later by the six Furies led *en route* by Wing Commander Cedric Hill in one of the spare aircraft.

The Furies approached Zurich's Dübendorf airfield on Saturday, 24 July. The same four young pilots who had, just one month before, enthralled the crowds at Hendon – Donaldson, Boxer, Walker and Hanks – made a couple of wide circuits, picking out the landmarks that would assist them in their formation breaks, turns and form-ups.

Top Boxer flew in the No. 2 position on Teddy's starboard wing, while Johnnie Walker held the similar No. 3 position to port. Hanks flew line astern on his leader in the new and somewhat controversial 'box' position. Some mystique had been woven by the press about the problems of flying in the box which is, if anything, slightly easier than in the two echeloned positions. Young Prosser Hanks made it seem quite effortless.

Led by Teddy, the No. 1 Squadron team put on a breathtaking display in practice on the afternoon of the day they arrived, and then executed an equally impressive programme the next day, 25 July, during the opening Sunday of the show. It was estimated that almost half of Zurich's population turned out at Dübendorf on that first public day. The team's near-perfect display drew tremendous admiration from the crowd and the international press. Throughout the week, they continued to match the finest that Europe could produce, drawing considerable open praise in the process from their rivals.

As the week progressed towards the climax on the final Sunday, it was noticeable that the opposition was becoming increasingly daring in their efforts to outshine No. 1 Squadron. The Italian display team, in particular, were getting visibly more adventurous in their Fiat CR42s as the weekend approached. They were not called the 'stunning bachelors' for nothing!

There was no display on the Friday as the airfield was being prepared for the weekend, and most of the participants had taken the day off, but not Teddy's pilots. The RAF team had been given a car to take them to Lucerne for the day, but did not leave until Teddy had led them through their routine once more immediately after breakfast. This amazed their rivals, most with hangovers, who had last seen Teddy's boys whooping it up at a party into the wee small hours.

The weather was fine for Saturday's display, when the Furies shared the honours with the Italian team. The 'stunning bachelors' put on the most exotic show, with a lot of low flying, side-slipping and noise, which pleased the crowd. The German solo artist was not only equally impressive but also hugely daring. He began his display with a loop that led into an inverted dive which he bunted out of with his tail fin about 10 ft off the grass.

The scene was now set for lively and competitive displays on the final Sunday, 1 August, but the weather was threatened by thunderclouds lurking ominously in the hills. The programme showed that the RAF aerobatic team was due to provide the finale, following on from the French and the Italians. The Italians had tried throughout the week to out-fly the RAF but had so far failed. Their captain therefore approached Teddy and asked if they could swap their mid-afternoon slot for the RAF's final one, with the 'stunning bachelors' hopefully getting the kudos they yearned for by providing the closing climax to the show. Teddy agreed – it proved to be a master-stroke.

The storm held off for the first part of the show but, as the day wore on, it became obvious the weather was closing in, with heavy thundery rain and a low cloud-base. By mid-afternoon, the skies were black and the cloud-base was, in places, down to 200 ft. The organizers therefore approached Donaldson with a view to cancelling the rest of the flying programme. Teddy looked over to his men who, such was their team spirit and faith in their leader, responded: 'If you want to lead, then we'll follow you, Teddy.'

And so it was that the four Hawker Furies took off in a near blinding storm, rain blurring their goggles so they could hardly see their own wing tips, never mind the aircraft they were forming up on. Teddy somehow threaded his team in and out of the bad weather, looping and rolling as and when he got the opportunity. The four pilots, two of whom had only been in the RAF for barely a year, went on to complete their entire advertised sequence with apparent total disregard for the elements, and stage one of the best displays ever witnessed. The crowd below could only watch and marvel in stunned silence.

After the Furies had landed and bounced to a halt, the pilots alighted to a tumultuous applause and were almost immediately mobbed by the admiring crowd. Teddy recalled that the team met the same warm greeting later wherever they went in Zurich, being fêted as heroes.

The rest of the programme was abandoned. The authorities suspended all further flying after the Italian and French teams realized that the weather was simply too bad. This was particularly galling for the Italians, who had asked to delay their appearance to provide the grand finale, but the Fiat pilots were the first to offer their warm congratulations to the RAF team. And so, despite the German victories in the timed competitions, the British had stolen the show with their outstanding aerobatic performances; raw courage had won out over speed and efficiency.

The party returned, via a memorable night in Paris, to a tremendous reception at Tangmere and the adulation of the British press. For a public worried about the growing strength of the *Luftwaffe*, here was proof that at least one RAF squadron could take on the best and fly the pants off them.

As team leader, Teddy later received a letter from the Air Council congratulating him on 'the excellent efficiency and training skill the display had shown'. Furthermore, it said 'their exemplary bearing created an impression which has rebounded to the credit of the RAF'.

The magazine *Flight* reported the events in the following terms:

> The well-known merits of the Italian squadron and the French *Ecole de Perfectionement d'etampes* had raised some doubts in the British minds whether our formation of seven-year-old Furies could be as impressive with less than half the number.
>
> There need have been no doubt at all. The reaction of spectators, knowledgeable and otherwise, nationality no object, was really enthusiastic and the superb precision and finish of the British performance made up for any shortcomings in number or noise.

The official report from the Air Attaché in Paris was similarly full of praise.

> The flight gave a magnificent show under what must have been almost impossible conditions. The formation flying was just as accurate as it was when weather conditions were perfect. The British flight provided the culminating and final act of the Meeting.
>
> Flights of Italian and French military aircraft had been giving demonstrations of formation flying during the week, but it was quickly recognized by the instructed portion of the public and by all the military aviators present, that the British exhibition was of a far higher order of accuracy and good training.

General Erhard Milch, then Goering's deputy as State Secretary in the Reich Air Ministry and a close friend of Adolf Hitler, personally congratulated Teddy and his team, echoing the praise of others, saying simply: 'I have never seen flying like that in my life.'

His words were widely quoted in the British press. It was Milch, of course, who had been the architect of the secret rebuilding of the German air force under the cover of the civilian airline Lufthansa.

Of the display, Teddy simply recorded in his log book: '25 minute display at 1,000 ft. Bad weather.'

However, those 25 minutes were to provide lasting impressions of the high levels of skill and training within the RAF that would have a significant bearing on how the service was perceived by other nations, particularly by Germany.

Glowing though the praise for the display team was, the RAF's presence at the Zurich meeting had another, more important purpose.

Even before Hitler's open defiance on the Versailles Treaty, British intelligence had reported on the Nazis' development of non-civil aircraft, including bombers, fighter-bombers and single-seater fighters, as part of a rearmament programme. The pilots who would fly these aircraft in Spain and during the early stages of the Second World War were being trained through gliding clubs and Lufthansa. Ironically, many of their leaders were trained in Lipzek, under a still secret treaty with Stalin. In response to their own woefully small number of trained pilots, the British had just created the RAFVR in April 1937, which was set the target of training 800 pilots a year.

British intelligence and the RAF were trying to build up a picture of the German rearmament programme. Prior to setting off for Zurich, Teddy was summoned to the Air Ministry for a special briefing, during which the Air Council's willingness to send the RAF team to Zurich became apparent. His 'mission' was to gather data on the new Messershmitt Bf 109, the fighter that was to provide the RAF's greatest threat during the Battle of France and later in the Battle of Britain.

During his day at the Air Ministry, Teddy was shown the existing top-secret dossiers on the Messerschmitt Bf 109. The boffins had already projected performance figures based on evidence from the world speed record and from covert sources. However, what they desperately needed was a pilot's perspective of how it compared with existing RAF fighters. As well as air speed, climb rate, ceiling height and armament, the Air Ministry needed to know about the standard and length of pilot-training courses. These figures would be almost as crucial in assessing the readiness of the *Luftwaffe* for all out war.

When Teddy asked how he was meant to get this information out of ardent Nazis, he was simply told to talk about anything but the Bf 109 and then ply the pilots with drink until their arrogance came to the fore.

Teddy tried this tack but found that once they had downed the free drink, the Germans left, so a new tactic was needed. This involved getting the Germans to buy the first drink, which encouraged them to wait for Teddy to reciprocate.

It was with First World War ace Major-General Ernst Udet that Teddy struck gold. This arrogant head of the technical branch of the German air force was a former member of the Red Baron's Flying Circus, and he enjoyed his wine.

Udet, who had sixty-two 'kills' to his name, was scathing of the brave British pilot who took on whole squadrons of German fighters. 'Typically British,' he remarked. 'I suppose you would think that brave. I call it damn stupid, just like your display today. A damn show-off. Typically British. I suppose you thought it clever but I would have thought no one but a fool, or a Britisher, would fly in weather like that and do the things you did.'

The *Luftwaffe* would, to their cost, come up against this 'typically British' spirit again over northern France, the Channel and the Home Counties in the years to come. The RAF pilots would be aided by men from all around the Empire as well as from Poland, Czechoslovakia, Belgium and France, all of whom by then would have tasted Nazi brutality.

The German pilots were keen to learn about the new Hawker Hurricane, of which they seemed already to know a great deal. In fact, Teddy had not even seen a Hurricane, never mind flown one. 'Absolutely terrific,' he said. 'Best fighter in the world.'

The first production Hurricane had not come off the line yet, but he used their interest in the Hurricane to goad information about the Bf 109 out of the boastful pilots.

'Rubbish!' he was told. 'Your best fighter must be these old Furies, otherwise you'd have sent the Hurricane here. And anyway, you haven't got very many of them.'

The latter statement was, of course, true. The Hawker Hurricane was one of two designs submitted to the Air Ministry by Sydney Camm, chief designer of Hawker Aircraft Limited, in the early 1930s. Both were rejected but Hawker decided to go ahead with the project, which was modified and eventually picked up by the Air Ministry (Air Ministry Specification F.5/34 issued in November 1934). The Hurricane first flew at Brooklands on 6 November 1935. Production time was twice as quick as for the Supermarine Spitfire, and so it was the Hurricane that domi-nated the events of 1940.

The German pilots left Teddy with a warning: 'You wait until September 1939. Once the harvest is in, you British will get the biggest thrashing you have ever had.'

'What do you mean?' asked Teddy.

'Never you mind. Just wait and see,' came the ominous reply.

On his return to England, Teddy submitted a report to the Air Ministry, bringing the profile of the Messerschmitt Bf 109 up to date. The findings astonished even Teddy. One of his most important pieces of information was that it had a cannon that fired through the propeller boss. This 37mm gun was of such a high calibre that at the time no one in Britain believed it could be mounted in any type of aircraft. It made the Messerschmitt Bf 109 a formidable foe.

CHAPTER SEVEN

Storm Clouds
Over Europe

Back in England, following his triumph over the elements, Teddy resumed his day-to-day flying, polishing up on air-to-air firing and fighter attacks in preparation for his squadron's fighter attack competition against No. 43 squadron. For the rest of the Squadron, the Zurich period had been one of business as usual. The four members of the team soon settled back into the less glamorous routines of training, but not before they had accounted between them for several pages in the squadron 'linebook'.

During the 1930s a healthy rivalry had developed between the two Tangmere-based squadrons, with No. 43 gaining an equally outstanding reputation for formation aerobatics at the annual Hendon displays. Teddy was as keen as ever to uphold No. 1 Squadron's motto, *In omnibus princeps* – 'First in all things', and was justifiably proud of its heritage as one of the three founder squadrons of the Royal Flying Corps.

No. 43 Squadron's motto was just as taunting, *Gloria finis* – 'Glory is the end'. Its badge, a black gamecock approved by King Edward VIII in July 1936 and developed from an unofficial design produced in 1926 when the squadron was equipped with the Gloster Gamecock, led to No. 43 Squadron becoming known as 'The Fighting Cocks'. Teddy's respect for his rivals was reflected in later years by one of his more endearing welcomes – 'Watcha Cock'!

The competition combats took place on 28 September 1937 between Selsey Bill and Tangmere, resulting in victory for No. 1 Squadron. Further air attack practice marked the build up to the Sir Philip Sassoon Flight Attack Competition at Northolt a few weeks later, on 11 October, Teddy once more leading six aircraft from the squadron to glory.

In October, Teddy again served as Acting CO of No. 1 Squadron, this time during the brief absence of Squadron Leader F.R.D. Swain AFC.

On 4 February 1938, he was posted, rather surprisingly for such an exceptional fighter pilot, to No. 30 Squadron of Bomber Command, then based at RAF Hanaidi, just outside Baghdad in Iraq. It was hard luck that he should be sent to one of the few unaccompanied stations in the RAF so soon after his marriage. As ever, however, duty came first and his piloting skills were once again rated as 'exceptional' on his log summary. Fortuitously, this bizarre posting was almost immediately cancelled and Teddy was back flying with No. 1 Squadron by the 28th. The reason for his quick return soon became evident. It was considered that a showcase display should be given to honour the visit of King Carol of Rumania to Britain. Teddy was ordered to commence aerobatics practice from 15 March, and the four Hawker Furies performed before King Carol a few days later.

Despite his former CO's threats, and much to his relief, pride and delight, Teddy was granted a permanent commission in the rank of flight lieutenant on 29 March 1938.

On 1 May, now 26, he was sent on an instructor's course at the Central Flying School, gaining a B1 rating as 'above average'. On qualifying as an instructor, he was posted to No. 6 Flying Training School (FTS) at Netheravon on 16 July. Having taken up the posting, he was apparently not required and therefore did not fly there at all; instead, he was re-posted north in mid-August to No. 7 FTS at Peterborough. Here he had six Hawker Harts in which he taught advanced flying. Barely three months later, his destiny was put firmly back on course when, on 14 November 1938, he was given command of No. 151 Squadron, a Fighter Command squadron in No. 11 Group, based at North Weald to the north-east of London. Promotion to Acting Squadron Leader was immediate and the rank was confirmed as substantive on 1 December 1938.

Teddy was thrilled, especially as he had already served as the squadron's temporary CO from 22 September to 2 October 1936, not long after it had been re-formed from a flight of No. 56 Squadron's Gloster Gauntlets. The Gauntlet was introduced into production in 1934. A single-seat biplane, it had a 605 hp Mercury VIS engine with a maximum airspeed of 230 mph. While it was highly manoeuvrable, it only had two .303 inch calibre machine-guns and took an agonizingly long nine minutes to climb to 20,000 ft.

After being disbanded in September 1919, No. 151 Squadron had remained as a number only in Air Ministry Records. Nevertheless, from this inglorious past, Teddy saw his new command as an opportunity for the challenges ahead.

No one knew what kind of confrontation might ensue, nor would anyone dispute that it was an unstable period. The political situation in Europe had deteriorated alarmingly, with the Germans gaining military strength. There was unrest and mistrust amongst the main powers, and this led to a rethink in terms of the requirements and general armaments for all three Services.

The First World War had shown the importance of air power, both as a strategic force and as a supporting tactical force for army operations. Unfortunately, it had been assumed that the Armistice meant everlasting peace, but as with all 'pieces of paper' this was to prove a fallacy.

With a trade recession biting hard into the country's economy, and with opposition from pacifist and other political factions, there had been a reluctance to spend money on armaments in general. However, there was clear thinking by some industrialists and, fortunately for the world at large, the Hawker and the Supermarine companies were working hard on designs of revolutionary aircraft for defensive roles. Not unexpectedly, Germany was working along similar lines, although the Jumo engine was not ready for fitting to their more developed airframes. To meet their programme, Germany had purchased Rolls-Royce Kestrel engines between 1931 and 1934, and it turned out that these were used in some of the *Luftwaffe's* Messerschmitt Bf 109 aircraft.

It was against this background, and the increasing uncertainties of 1938, which culminated in the so-called 'Munich Crisis', that the Service chiefs were spurred into action, despite the fact that the Prime Minister had returned on 30 September with an agreement signed by Hitler which, he claimed, meant 'peace in our time'. The price was to allow Germany to absorb the ethnic German areas of Czechoslovakia, known as the Sudetenland. In the event, Britain would not immediately go to war, and the nation began to breathe again. For the RAF, Munich provided the time for its vital re-equipment and gave another year of life to its young men. With the benefit of hindsight, Teddy firmly believed that Chamberlain's act of appeasement, so often reviled by many, undoubtedly saved Britain from a terrible defeat.

The effect of placing No. 151 Squadron under the command of the hugely talented Squadron Leader Donaldson at the end of that tumultuous year was soon to be seen. Equally significant was the end of all the rumours about the re-equipment programme for frontline squadrons. By the end of the year, and coinciding with the arrival of its new CO. No. 151 Squadron began to take delivery of its first Hawker Hurricanes. These aircraft were basically fabric-covered monoplanes with a metal-covered front fuselage, following the well-proven construction features of the Hawker biplanes of the day. The engine powering the Hurricane Mark 1s was the Rolls-Royce Merlin II engine, this being a natural development of the Kestrel. Its power was 1030 hp, giving the Hurricane a top speed of 312 mph, but an early model had achieved a record-breaking run in flying from London to Edinburgh at an average ground speed of 415 mph. The first Hurricanes were fitted with the Watts fixed-pitch propeller.

November 1938 saw the first of the new eight-gun Hawker Hurricanes arrive at North Weald, just a year after they first came into military service with Treble-One Squadron at Northolt. Teddy took his first flight in the fighter on 1 December, the day his substantive promotion came through, collecting L1724 (GG-M) from the makers at Brooklands, and L1748 two weeks later.

There were to be twelve Hawker Hurricanes on Squadron charge with two on immediate reserve and four more on Command reserve. The Squadron letter codes were originally GG, but were later changing to DZ.

Taking on board a completely new aircraft, a monoplane as opposed to a biplane, with four times the engine power, and what was then considered to be first-class armament of eight forward-firing .303 machine-guns (four in each wing), led to a very intensive training programme, especially as war with Germany was now felt to be both inevitable and imminent.

Between 1936 and 1939, the RAF's front-line fighter squadrons carried out many interception exercises in conjunction with Bomber Command, as it had been accepted by the then Prime Minister, Stanley Baldwin, that 'bombers would always get through'. With this philosophy, which had been proved correct in Ethiopia and in the Spanish Civil War, it had been nearly impossible for Dowding to convince the Air Staff that the role of the fighter for the protection of the United Kingdom should be the dominant factor in Britain's defence policy. France had, on paper, the strongest army in Europe, and it seemed to many inconceivable that they could ever be overwhelmed by a German aggressor. The Air Staff's belief was that if war with Germany came, it would be fought in continental Europe like the First World War, in which many of them had fought and during which raids on England had been nothing more than a political embarrassment.

During this period, however, Germany had significantly increased the size of its own bomber force, and had proved its capability in Spain to such an extent that it seemed impossible for Britain to be able to catch up. With such a large force, Germany might overwhelm their opponents with sheer weight of numbers. So, in December 1938, with the growing might of the *Luftwaffe* apparent to all, Sir Thomas Inskip, the Minister for Co-ordination of Defence, whilst proposing that more fighters than bombers could be built for a given expenditure, issued a memo which was to turn the prominent responsibility of the RAF from attack to defence: 'The role of our Air Force is not an early knock-out blow – no one has suggested that we can accomplish that – but to prevent the Germans from knocking us out.'

Consequently, on the eve of the Second World War, no fewer than seventeen squadrons were to become fully operational with Hurricanes. In contrast, only seven would have Spitfires, four the fighter version of the Blenheim light bomber, and the remaining six would still be flying Gladiators, Gauntlets or Hinds!

It later transpired that, at the beginning of the war, the RAF's successes regularly made headline news. The public believed that the new monoplanes had the measure of anything the Germans could produce. Teddy in his Hurricane, however, quickly found out that, despite the pilot's good all-round visibility and the aircraft's tight turn, it lacked speed and could be out-run and out-climbed by all the *Luftwaffe*'s fighters and fighter-bombers, as well as by some of their bombers too. 'You couldn't run away,' he would say. 'You just had to be bloody brave, daring or dead!'

Nevertheless, he found it a very forgiving aircraft which could take a lot of punishment. He was later to discover that this extended to combat damage too. With a stable gun platform and being relatively easy for the squadron 'erks' to repair, it was to be the workhorse of the Battle of Britain.

North Weald aerodrome, Teddy's home base for the remainder of his tour of combat, lies to the west of the small village on the north side of the Epping to Ongar road. The hangar occupied by No. 151 Squadron was located close to the road and, conveniently for the pilots and 'erks' alike, to the Kia-Ora café which was run by a lady from New Zealand. A hole in the hedge adjacent to the Squadron hangar led straight to the café.

Teddy's Squadron was to share North Weald with No. 56 Squadron, led by Squadron Leader E. V. Knowles. Teddy Donaldson and Knowles encouraged a healthy rivalry between the two Hurricane squadrons, competing to better each other's performance in attack exercises and 'scrambles'. Every aspect of the squadron's performance was timed and rated. Teddy was particularly keen to use this competitiveness to hone the Squadron's gunnery skills

It was in May 1939 that No. 17 Squadron arrived at North Weald, swapping their Gloster Gauntlets for No. 56 Squadron's Hurricanes before moving on to Debden, thus temporarily bringing to an end the battle-climb and other competitions until the squadron was re-equipped with new Hurricanes later that month.

Teddy recalled that, among the many fine pilots flying with No. 151 Squadron, was a fellow sportsman, Pilot Officer Jack Hamar. Jack was a weight-lifter and, like Teddy, a natural pilot. Born in Knighton, Radnorshire, Jack had earned a reputation as a daredevil in his neighbourhood with his motorcycle riding. Two of Jack's uncles had flown in the Great War, one being killed in combat the other dying in a flying accident in Canada while training as an Observer.

Teddy soon recognized Hamar's natural flying ability and exceptional gunnery skills, and he was to become his CO's number two, his 'wingman', flying cover for Teddy on his starboard side in training and later when they went into combat.

In January 1939, Teddy went on a three-week secondment to

command an air-firing instructor's course at Sutton Bridge. This included experimental firing on both the Spitfire and the Hurricane. Having been twice winner of the Brooke-Popham Air Firing Trophy in the mid-1930s, Teddy remained one of the best shots in the RAF, arguably only bettered by Harry Broadhurst who took the title off him, winning it three times in a row. Teddy's experience was passed on to the new generation of instructors who, in turn, were to train hundreds of Battle of Britain pilots.

On the political scene, Prime Minister Neville Chamberlain announced in Parliament that he had made a promise to the Polish government that Britain and her ally France would go to war to defend Poland's borders.

Back with No. 151 Squadron, Teddy began putting his men through their paces with formation flying and practice attacks. He ensured that his men were to be among the best prepared for war should war come. Once again he was called upon for aerobatics duties, giving a number of displays, including amazing the crowds in an Avro Tutor (the AOC having, for some reason, forbidden aerobatics in Hurricanes) on 22 May, the last Empire Day before the war. Among the exercises Teddy flew were mass flights not unlike the so-called Big Wing later promoted by Douglas Bader.

Teddy maintained No. 151 Squadron's high level of readiness with regular exercises and mock combats. Meanwhile, he arranged for the approaches to North Weald's satellite airfield at Stapleford to be improved, flying several trips to check on progress in removing flying hazards such as trees and other obstacles.

Stapleford Tawney lies to the north-east of London, between Chigwell and Ongar. The airfield was opened in 1934 by a small charter company and included three hangars and a concrete apron. With the death of its founder, Edward Hillman, the company was taken over and eventually merged to form British Airways, but the new company used Heston as their main operating airfield. Taken over by the Air Ministry in 1938, the airfield was used by No. 21 Elementary and Reserve Flying School, training the men of the RAFVR. On the outbreak of war it was expanded and became a satellite of nearby North Weald and would be used by both Nos. 56 and 151 Squadrons.

In early July, Teddy was given leave. He drove down to the south of France and spent an enjoyable time in Monaco, including a little gambling after joining the Casino de Monte Carlo. There was time too for socializing in the officers' mess and for visits to the other No. 11 Group stations in Essex. At Debden, Teddy became great friends with Squadron Leader Eric Stapleton, and was introduced to his beautiful Norwegian fiancé Anne Sofie.

On his return, he lost no time in stepping up the training programme for all his pilots, working on interceptions and attacks as well as formation flying. Staying close in on a leader required great skill, not to mention alertness. Teddy's men practised until their skilful use of throttle, stick and rudder became second nature. Gunnery skills too were honed.

As the summer drew to a close, the political tension in Europe rose even further, with the surprise signing of the Nazi-Soviet non-aggression pact. The British government responded by reaffirming with France the agreement to come to Poland's assistance should she be invaded.

Invasion came in the early hours of 1 September. A group of Germans, dressed as Polish soldiers, launched a raid on one of their own radios stations. This staged 'invasion' of German territory was Hitler's excuse to his own people for the outbreak of the Second World War.

Polish resistance to the German blitzkreig was brave but in the end futile, with the Russians later invading from the east and creating a war on two fronts. The British Government was initially in shock but at length an ultimatum was sent to the Germans, demanding a withdrawal or Great Britain and her dominions would be in a state of war with Germany.

North Weald was put on war alert, the Hawker Hurricanes being dispersed around the airfield, while tents sprang up around dispersals, being used as temporary crew rooms. Meanwhile the operations room was linked up to the makeshift dispersals, with tannoy loudspeakers being set up to speed up the pilots' and ground-crews' reaction time to a possible scramble.

Both Nos. 56 and 151 Squadrons were ready should war come, as come surely it now must.

CHAPTER EIGHT

War – Early Incidents and a Tragic Loss

The morning of 3 September was bright and sunny but the dark spectre of hostilities was on the horizon. Britain stood on the verge of war after Hitler's forces had violated Poland's borders. At 1000 hours the BBC told its listeners to stand by for an announcement of 'national importance'. Squadron Leader Teddy Donaldson gathered his pilots in the officers' mess, where they listened intently, awaiting the news. All talk on the squadron, and across the nation, had been of war since Hitler's forces had invaded Britain's ally in the early hours of 1 September.

Every fifteen minutes listeners were told that the Prime Minister would make an announcement at 1115 hours, some fifteen minutes after the ultimatum to Adolf Hitler was due to run out. A musical selection from Princess Ida was followed by Parry Jones singing 'The Passionate Shepherd', all punctuated by a pre-recorded talk entitled 'Making the Most of Tinned Foods'. Then came the long-awaited announcement by Neville Chamberlain.

I am speaking to you from the Cabinet Room at No. 10 Downing Street. This morning the British Ambassador in Berlin handed the German government a final note stating that, unless we heard from them by eleven o'clock that they were prepared at once to withdraw their troops from Poland, a state of war would exist between us. I have to tell you now that no such undertaking has been received and that consequently this country is at war with Germany. Now may God bless you all. May He defend the right. It is the evil things that we shall be fighting against, brute force, bad faith, injustice, oppression and persecution and against them I am certain that the right will prevail.

As those assembled stood to the strains of the National Anthem, a thousand thoughts ran through their heads. Theirs was the first generation

53

to hear, first hand, a formal declaration of war. No one could have suspected that it would be six years of great sacrifice and hardship before peace once more reigned; not a single man ever considered that they might lose the war. Many of those gathered alongside their CO would be killed, wounded or taken as prisoners of war. Most flew with Teddy in the Battle of France, and later in the Battle of Britain, earning the eternal gratitude of a nation and the free world.

No sooner had the Prime Minister finished speaking than the sirens droned out their warning tone. The alarm turned out to be false, but all were suddenly aware that this war would be waged against civilians in the Home Counties as much as against soldiers, sailors and airmen.

Acutely aware that he had in his hands a historic document Teddy recorded the names of the combatants in the great battles to come, writing in bold letters across the pages of his Service log book:

**WAR DECLARED AGAINST GERMANY 11.00 HRS
ON 3RD SEPTEMBER BY THE RT. HON. NEVILLE
CHAMBERLAIN PRIME MINISTER OF GREAT BRITAIN**

MEMBERS OF No 151 (Fighter) SQUADRON

S/L Donaldson	F/O Walsh	F/O Atkinson (adjutant)
F/L Thompson	P/O Lovell	P/O Hamar
F/L Ives	F/O Allen	P/O Milne (sick)
P/O Todd-White	P/O Ward	P/O Herrick
P/O Newton	P/O Courtney	P/O Wright

Sgt Pilot Currant   Sgt Pilot Atkinson
Sgt Pilot Muirhead   Sgt Savill
Sgt Pilot Badger
Sgt Trice
Sgt Aslin

Posted 1st month APO Hancock
    1940 May 20th   F/O Blomeley
                     F/O Blair
                     F/O Forster
    1940 July   Sub Lieut Biggs
                     Midshipman Wightman

Teddy was later to annotate the entry with the fate of each of his pilots.

Since assuming command nearly a year earlier, Teddy had ensured that the pilots of No. 151 Squadron gained vital experience in flying the new Hawker Hurricane on squadron intercepts and co-operation missions with Bomber Command. However, like the rest of Fighter Command, they still lacked actual combat experience. Meanwhile the *Luftwaffe* had already tested many of their front-line aircraft against lesser machines in the Spanish Civil War. Combat experience was everything. Most pilots survived their first two or three dog-fights through a combination of flying skill and good fortune. Once they had been 'blooded' they stood a fair chance of surviving until fatigue set in or they could be rested, whichever happened first – it was a fine balance.

The standard patrol formation within the RAF was to fly in a 'vic' of three – 'vic' being the abbreviation for a 'V' for 'Victor' formation. Teddy, already an innovator in aerobatics formations, broke with the RAF's Fighter Manual and instead flew No. 151 Squadron in pairs, a system already favoured by the *Luftwaffe*, and one which was to serve his pilots well. Each pilot flew with a wingman protecting him from surprise attacks, allowing the leader to concentrate not on maintaining formation with his wingman, but on navigation and on searching out his enemy.

Teddy also taught his pilots how to work out the range of their target more accurately – a German bomber would fill the sights at 500 yards, a single-seater-fighter at 250 yards, the optimum firing distance and the range at which the Hurricane's guns were harmonized for maximum effect.

Despite the rather belated change in policy at the Air Ministry in favour of Fighter Command, Dowding still found he had to fight for resources. His request for bullet-proof canopies was initially denied, while armour plating to protect the pilot from the rear was still not available. Similarly, Fighter Command's landing strips were simply grassed fields. This meant that the pilots could easily fly from small private airfields if North Weald was temporarily put out of action by bombing, as they were used to grass fields. However, what would happen if German aircraft were able to take off from dry grass or from concrete airstrips, and the RAF's landing grounds were waterlogged? This problem had still not been resolved by the following summer which, fortunately for the RAF and the nation, proved to be one of the driest on record.

No. 151 Squadron flew its first war operation on 4 September but without making contact with the enemy. On their first patrol over the Thames Estuary two days later it became involved in what was to become known as the Battle of Barking Creek.

The tragedy of 6 September involved a series of minor errors each of which had a knock-on effect, resulting in the controllers from neighbouring Nos. 11 and 12 Groups vectoring their aircraft on each other. The events began innocently enough with a searchlight crew reporting a

possible raid to the south of Colchester. No. 11 Group was informed and
Uxbridge scrambled Teddy's No. 151 Squadron.

Teddy led the squadron on the intercept, being directed to their target
by No. 11 Group controllers. They were followed by two Hurricanes of
No. 56 Squadron. Meanwhile, anti-aircraft gunners along the Thames
Estuary began to open fire almost indiscriminately, adding to the con-
fusion, while both Debden and Duxford sent fighters up and vectored
them on each other. Spitfires of No. 74 Squadron were scrambled from
Hornchurch, and vectored not onto the original 'bogey' but onto the
North Weald Hurricanes. No. 74 Squadron pilots Pilot Officers John
Freeborn and Paddy Byrne made contact with the Hurricanes and
radioed for confirmation, upon which they were given the order to carry
out an attack. The resulting pass left two Hurricanes destroyed with Pilot
Officers Montague Hutton-Harrop (L1985) killed and Frank Rose
(L1980) forced to crash land.

On 7 September, Group Captain M. B. Frew became Station
Commander at North Weald. Frew's first task was to file a report
outlining the circumstances behind the previous day's disaster.

A court of enquiry found that Freeborn and Byrne had acted within
their orders and were not to blame for the incident. But the lessons had
to be learned if Fighter Command were to stand any hope of defending
the country against the threat of the *Luftwaffe*.

In October, No. 56 Squadron moved from North Weald to Martlesham
Heath, a detachment remaining at their former station, which they
shared with No. 151 Squadron and No. 604 Squadron's Bristol
Blenheims. In January No. 604 Squadron would be replaced by No. 25
Squadron who also flew the slow twin-engined aircraft.

During the autumn of 1939 No. 151 Squadron was mainly employed
in the day-fighter role in what Teddy called 'the Battle of the Home
Counties'. Unlike the British Army, who were engaged in the 'Phoney
War', the Royal Navy and the RAF's Bomber and Fighter Commands
were already seeing action over both Britain and the Channel shipping
lanes. There were minor raids and the first German bomber was shot
down over British soil by Spitfires of Nos. 602 and 603 Squadrons on
29 November, but this was something of an isolated incident.

Teddy spent the time sharpening the squadron's combat techniques
and formation flying skills, establishing an unofficial display team which
included Pilot Officer Ward and Sergeant Pilot Badger.

With heavy snow heralding in the New Year, there was little flying
and the Hurricanes remained idle, the aerodrome being covered by a
blanket of white, criss-crossed by hand-cleared trails linking the network
of buildings, hangars and workshops. As soon as he was able, Teddy had
the grass landing strip cleared and commenced flying with a renewed
sense of urgency.

The convoy patrols of late 1939 continued into the following year but no enemy aircraft were seen. Despite this, convoy patrols were fraught with danger. Once the squadron had sighted the convoy they would approach to a safe distance before firing a combination of flares which corresponded with the colours of the day. Frequently, sailors fired regardless at anything that flew too close, their training in aircraft recognition often being very poor. Later in the war the Channel convoys carried an RAF squadron leader to act as a liaison; nevertheless, losses to 'friendly fire' continued to occur.

The squadron suffered its first casualty of the war on 2 April 1940. The incident did not involve contact with the enemy but was probably due to a mechanical failure. Pilot Officer Henry Fenton's Hurricane was seen to crash into the sea while on a convoy patrol. His body was never found. As there was insufficient room in the cockpit for an inflatable raft, all the pilots had was a dull green or sea-coloured life-jacket, known as a Mae West, which had to be inflated after they hit the water. Donaldson would later file a report with recommendations on the inflating procedure for the Mae West, following his own baling out into the Channel during the Battle of Britain.

In early April Teddy received a message from his elder brother, Squadron Leader John Willie 'Baldy' Donaldson (known to the family as 'Jack' but to his squadron as 'Baldy'), informing him of his squadron's imminent move overseas, the rumour appearing in the local press of a posting to the Near East. Baldy had earlier been awarded the Air Force Cross (AFC), the first of nine gallantry awards won by the three Donaldson brothers (awarded for gallantry in 1939, but not promulgated until July 1940).

No. 263 Squadron, which had been formed in September 1918 and disbanded in May 1919, was re-formed in the fighter role at Filton on 2 October 1939 equipped with Gloster Gladiators. Baldy Donaldson had been give command of No. 263 (Fighter) Squadron on its resurrection when its prime responsibility was the defence of Bristol. Significantly, its old-fashioned biplanes formed the only front-line Gladiator squadron then based in the UK.

On 8 April 1940, Germany punctuated the 'Phoney War' invading Norway and Denmark to protect their supplies of iron ore, two-thirds of which came from Norway and Sweden. The key ports and airfields were soon in enemy hands. It was decided that the British and French would send an expeditionary force to stem the tide.

Within twelve hours of the invasion, an urgent signal had been sent to No. 263 Squadron ordering them to be brought up to operational strength. The choice of a Gladiator squadron as air support was based on the fact that the biplanes could land successfully on the frozen lakes. The Finns had already been fighting the Russians for several months prior to the squadron's deployment, the RAF shipping out a number of Gloster Gladiators which had been flown operationally with some success. The fact that there was a ready supply of spares and that the Gladiators were a match for the local flying conditions had swung the decision in favour of No. 263 Squadron's out-dated aircraft.

Allied landings were made at Namsos and Aandalsnes, with air support being provided by the eighteen Gloster Gladiators of Baldy's squadron. Flying off the deck of HMS *Glorious* on the afternoon of 24 April, the biplanes made the 180-mile flight through heavy snow-storms to a prepared landing ground on the frozen Lake Lesjaskog in Oppland in central southern Norway. The squadron took off in two flights, one at 1500 hours, the second thirty minutes later, each being escorted to the lake by a Fleet Air Arm Skua for navigation. All the aircraft had landed safely on the lake by 1800 hours. Within half an hour of landing, there was what turned out to be a false alarm. However, all eighteen aircraft had been refuelled and were ready to take off. Later, at 2130 hours, a pair of aircraft were intercepted by two of the squadron's Gladiators, although a third could not be started. They carried Norwegian markings but later speculation grew that they had in fact been flown by Germans. Certainly the enemy appeared to know the squadron's location by early the following morning.

That night, Baldy Donaldson had the Gladiators dispersed around the perimeter of the frozen lake, taking what cover they could from the surrounding woodland. Four Gladiators were arranged at intervals along the 700-yard cleared runway. The pilots themselves stood guard over their 'ships'.

The mission was, however, pretty much doomed from the beginning. The squadron was sent to Norway to provide air support for ground troops and to act as spotters for the artillery. However, the rapid collapse of the British Expeditionary Force's position and prevailing conditions meant that they were a lost cause before a single Gladiator had landed on the ice.

The mission did not begin well. It transpired that the ice at one end of the runway was beginning to melt and that the preparations to receive the Gladiators had already been seen by the enemy. Moreover, not only did the temporary airbase on Lake Lesjaskog have no air defences, but it also did not have any form of advance warning system of incoming raids. This meant that the only way of protecting the makeshift airstrip would be to mount standing patrols.

There were technical problems, too. There was no acid for the starter trolley batteries which meant that the Gladiators could only be started up using their internal batteries. Furthermore, with no fuel bowsers, the pilots and ground crew, assisted by a handful of Norwegians, had to refuel the aircraft manually using 4-gallon tins dragged across the ice on a sleigh. This was a highly dangerous and laborious procedure under combat conditions, made more difficult by the fact that there was no ground echelon; after the first strafing of the landing strip when most of the locals disappeared, the pilots would have to refuel and maintain each other's aircraft between sorties. They only had one qualified armourer, and he was responsible for rearming seventy-two Browning machine-guns as well as ensuring that they did not freeze up or jam as soon as they were fired. Sergeant Pilot E. F. W. Russell was to be recognized for his gallantry in rearming the squadron's Gladiators under intense bombing and machine-gun fire.

Baldy gave orders that from 0300 hours until dusk one section should be on patrol over the base at 6,000 ft providing aircover. Each patrol would be of two hours' duration, with the relief taking place in the air. Two more sections were on the ice at readiness, while the forth section would be on fifteen minutes' standby.

Early on the morning of the first day, 25 April, and after a severe overnight frost, two Gladiators eventually took off at 0445 hours for the squadron's first patrol over the lake. Within fifteen minutes, a Heinkel He 115 appeared. It was immediately attacked and destroyed. Meanwhile a Heinkel He 111 pilot, seeing the patrol preoccupied elsewhere, dropped a stick of bombs on the lake. This initial attack destroyed four Gladiators and injured three pilots, including Donaldson, who suffered from concussion and Pilot Officer Purdy who received facial burns. The attacker was one of a pair from Stab/LG1, which reported seeing fifteen biplanes and several other aircraft on the ground.

Flight Lieutenant 'Milly' Mills took off at about 0900 hours, giving cover for six more Gladiators to be launched into the air. He sighted a formation of six heading for the landing strip; he quickly engaged the intruders, destroying one enemy aircraft and preventing the remainder from making a bombing run.

Another of the squadron's aircraft was lost during Sergeant Forrest's standing patrol at 1100 hours after his Gladiator had suffered engine failure. An hour later, Pilot Officer McNamara destroyed a Heinkel He 111 which crashed near the lake.

At Lesjaskog four more frozen Gladiators were destroyed by air attack at 1305 hours, but two others then got off, flown by a recovering Baldy and Flight Lieutenant Mills. Over the next two and a half hours these two engaged in six major combats within full view of the lake, fighting off raid after raid. First, at 1400 hours, both pilots attacked a Heinkel He 111 of Stab/LG1 and brought it down to crash land south of Vinstra, near Dombås. The crew set fire to the aircraft, in which the badly injured wireless operator had shot himself. The survivors were subsequently captured, and the wreckage of this bomber was later inspected by British troops.

Both pilots then attacked another Heinkel, which was damaged, but made it back to Fornebu, just outside Oslo, with two wounded aboard. Baldy quickly turned his attention to a formation of three more Heinkel He 111s making a head-on attack, sending them all in different directions.

Baldy and Mills were still in the air at 1445 hours. They sighted two Heinkel He 111s, one approaching the lake from the west, the other from the east. Both were fended off. With little fuel remaining Mills landed his Gladiator while Baldy gave him cover. Baldy spotted four Junkers Ju 88s which he engaged with ammunition remaining in only one of his four machine-guns. Just at the crucial moment he had to switch to his reserve tanks. The advantage was lost and he was forced to fight for his life, using every move he could to put the enemy to flight. The combat lasted ten minutes but saw the enemy turn and run in the face of Baldy's dogged determination. In the meantime Mills had landed and taken off almost in the same manoeuvre, taking on a second Junkers Ju 88 formation lining up to bomb the Gladiators on the lake. He engaged seven Junkers Ju 88s but without claiming a 'kill'. He did, however, break up the formation before eventually having to land short of both fuel and ammunition. As he was examining his Gladiator for damage, a formation of Heinkel bombers appeared and destroyed it. Mills could only look on but he had sacrificed his aircraft to protect the squadron's base. By this time, the squadron had lost ten aircraft.

The Germans raided the squadron almost continuously until about 2000 hours. During the mêlée two more Gladiators froze on the ice and could not be brought into action.

By nightfall only five Gladiators remained; they had been withdrawn from Lesjaskog and flown north to another temporary landing ground which had been prepared at Setnesmoen, just outside Aandalsnes. From here Baldy was scrambled to destroy a Heinkel He 111 which was lining up to bomb a steamer near Aandalsnes. This aircraft was believed to have been shot down into a ravine, but it was later discovered that the badly damaged bomber had almost made it back to Fornebu before the engines failed and the crew baled out.

A further Gladiator was lost on the following day when Pilot Officer Craig-Adams's engine seized and he was forced to take to his parachute.

More enemy aircraft fell to the guns of No. 263 Squadron, bringing their tally to six enemy aircraft destroyed and eight probably destroyed. The squadron's remaining Gladiators had to be destroyed before the pilots and ground crew were withdrawn, later embarking on the cargo ship *Delius*. The danger was, however, far from over and the men spent six hours under nearly continuous attack from German dive-bombers.

The squadron's exploits were reported in the newspapers on 9 May, drawing on a description of the events given to the House of Commons by Sir Samuel Hoare, Secretary of State for Air. He explained that on one day no less than forty sorties were flown and thirty-seven enemy aircraft engaged. Meanwhile between eighty and ninety bombers had attacked the makeshift aerodrome with 132 craters counted. Combat victories were recorded as fourteen destroyed and fifteen unconfirmed destroyed, while officially only six enemy aircraft were credited as having been destroyed, with a further eight remaining unconfirmed destroyed. Remarkably, although the squadron had lost all its eighteen Gloster Gladiators, none had actually been shot down in combat.

In recognition of the courage displayed during these actions, a number of gallantry awards were made to Squadron Leader J. W. Donaldson and his fellow pilots. These were announced in the *London Gazette* of 10 May 1940. John Willie, as Squadron CO, was awarded the Distinguished Service Order (DSO), while three of his pilots were awarded the Distinguished Flying Cross (DFC): Flight Lieutenant Randolph Stuart Mills, the A Flight Commander, and Pilot Officers Sidney Robert McNamara and Philip Hannah Purdy. In addition, Sergeant Pilot Ernest Russell was awarded the Military Medal (MM).

No. 263 Squadron was quickly re-equipped at Turnhouse in Scotland, and sent back to Norway on 14 May in order to give air cover for the British forces at Narvik in the north. Baldy Donaldson and his pilots embarked on HMS *Furious* on the River Forth while Fleet Air Arm pilots flew their eighteen replacement Gladiators Mark IIs onto the carrier. This time they would be supported by ground staff and kept well supplied with fuel, ammunition and spares, the main ground echelon sailing in the SS *Chroby*, while seven replacement pilots would join them via the SS *Sobriesti*.

On 21 May two sections of the squadron's Gladiators took off from the *Furious* for their temporary base at Bardufoss to the north of Narvik; they were each led by a Swordfish. One section, faced with deteriorating visibility, managed to return to the carrier and land safely. The Swordfish of the other section got lost in heavy sleet and flew into a mountainside at Soreisa, followed instantly by two Gladiators. Pilot Officer Walter Philip Richards was killed, while Flight Lieutenant Mills, although critically wounded, survived, eventually to return to England on the merchant vessel *Arandora Star*.

The following day eight Gladiators took off from the deck of HMS *Furious* and managed to reach the landing strip at Bardufoss. Operations began on 23 May when the remaining Gladiators arrived from the *Furious*. This brought the squadron's strength up to fourteen serviceable aircraft, one of which was lost when Sergeant Pilot Whall engaged a Dornier Do 17, which he destroyed; he was, however, forced to abandon his own aircraft when he ran out of fuel. Pilot Officer Craig-Adams was killed in action on his first sortie. It is not clear whether he was shot down by return fire from the Heinkel He 111 he destroyed, or whether the two aircraft collided during the mêlée. A total of fifty-four sorties was flown during this first day of operations.

The squadron could only add one Heinkel He 111 to their tally on 24 May, a second being claimed as damaged, while three Junkers Ju 90s fell to their guns on the following day.

On 26 May No. 263 Squadron was in action once more, with seven enemy aircraft falling to their guns and a further two being damaged. One pilot, Flying Officer Riley, was wounded by return fire from the Heinkel He 111 he claimed as a shared 'kill'. Flight Lieutenant Caesar Hull and Lieutenant Lydekker, a Fleet Air Arm pilot of No. 802 Squadron seconded to replace the wounded Pilot Officer Wyatt-Smith, were both wounded on 27 May while destroying two Junkers Ju 87s. A Heinkel He 111 was damaged on the following day, after which there was a dramatic decrease in activity until 2 June when the evacuation of Norway began.

Three Heinkel He 111s, out of a formation of fifteen, were destroyed by Flight Lieutenant Williams and Sergeant Kitchener, the remainder being dispersed. The pair's sortie was not yet over and they broke up a formation of Dornier Do 17s before taking on and destroying a Junkers Ju 87, although a second escaped. One further Heinkel He 111 was attacked but the results were inconclusive.

In the early afternoon of 2 June, Pilot Officer Wilkie was killed while attacking a pair of Junkers Ju 88s with Pilot Officer Jacobsen. During what was to be 263's last engagement with the enemy in Norway, Jacobsen went on to fight a titanic single-handed struggle among the Arctic mountains between the Norwegian coast and the Swedish border. Finding himself up against vastly superior numbers, constantly subjected to head-on attacks and occasionally surrounded by massive enemy formations, Jacobsen destroyed three Heinkel He 111s, probably destroyed a Junkers Ju 88 and possibly many more that were never found in that hostile terrain. By evasive tactics and perilously low flying, with his ammunition exhausted and fuel almost gone, he managed to make it back to base. Baldy Donaldson recommended the young pilot officer for an immediate DFC although, if the precedent set by the award of a Victoria Cross (VC) to Major William Barker for his marathon single-handed air battle over France in October 1918 had been followed, he might well have received the highest honour for valour in war.

Together with the Hurricanes of No. 46 Squadron, RAF fighters destroyed forty-seven enemy aircraft during the second Norwegian campaign, thirty-six of which were believed to have fallen to the guns of the Gloster Gladiators. Of perhaps even greater significance was that the number of enemy aircraft officially credited as being destroyed by No. 263 Squadron during both its visits to Norway was fifty, against which only two Gladiators were shot down in air combat and two pilots killed in action throughout the entire campaign.

The losses in France meant that the Allies' position in Norway became untenable. No. 263 Squadron was ordered to leave and the ten remaining serviceable Gladiators successfully landed on the deck of HMS *Glorious* on 8 June. All of 263's RAF pilots that day made their first ever deck-landings in order to save their aircraft. Orders were given to destroy the Hurricanes of No. 46 Squadron. The pilots were reluctant to wreck perfectly serviceable aircraft and asked to be allowed to try to save their Hurricanes by also making a deck landing on the carrier, something that had never been done before. Without arrester hooks to catch them on landing, the pilots devised the idea of suspending a sandbag below the tail for added drag. All landed successfully.

During the return voyage, HMS *Glorious* and her escort of two destroyers were cornered and sunk by the German battle cruisers *Scharnhorst* and *Gneisenau*. She went down with the loss of most of her crew, along with the ten pilots of No. 263 Squadron. The loss of life included 1,474 Royal Navy crew and forty-nine RAF men, qualifying the incident as one of the worst naval disasters of the Second World War.

There were only thirty-nine survivors, including just two pilots from No. 46 Squadron, including its OC, Squadron Leader 'Bing' Cross. Scrambling aboard a Carley float together with the thirty-seven others, the two airmen drifted for three days and two nights before being rescued by the Norwegian trawler SS *Borgund* and taken to the Faeroes. From there they were transferred to Rosyth aboard HMS *Veteran*. Bing Cross later rose to become Air Chief Marshal Sir Kenneth Cross KCB CBE DSO DFC.

John Willie died leaving a widow, Sheila (née Atchley) and their 11-month-old son, Antony, who were living with the indomitable Gwendoline Donaldson at Selsey.

Following the squadron's second campaign in Norway, four more gallantry awards were made, DFCs being awarded to Flight Lieutenant Caesar Barrand Hull, Flying Officers Alvin Thomas Williams and Herman Francis Grante-Ede, and the heroic Pilot Officer Louis Reginald Jacobsen.

On reflection, it was not so much a case of all the decorations awarded during the two Norwegian campaigns honouring No. 263 Squadron, but more a matter of the squadron, pilots and ground crew, honouring the awards.

Of all the 263 Squadron pilots who had been decorated for their air actions over Norway, only the two flight commanders, Milly Mills and Caesar Hull, escaped death with the sinking of HMS *Glorious*. Mills returned to England with the ground echelons and a handful of other pilots; he left the RAF in 1956 as a wing commander, retaining the rank of Group Captain. Hull was evacuated back to the UK in a Sunderland flying boat; he was subsequently killed in the Battle of Britain when, as CO of No. 43 Squadron, his Hurricane was shot down on 7 September 1940 whilst attacking German bombers as they ran up to bomb London's Dockland.

No matter how one measures the success of a squadron in action, the two campaigns fought by the pilots of No. 263 (Fighter) Squadron in Norway from April to June 1940 probably rank amongst the greatest epics in the history of the RAF. Baldy Donaldson had been an inspirational leader. Widely recognised as a truly outstanding pilot, his skill and gallantry had set an example worthy of the highest traditions of the Service.

John Willie was later awarded the Air Force Cross, the award being announced in the Supplement to the *London Gazette* of 11 July 1940.

Teddy was immensely proud of his brother and his death hit him hard. It was a sombre Teddy who added the press notification of his brother's death into his 'line book'. But there was no time to grieve, he had a responsibility to his own pilots.

CHAPTER NINE

Blitzkrieg on France

S ince the outbreak of the war it had been clear that both France and
Britain would be targets for subjugation by Germany. Both, if
conquered, would bring with them vital trading monopolies and
extensive colonies. The strategic planners in Bomber Command had
decided that German targets, including those in the Ruhr, the industrial
heartland of the country, could be reached by short-range bombers
based in France. These battle squadrons and the ground troops would
be given air cover by the faster single-seater Hawker Hurricane fighters.
Initially it had been decided that no Spitfires would serve in France; they
would be reserved for Home Defence.

The structure of the RAF in France comprised the Advanced Air
Striking Force (AASF) and the Air Component of the British
Expeditionary Force (BEF). The AASF, commanded by Air Vice-Marshal
P.H.L. Playfair at Reims, originally consisted of ten Blenheim and Battle
light-bomber squadrons, while the Air Component, under Air Vice-
Marshal C.H. Blount, included the four Hurricane squadrons stationed
on the Channel coast. Both came under the command of Air Marshal
'Ugly' Barrett as Commander-in-Chief (C-in-C) British Air Forces in
France (BAFF).

Initially the RAF squadrons were confined to flying within French
airspace owing to Belgian and Dutch neutrality. And while the Hawker
Hurricanes were to prove nimble fighters, the Fairey Battles were hopelessly slow and lacked either defensive firepower or a viable payload.
This was clear from the out-set. On 30 September 1939 a formation of five
Battles had been engaged by the enemy, but only one survived the brief
combat. The early lessons of this contact with the enemy were not
learned and the pilots and aircrew of the Battle squadrons were to be
sacrificed in the vain hope of slowing the German advance.

The so-called 'Phoney War' was to end in dramatic style with
Hitler's forces being deployed rapidly in a Blitzkrieg, preventing
British and French troops from entering the Low Countries, from where
they might have threatened Germany's borders; despite the fact that a
copy of the German plan of attack had fallen into the Allies' hands as

early as 10 January 1940 following the crash of a German light plane carrying two officers who had a copy of the operational plans in their possession.

Like the Von Schlieffen Plan in August 1914, the battle plan devised by Eric von Manstein and Heinz Guderian required the element of surprise if it was to succeed with the minimum cost to the *Wehrmacht*. It would involve a race to cross the Ardennes Forest and reach and bridge the River Meuse at Sedan before the British and French could react. Sedan, they had calculated, marked the weakest point along the French front, being the hinge between the 2nd and 9th French Armies.

At 0300 hours on 10 May Adolf Hitler arrived at his bunker near Aachen, from where he was to direct operation *Fall Gelb* ('yellow case'). An hour later German forces began operation *Sichelschnitt* ('sickle stroke'), the surprise assault against Holland, Luxembourg, Belgium and France. Thirty minutes later, in accordance with the battle plan, fleets of *Luftwaffe* bombers and fighters took off to attack their designated targets, including Allied airfields, railway junctions and other strategic targets.

During the afternoon, thirty-two British Battle light-bombers of the AASF went on the offensive and attacked German columns in an attempt to staunch the flow of their advance through Luxembourg. Thirteen were shot down and the remainder damaged, eleven beyond repair.

This was to be the first real test of the RAF's new fighter. And what a test it would be with 100 Hawker Hurricanes of the AASF and Air Component facing odds of ten to one. Amazingly the RAF fighters accounted for half their own number on the first day of the blitzkrieg, loosing less than ten aircraft, three pilots being wounded. For the time being at least the AASF would hold out but they would soon desperately need help, with replacement pilots, and later whole squadrons, rushed to France to support them at a cost to Home Defence.

Half a dozen Hurricane squadrons had been sent to France to strengthen the Allied air forces in northern Europe. They were to face the might of the *Luftwaffe* which had nearly 1,000 Messerschmitt Bf 109s alone. Teddy Donaldson's No. 151 Squadron, however, was to remain in the UK, much to his disappointment, but his Hurricanes were scrambled on an interception during the day, with a possible raider being reported off the coast. Teddy's log book hid his frustration and read simply: 'Missed enemy.'

Neville Chamberlain's government was facing a crisis. The Norwegian campaign was on the point of collapse, while the Allies' defensive lines in north-western Europe were being swept away as German armoured units advanced through the Ardennes outflanking the Marginot Line on the French-German border. The blitzkrieg that had claimed Poland, Denmark and Norway would lead to the loss of

Luxembourg before the end of the day and was already heading through the Low Countries and France.

Leopold Amery, leading the attack on the Prime Minister in the House of Commons, quoted the great defender of Parliament, Cromwell: 'Depart I say, and let us have done with you. In the name of God, go!' Chamberlain was shaken. He began to consider the need to form a government that incorporated both Labour and Conservative members for the duration of the war. Despite Churchill's acceptance of blame as First Lord of the Admiralty for the Norway débâcle and his culpability in the Gallipoli Campaign a quarter of a century earlier, he was summoned to Buckingham Palace at six o'clock that evening and asked to form a government. By midnight Prime Minister Churchill had formed his coalition government.

The RAF continued to take the war to the enemy in the hope of halting the Germans and giving the men of the BEF some respite.

On 11 May, eight more Battles attacked German columns entering Luxembourg in what was to prove a suicidal attack. Seven were shot down. Three more Battles were lost around St Vith, and another at Ecury-sur-Coole. Hurricane squadrons meanwhile accounted for around thirty-five enemy aircraft for the loss of fifteen of their own fighters, with two pilots killed and one wounded.

The RAF's losses mounted sharply on 12 May when only one out five Battles returned to base after another disastrous bombing raid on vital bridges. Even worse, seventeen out of thirty-three Blenheim bombers were shot down while attacking bridges, roads and a German column near Maastricht, close to the Dutch-Belgian border. Significantly during the day General Erwin Rommel's 7th Panzer Division reached the Meuse River in France.

It was a frustrated Teddy who learned of the previous day's events. He was eager to get his squadron into action; this was what they had trained for. Early on the morning of 13 May No. 151 Squadron's Blue Section, consisting of Flight Lieutenant Ives, Flying Officer Ward and Sergeant Atkinson, took off from North Weald for Martlesham Heath ready to fly a dawn patrol off the Hook of Holland. The Hurricanes encountered a 'vic' of Blenheim IVs and patrolled alongside them for a while, giving air cover for a cruiser and four destroyers below. Later during the patrol the pilots observed around fifteen burnt-out Junkers Ju 52s on an aerodrome to the south-west of the Hook, a rare sight of German losses. On their return there were sorry tales of the full extent of the enemy's advances.

The Battle of France took its first toll on the squadron on this day when they lost the first of a number of trained operational pilots on second-ment to combat-depleted units. Flying Officer Ken Newton and Pilot Officers 'Buck' Courtney and David Blomeley were all sent to reinforce

No. 607 Squadron in France, only to return to England on 20 May. When they landed it was discovered that their Hurricanes were so badly shot up that they were immediately removed from service. Another pilot, Flying Officer Leonid Ereminsky, landed at Merville on secondment to No. 615 Squadron. His first real baptism of fire came on 16 May when he was posted to No. 87 Squadron, then serving with the Air Component of the BEF in France. Five days and many bitter actions later he withdrew to England with the survivors, and on 4 June rejoined No. 151 Squadron at Martlesham Heath.

Teddy must have been dismayed to see four of his finest pilots leave the Squadron. He had spent months binding the men into a tight fighting force and each of them would have followed Teddy to hell and back. They had expected to fight, and if necessary to die together.

Teddy later recalled that in his own darkest hours he gained tremendous inspiration from listening to the words of Prime Minister Winston Churchill. On the evening of 13 May Churchill's speech to Parliament was broadcast to the nation. In it he set out his stall:

> In this crisis I think I may be pardoned if I do not address the House at any length today, and I hope that any of my friends and colleagues or former colleagues who are affected by the political reconstruction will make all allowances for any lack of ceremony with which it has been necessary to act.
>
> I say to the House as I said to ministers who have joined this government, I have nothing to offer but blood, toil, tears, and sweat. We have before us an ordeal of the most grievous kind. We have before us many, many months of struggle and suffering.
>
> You ask, what is our policy? I say it is to wage war by land, sea, and air. War with all our might and with all the strength God has given us, and to wage war against a monstrous tyranny never surpassed in the dark and lamentable catalogue of human crime. That is our policy.
>
> You ask, what is our aim? I can answer in one word. It is victory. Victory at all costs – victory in spite of all terrors – victory, however long and hard the road may be, for without victory there is no survival.
>
> Let that be realized. No survival for the British Empire, no survival for all that the British Empire has stood for, no survival for the urge, the impulse of the ages, that mankind shall move forward toward his goal.

The pace of the war quickened over the next few days. On 14 May, while German aircraft were bombing Rotterdam, killing 30,000 civilians, sixty-three Battles and eight Blenheims raided German pontoon bridges crossing the Meuse River. Once again the RAF suffered a terrible casualty rate, with thirty-two Battles being shot down in an hour, while only three Blenheims returned.

Combats were not confined to the skies over France; a number of raiders were also engaged over the Channel. Jack Hamar was in combat over Dover, sighting at least a dozen enemy aircraft flying at about 10,000–12,000 ft. The whole action took place between 1515 and 1520 hours, five minutes of frantic combat followed by calm. For Jack and the other pilots it must have seemed quite surreal.

As always Jack was acting as Red Two, although on this occasion Flying Officer Milne led the squadron. As Red Two it was Jack's job to keep the German fighters off his leader's tail. Despite this Jack was still able to get a crack at the enemy to good effect. The combat report (Form F) was filled in by Jack himself, as is evident from the handwriting.

At 1500 hours on the 14.5.40 the Squadron was ordered off from Rochford to intercept E/A [enemy aircraft] south of Dover. At approx. 1520 hours a bunch of Me109s were sighted about 5,000 ft. above our formation. I was Flying Red 2 in the formation. As it looked as though the E/A were about to attack us Milne leader immediately ordered our defensive line astern tactics. As we turned sharply to port 2 Me 109s were seen diving to attack the lead aircraft of our formation. Milne leader attacked the leading Me 109 + I attacked the second. I turned inside the E/A which had pulled up into a steep left hand climbing turn. I closed rapidly + opened fire at about 250 yards with a 45 degree deflection shot. The E/A seemed to falter + straightened out into a dive + I placed myself dead astern at about 50 yards + opened fire close to almost no distance. I saw a large explosion just in front of the pilot + a large amount of white smoke poured from the E/A which was by this time diving steeply. I was then forced to break away quickly due to fire from rear + lost sight of E/A therefore did not see it crash. This action was also seen by F/O Forster of 151 Squadron.

I fired two bursts of about six seconds each at E/A. I turned to base to refuel and rearm.

Flying Officer Anthony Douglas 'Bunny' Forster had destroyed a total of four enemy aircraft while in France with No. 607 Squadron, and two with No. 151, for which he was subsequently awarded the DFC.

Fighter pilots rarely had time to watch their victims crash, falling several thousand feet or limping through cloud before hitting the ground or plunging into the English Channel. Any pilot who maintained a straight and level course for more than a few seconds in a combat zone was liable to find an assailant on his tail. In these circumstances, pilots had to spend 90 per cent of their time watching what was behind them, not in front.

The south coast was under threat of raids for most of 15 May, and No. 151 Squadron was placed on a state of fifteen minutes' readiness from 1300 hours; it remained at this state until dusk when it was stood down for the night. Two new Rotol Hurricanes were collected from North Weald by pilots from A Flight. This meant that the squadron now had twelve available for air operations if required.

Despite heavy losses over the previous five days (No. 2 Group lost a further six Blenheims destroyed and two more damaged beyond repair), the War Cabinet, at its meeting on 15 May, gave Bomber Command permission to bomb the Ruhr area of Germany, east of the Rhine. The badly mauled squadrons of the AASF were to spend the next few days relocating.

Meanwhile, the French premier, Paul Reynaud, now facing defeat, asked the British prime minister for all the troops and planes he could make available. Recognizing that the war would be a lengthy one, Churchill sent US President Roosevelt a telegram asking to buy moth-balled ships, aircraft and munitions.

Early the following morning, 16 May, Churchill took a great personal risk and flew to Belgium where the French General Gamelin, who had already ordered a retreat of his forces from Belgium, announced that the ground battle was lost. In response, Churchill agreed to provide an extra ten fighter squadrons to help France, with six operating out of Kent. One of these was to be No. 151 Squadron, flying from Manston. Churchill flew back to Britain that evening, dejected by the situation on the continent, and the apparent collapse of the French army, only months earlier recognized as the strongest in the world.

At 1230 hours the station scramble bell was rung and Blue Section, who were on 'Readiness', were given the order to scramble. Flight Lieutenant Ives and his section raced to their Hawker Hurricanes and took off to make an interception of the unidentified aircraft. Teddy was leading, as he was to do on nearly every mission the squadron flew for the next three months. Having sighted the bombers, Teddy searched the sky for any signs of fighter cover, aware that the bombers might be bait. Having placed his section in the best possible position to strike, he led them in to the attack. As they dived ever closer, Teddy suddenly recognized the outlines as Blenheims. 'Break! Break!' he screamed over the radio. 'Don't fire! Don't fire!' As he and the remainder of the squadron peeled away, he looked on in horror as two Spitfires took their place with guns blazing, tearing into the Blenheim formation. The fighters broke off their engagement and the formation limped on.

Partly in response to the second incident of misidentification of friendly aircraft, Teddy had all his pilots work on their aircraft recognition, while he had red, white and blue roundels painted onto the undersides of their wings to aid recognition of his own squadron's aircraft from below.

The squadron's diary records its composition since the loss of a number of pilots to squadrons in France:

Red	S/Ldr. Donaldson	P/O Hamar	Sgt. Badger
Yellow	Fl/Lt Ironside	F/O Allen	P/O Bushell
Blue	Fl/Lt Ives	P/O Wright	Sgt. Atkinson
Green	F/O Ward	F/O Milne	Sgt. Trice

Non combat trained pilots:	F O Atkinson	P O Pettigrew
	Sgt Aslin	Sgt Seabourne.

However, late on 16 May an order arrived at No. 151 Squadron posting several of its pilots away to join No. 87 Squadron at Lille-Seclin. That squadron had taken the brunt of much of the action thus far and had lost two pilots killed and another two wounded. Those posted were Flying Officer J. H. Allen (killed following air operations near Dunkirk), Sergeant A. N. Trice (killed later the same day while in combat with Bf 109s), Flight Sergeant I. J. Badger and Flying Officer D.W. Ward. This brought the total of operational pilots lost to combat-depleted squadrons to nine. Both Badger and Ward were taken onto the strength of No. 87 Squadron and served with them throughout the Battle of France and later the Battle of Britain.

No. 151 Squadron was thus reduced to three sections with only nine pilots. In order to make up the squadron, Aslin flew with Red Section, Milne with Yellow, while Green Section ceased to exist. Teddy would put the replacement pilots through an intensive training programme in order to bring them up to operational status.

No. 87 Squadron's Diary records events from their perspective.

Six aircraft and pilots arrived early one morning from Amiens. No spare pilots available so the ferry pilots, who had no definite orders, elected to stay. Some were squadron pilots, some straight from FTS and some with no previous experience on Hurricanes. Names not recorded, but only two returned to the UK. They went into action almost immediately and joined the mass patrols carried out by 87 and 504 Squadrons. It is safe to say they achieved some success before they themselves went missing.

As the AASF and Air Component had been under great pressure since 10 May, severely mauling the *Luftwaffe* but sustaining losses themselves and becoming badly under strength, Air Chief Marshal Dowding decided, after Churchill's pronouncement, to deploy elements of No. 11

Group to France, including Nos 17, 32, and 151 Squadrons, along with units composed of half of Nos 56/213, 25/111, and 145/601 Squadrons, on daily detachments. They would operate from their French bases up until noon, before flying back to the UK after being relieved by three other squadrons, in order to give the pilots some chance to rest and also to prevent whole squadrons from being wiped out.

Shortly before dawn on 17 May, No. 151 Squadron took off from Martlesham in Suffolk and reported to the coastal airfield at Manston in Kent, the closest RAF station to continental Europe, where their CO received his orders. Teddy recalled that on landing he was told: 'It's France for you. Report to Abbeville.'

It was the news the whole squadron, all eager for action, had wanted to hear for months. But there was a tinge of disappointment that they would not go as a whole unit, with so many pilots having already gone to France as replacements to Nos. 615, 607, and 87 Squadrons.

As Teddy climbed into his Hurricane, his old friend from No. 1 Squadron, Wing Commander McEvoy, now a staff officer, climbed up onto the wing root. Gripping Teddy's shoulder hard he said; 'I have every faith in you Teddy. With pilots like you I've every confidence in the future. Good luck!'

The Squadron Diary recorded the names of the pilots who accompanied Teddy that fateful day:

The following pilots took off and flew to Abbeville aerodrome.
Red Section.   S/Ldr. Donaldson P/O Hamar Sgt. Aslin
Yellow Section.   F/Lt. Ironside F/O Milne P/O Bushell
Blue Section.   F/Lt. Ives P/O Wright Sgt. Atkinson

Red, Blue, and Yellow Sections took off from Manston at 0730 hours, proceeded to Abbeville, near the Somme Estuary, and arrived some forty-five minutes later.

Teddy found Abbeville to be chaotic and his position awkward, with no really clear orders. Furthermore, he had continually to ask permission for his pilots to mount sorties.

At 1000 hours the squadron was ordered to take off and fly an offensive patrol between Lille and Valenciennes. The flying was over unfamiliar terrain which Teddy found taxing, and about an hour into the patrol he found himself lost 12,000 ft over German-occupied territory. At this low point Pilot Officer Jack Hamar caught sight of two Stukas (two Junkers Ju 87s of III/St G51 distinguished by yellow roundels with faint black crosses on the fuselages and wings) way off to the south-east.

Teddy established Yellow and Blue Sections as top cover, while he led Red Section to investigate. Closing in, the Stukas were found to be practising dive-bombing over woodlands.

They thought the Hurricanes were friendly until it was too late. Close enough to strike, a further twenty Junkers Ju 87s had been sighted taking part in the same training exercise. Teddy gave the order for a No. 1 attack, calling down Yellow and Blue Sections to join in the action.

Diving in, the pilots selected the booster on their throttle control which gave them additional speed over a short period of time. The booster was protected from accidental use by a thin wire which had to be broken first. This done, combat was joined.

During the ensuing battle, which took place between 300 and 20 ft, at least six Junkers Ju 87s were destroyed without loss to the Squadron. As Teddy recalled; 'It was fairly easy as the Germans were grossly over-confident.'

His log book records that his squadron's nine Hurricanes destroyed eleven enemy aircraft, with Teddy claiming two shot down (one in flames) and a third forced to dive into the ground.

The squadron's claims were:

Sqn Ldr Donaldson	2 Ju 87s Confirmed and 1 Ju 87 Unconfirmed
Flt Lt Ives	1 Ju 87 Confirmed
Fg Off Milne	1 Ju 87 Confirmed
Plt Off Bushell	1 Ju 87 Confirmed
Plt Off Wright	1 Ju 87 Confirmed
Plt Off Hamar	1 Ju 87 Unconfirmed
Flt Lt Atkinson and Sgt Aslin	1 Ju 87 Unconfirmed shared
Flt Lt Ironside	1 Ju 87 Unconfirmed with the air gunner killed

On landing, every pilot who had fired his guns had to file a combat report and these were studied before any 'kill' was allowed. It was important that each aircraft destroyed by a pilot was properly attributed otherwise everyone who fired in its general direction might claim a plane rather than just the pilot who fired the decisive burst. Thus the squadron would not accidentally over-claim.

The combat reports for No. 151 Squadron survive at the Public Records Office at Kew. Sergeant Atkinson wrote confirming Flight Lieutenant Ives's Junkers Ju 87:

I followed Flight Lieutenant Ives down and approximately 200 yards behind him. His first target crashed and burst immediately into flames. He broke away and commenced attack on the second aircraft. His attack was short and I followed up immediately he broke away. I opened fire at 150 yards. The second burst was delivered at approximately 80 yards. The e/a did not employ evasive tactics.

Flying Officer Richard Maxwell 'Dickie' Milne destroyed another of the dive-bombers, silencing the rear gunner before the aircraft crashed.

> I closed on one which immediately commenced evasive tactics, doing vertical left turn and stall turn. The rear gunner commenced firing before me, his tracer bullets passing across and then beneath me. The gunner ceased firing when I was approximately 100 yards away. I clearly saw fabric and other pieces ripping away. I overtook, breaking to starboard, and on turning observed e/a fall in a straight line. It fell in the middle of a large field and was completely destroyed.

Pilot Officer Les Wright's Junkers Ju 87 was hit at short range and hit the ground in flames: 'I followed him and as he levelled up, I gave him a burst of three seconds from 50 yards. The e/a dived into ground and burst into flames.' He also witnessed Pilot Officer John Bushell's combat, which nearly ended with a mid-air collision with his victim. Bushell reported:

> I got on the tail of a Ju 87. E/a dived from 500 ft to ground level and flew almost straight. Its rear gunner opened fire at approximately 400 yards with tracer, but it all passed to the port of me. I closed to 200 yards and opened fire, closing rapidly to 50 yards. E/a caught fire under port wing root. I had to pull up smartly to avoid ramming e/a [which] was observed to crash by Pilot Officer Wright.

Sergeant Aslin used all his ammunition on one Junkers Ju 87, claiming a probable: 'An e/a went past me on port quarter and I engaged it. I saw no reply from the rear gunner after my first burst. I gave six bursts of between two and three seconds. I saw streams of white smoke.'

Flight Lieutenant Harry Ironside damaged one Junkers Ju 87, silencing the rear gunner; a second came into his sights but was shot at without being hit:

> I engaged a Ju 87 from astern at about 200 yards. After two short bursts the rear gunner ceased firing and slumped down in the cockpit. Noticed considerable damage to the e/a. I also attacked another e/a, finishing my ammunition, with no noticeable result.

Jack Hamar's combat report confirms his initial sighting of the enemy and explains more fully the details of the ensuing mêlée.

> On sighting two Ju 87s on port quarters I informed the leader who ordered the Red Section to attack with leader + the Yellow + Blue

Sections to remain above. On confirming the aircraft were definitely enemy the leader ordered a No. 1 attack. As the leader attacked
the first enemy, who were turning and diving in line astern, I saw
smoke start pouring out from this a/c. As I was in a good position,
I also gave it a short burst and as I turned away, saw it crash. By
this time we were nearly at ground level and the next enemy was
dead ahead + as I had little chance to break away I attacked this
enemy. He went into a steep left-hand turn and I could only get a
deflection shot. Apparently I allowed too much deflection + I saw
my burst enter the nose of this e/a and white vapour started
coming out. As I broke away I received a fair burst from the rear
gunner. As I turned around I tried to catch any further sight of this
e/a but saw the leader following another e/a down which crashed.
I also saw to the South + higher a formation of seven Me 110 but
these did not attack + as I had been shot about made for home
although I had some ammunition left.

The markings on e/a were small black crosses on yellow
roundels.

I had fired approx. half my ammunition.

German records reveal that, on 17 May 1940, III/StG51 lost seven Junkers
Ju 87s aircraft shot down, with the loss of all their crews, including the
Gruppenkommandeur, Major Heinrich von Klitzing.

These combats were made all the more eventful as many of the No.151
Squadron pilots were forced to land away from Abbeville. A combination of the deep intruder raid and flying back over unfamiliar terrain
meant that, looking at the needle on the fuel gauge resting on the bottom,
they headed for the nearest airstrip or field.

Having survived their baptism of fire, the squadron re-formed and
returned to Manston, as Teddy explained.

We had several damaged Hurricanes and no ground crews to
mend them. Next day we were back to France and this continued
every day because our airfields in France were heavily bombed.
Whilst pilots could get away to sleep off the airfields, the
Hurricanes would take a terrific beating on the ground.

On arrival back at Manston it was discovered that Pilot Officer Hamar's
aircraft had sustained eight bullet holes (hit by return fire from a Junkers
Ju 87 of IV(St)/GL1), including three in the port wing petrol tank. His
and other damaged aircraft (P3316, flown by Teddy, and P3315, flown
by Sergeant Atkinson), were sent to North Weald for repair, one having
four holes, including one which split the corner of the gravity tank,

while four other Hurricanes had sustained one or two holes each. If Jack had been lucky then so had Ironside, who had had a bullet pass through the right sleeve of both his Irvin flying jacket and his tunic.

Manston was the closest mainland RAF base to occupied Europe, and on a clear day the pilots could climb a nearby hill and look out over the English Channel to France and see Calais and Boulogne. Its location made it an easy target for the *Luftwaffe* for a primary or secondary bombing or strafing attack. At the height of the battle the base was being hit several times a day, the aircrews and ground staff of No. 600 (City of London) Squadron winning the admiration of the whole of Fighter Command for the way they fought on regardless.

Combat reports filed, Teddy was able to report to North Weald, who passed on the details to Group. The results soon reached the Air Ministry, resulting in a Mention-in-Dispatches for Teddy's outstanding leadership during the action.

The press, eager for good news, reported the squadron's successes on 17 May:

> The Squadron Leader, who in peacetime was a crack shot, led the first section, selecting his quarry, and at once sent him down in flames.
>
> Immediately he swung onto a second and sent that crashing to the ground. The engagement became general and the German bombers swooped to within 30 ft of the ground in their frantic efforts to avoid the British fighters.
>
> Four Hurricanes accounted for one enemy each and three jointly finished off another, bringing the total to seven. Then the patrol turned on the others, tore the fuselage off one and sent another down in a column of black smoke.
>
> Finally the Squadron Leader found another Ju 87 beneath him, dived, put in a long burst and saw the enemy break up as he crashed to the ground. The Germans were utterly routed and the Hurricanes withdrew.
>
> One British pilot had a bullet through his sleeve which did not touch his arm and this was the nearest approach to a British casualty.

While that day the AASF and Air Component Squadrons lost six Hurricanes shot down with a further twelve damaged or obliged to make a forced landing, they claimed a total of thirty-six enemy aircraft destroyed and a further fourteen probably destroyed and four damaged. However, the light and medium bomber squadrons continued to take heavy casualties. Twelve Blenheims were ordered to attack German

Panzer movements near Gembloux. Their fighter escort failed to rendezvous with the poorly armed light bombers, which came up against a flak barrage and a protective cover of Messerschmitt Bf 109s. Only one aircraft returned.

CHAPTER TEN

Forward Operations and Escape from Vitry

On 18 May, the squadron's day began, as usual, before dawn. The pilots, however, were excused flying duties in the morning as they were due to be on operations in the early afternoon. News was filtering through that the German advance through France was faster than anyone could believe, and that a column of French tanks had been seen charging through villages with guns pointing firmly rearwards. It was going to be a challenging day.

At 1400 hours, Teddy led nine pilots of No. 151 Squadron from Manston to their advanced landing ground at Vitry, touching down an hour later. Here their aircraft were refuelled in preparation for the sorties ahead. While the Hurricanes were still being made ready, more than twenty Messerschmitt Bf 109s appeared overhead, sending men scattering in all directions, some to makeshift shelters, others to their battle stations. The accompanying bombers were quickly met by ground fire and by Hurricanes of another squadron, which were acting as temporary air cover. The pilots of No. 151 Squadron viewed the battle as frustrated and frightened spectators. A squadron patrol was mounted as soon as possible, and was launched at around 1540 hours. Flying in the vicinity of the airfield, Blue Section sighted two Heinkel He 111s which had overflown the airfield. These bombers were chased and engaged.

Sergeant George Atkinson of Flight Lieutenant Ives's Blue Section later reported:

> Leader went in and attacked. Pilot Officer Wright pulled to starboard and made a No. 2 attack. I followed up and gave one burst of two seconds at about 25 yards and broke away to port. I met three more He 111s flying east on my starboard side. I attacked the port aircraft. I saw him go down in a dive, flames coming from the port engine. I lost the other two aircraft as they went into cloud.

Atkinson became separated during the combat and landed at Le Touquet and was unable to rejoin the squadron until noon the following day. He reported to the Intelligence Officer, who filed the following in his combat report:

> I then met Yellow Section and formed up with them. I heard leader order line astern attack on about twelve Me 110s one of which I saw exploded in the air. I attacked another Me 110 from port quarter, three-quarter deflection shot. I opened from 250 yards and gave burst of eight seconds without known result. I flew north-west looking for aerodrome. I hit the coast at Le Touquet and landed.

Flight Lieutenant Harry Ironside reported the destruction of another Messerschmitt Bf 110.

> I fired a short burst at one e/a with little result – another 110 flew across my sights and I gave him a three second burst. I saw the fuselage foremost of the tail unit crumpled and the tail unit began to break off. One member of the crew jumped by parachute and was shot by French AA [anti-aircraft fire] while descending.

This combat was witnessed by Milne and Ives who were able to confirm the 'kill'.

Flying Officer Dickie Milne had not been so lucky. Having shot at a Messerschmitt Bf 110 his Hurricane was hit by return fire. Ives was able to land safely, having claimed a Messerschmitt Bf 110 destroyed. This was later downgraded to 'unconfirmed'.

Pilot Officer John Bushell engaged another Messerschmitt Bf 110, the destruction of which he described in his combat report:

> I saw one of the Messerschmitt 110s dive away in a southerly direction. As he appeared to be under control and unfollowed, I gave chase and after pulling the boost plug and giving full throttle I gradually overhauled him. At 600 yards the rear gunner opened fire with tracer – apparently two guns. I opened fire at 300 yards and closed to 100 yards, when e/a caught fire under port engine. I was smothered in oil and smoke and broke off the engagement. The fire died down and e/a commenced to climb slowly. I attacked again at 150 yards when something, which looked like a wheel, fell away from port engine nacelle and fire burst out again. As I broke away the engine appeared to blow up with showers of sparks and e/a dived into a field and blew up. I observed one parachute descending.

A third Messerschmitt Bf 110 was claimed by Sergeant Aslin.

> I climbed to approximately 6,000 ft and saw a Messerschmitt 110 in engagement with another Hurricane about five miles on port beam. I turned towards it and dived with full throttle and got quarter attack developing into full astern. The e/a dived and pulled up into a climbing left-hand turn. I got in full deflection shot at about 50/60 yards. Continuously tracer from rear gunner of e/a, but inaccurate owing to violent manoeuvres of e/a. The port engine of e/a on fire, but flickered out again. The e/a levelled out and I started gentle dive. I got another burst in dead astern from about 100 yards and port engine caught fire again. The crew jumped (two first, then one) and the machine crashed. I feel sure that three crew jumped.

Meanwhile, Red Section joined with Yellow in an air battle with a dozen or so Messerschmitt Bf 110s, slightly evening up the odds. At least one Bf 110 fell to the guns of No. 151 Squadron during the general mêlée.

Later that day, at about 1615 hours, Blue and Yellow Sections joined B Flight of No. 56 Squadron in engaging three Heinkel He 111s of III/KG 54. During the ensuing battle Sergeant Atkinson got a probable Heinkel He 111, while Ives, Wright, and Atkinson attacked the same Heinkel He 111 which was damaged, each being given a 'share' to add to their tallies.

The Squadron was again caught on the ground at 1830 hours when six Do 17s made a low-level attack, destroying twelve Hurricanes as they sat on the airfield. Fortunately for No. 151 Squadron, none of their Hurricanes was damaged.

Teddy had seen the Dorniers passing the aerodrome about 5 miles to the south; they appeared to be turning in towards Vitry as they progressed. He had requested permission to scramble, but was refused and had to look on helplessly as the bombs fell all around. However, fifteen minutes later the squadron was in the air and in combat with Messerschmitt Bf 110s of II/ZG76 which were attempting a further surprise attack. These may have been the fighter cover for the earlier raid, taking the opportunity to attack while the remaining Hurricanes were still grounded. This time the airfield was undamaged and several enemy aircraft were destroyed. Teddy claimed one Messerschmitt Bf 110 damaged. Meanwhile Ironside, Bushell and Aslin destroyed one each. It was another good 'bag' for No. 151 Squadron.

Teddy's combat report included references to the build-up to No. 151 Squadron's scramble; no doubt, he wanted his earlier request recorded.

> At about 16.30 [corrected to the time of the combat, which was 1900 hours] we observed seven Do 215s [sic] passing the aerodrome

about five miles to the south. I requested permission to be allowed to take off as they appeared to be turning the whole time in the Vitry direction. My request was refused.

The Dorniers bombed the aerodrome with incendiary bombs in what Teddy described as a 'perfect low-level attack', resulting in the destruction of a dozen or so Hurricanes and one Blenheim. Teddy recalled that 'they came in at tree top height'. Nearby stood a soldier, momentarily paralysed with shock. Teddy grabbed his rifle and knelt down to get a shot. He picked out one Dornier Do 215. As it drew ever closer the bomb doors opened to release a yellow form turning over and over as it appeared to roll though the sky towards him, whizzing past his head before exploding.

Picking out the figure of a German in the nose of the enemy aircraft, Teddy squeezed the trigger. It was a clean chest shot, without the need for deflection. The fresh-face young pilot was mortally wounded but flew on straight and level. Honours even, Teddy dived for the nearest cover, explosions erupting all around him as debris and deafening noise filled the air.

Then, as quickly as they had arrived, they were gone. Teddy climbed from his shelter and dusted off his uniform as he took in the enormity of the raid. This had been his first experience of being on the receiving end of an air raid and he did not mind admitting that it terrified him. All around lay the burning wrecks of Hurricanes, lorries and other vehicles. Amazingly, none of No. 151 Squadron's aircraft were touched. Teddy was certain that the burnt-out Hurricanes saved his own Squadron's aircraft. Alarmingly, he then recalled: 'Not long after the raid I saw a German tank approaching the aerodrome perimeter. The commander must have believed the airfield to have been destroyed and evacuated.' Vitry airfield was not captured by the Germans until the following day. The tank may have been on reconnaissance duty.

Fearful of a second wave catching his fighters on the ground Teddy raced to a phone.

I immediately asked permission to take off again. This was granted and I yelled out 'Scramble whole Squadron.' I pulled the plug and climbed after two Me 110s which were the remains of six of the escort of the Do 215s (sic) which bombed the aerodrome. When I had climbed to 6,000 ft, the Messerschmitts attacked. They passed vertically down behind me and I was able to flick-roll in behind one of them, which dived to ground level into the smoke of the burning Hurricanes. I followed, pulled the plug but although I was doing over 400 mph I could not gain on him. At 800–600 yards he fired at me with what appeared to be cannon (his bullets were coming straight with no drop over the whole 800 yards so they could not have been ordinary M/G [machine-gun] bullets). At 600 yards I opened fire without a break. About half-way through my ammunition, the e/a's port engine caught fire and he slipped to the right. I finished the rest of my ammunition. I noticed that the smoke from the e/a's port engine got less and less. He did not crash.

Teddy's log book confirms that he shot at a second Messerschmitt Bf 110 during this combat, again damaging the enemy aircraft but not conclusively.

With the *Luftwaffe* holding so many landing strips, they could attack the RAF's temporary landing grounds almost at will. Without the same network of spotters and advanced radar that they enjoyed over the English coast, the RAF had no advance warning of an attack. Nor did they have the manpower or aircraft to mount standing patrols to defend their airstrips. While a patrol of a section could perhaps give a few minutes' warning of an impending raid if they were fortunate enough to spot an approaching force, they clearly could not be expected to defend the airfield other than by using scare tactics as best they could. The situation was hopeless and it was felt that it was only a matter of time before all the Hurricanes fell victim to either bombing raids or air-to-air combat.

The airfield at Vitry suffered two further raids on 18 May, one at 1900 hours and the next half an hour later. At 1930 hours, and much to everyone's relief, the squadron took off and flew back to Manston, using what fuel Teddy could scrounge. He felt badly about having to tell the ground crews to make their own way back with the retreating army before the airstrip was overrun. There were no spare Avro Ansons to fly over and pick them up. The German advances over the previous twenty-four hours had been too rapid and there was little time to coordinate a more measured retreat.

On their return, the Hurricanes were given a thorough check for combat damage. Remarkably, the only recorded problem was an armour-piercing bullet which had struck the aileron of Milne's aircraft.

The day's successes were measured against the loss of Sergeant Atkinson who, it was thought, had been shot down, and therefore posted as missing. To everyone's relief, however, he arrived back at Manston the following day, having set his Hurricane down at Le Touquet after he had destroyed a Heinkel He 111. Sergeant George Atkinson was later awarded the DFM, the award being promulgated in the *London Gazette* of 7 March 1941. Commissioned as a pilot officer in late 1941, he was killed in a flying accident on 1 March 1945, while serving as an instructor, only weeks away from the end of the war in Europe.

Jack Hamar's combat report for 18 May shows that he took part in one of the actions mentioned by others, flying in his role as Red Two. The exact time of the combats do not appear to tally with the squadron records, but this is not unusual due to the war conditions.

> I scrambled off the ground independently to engage 3 e/a which appeared to be escort of bombing attack. I climbed to 7,000 ft + attacked two Me 110s. I succeeded in getting on to the tail of 1 e/a + opened fire at 300 yards with a burst of 5 seconds, while closing in I noticed tracer passing over my head from behind + looking around found the other e/a on my tail. I immediately half-rolled away + noticed two Hurricanes chasing another e/a which was diving to ground level. I followed down after to gain on e/a. I got within 500 yards + I put in a 5 second burst. I saw my tracer entering the wings each side of the fuselage, but did not observe any damage. As my window screen was covered in oil from my own airscrew + sighting was impossible, I broke away + landed at Vitry.

CHAPTER ELEVEN

A Change of Attitude

Sergeant Atkinson's safe return to the squadron at Manston greatly heartened everyone. Since their first contact with the enemy they had accounted for at least ten enemy aircraft without the loss of a single pilot. Luck had been on their side too. Their Hurricanes remained undamaged among the bomb-craters at Vitry while all those around had been turned to burning wrecks.

During the previous twenty-four hours, however, the land war had continued to go disastrously for the Allies. The cities of Antwerp and St Quentin had fallen, along with Perrone.

Once again the squadron made their way over to France and landed at Vitry ready for the afternoon's sorties.

At 1330 hours on 19 May, the nine machines of Red, Yellow and Blue Sections, led by Squadron Leader Donaldson, took off from their advanced airbase to carry out an offensive patrol. As the Squadron Diary records: 'They patrolled between Tournai and Andenarde, and Courtai and Roubaix for about forty-five minutes, but no enemy aircraft were sighted and no action took place.'

As was so often the case, the squadron diary did not, however, convey the whole story. During this patrol there were a number of minor combats. Teddy's log book confirms that he managed to get onto a Junkers Ju 88, at which he fired but without observing any result. The squadron returned to Manston at 1530 hours having made contact with the enemy but without having any combat victories.

On the following day, the 20th, at 1030 hours, Teddy led a wing of twenty-seven aircraft composed of No. 151 Squadron, together with Nos 56 and 17. Their mission was to carry out a bomber escort patrol, linking up with Blenheims of Nos 21 and 107 Squadrons, led respectively by Squadron Leader Pryde and Wing Commander Embry, somewhere over Hawkinge. The wing successfully flew to their target at Marquion on the Courtrai to Arras road. Although the squadron diary makes no mention of a contact with the enemy, Teddy added the note 'No satisfactory results' to his log book, which would suggest once more that a contact was made but with no decisive outcome on either side. The aircraft came up against heavy flak, with a number of bombers suffering damage, although in sharp contrast to the events of 17 May, all of the aircraft and crew returned safely.

Back at Manston No. 151 Squadron were at readiness from 1500 hours, sending up a patrol at 1530 hours as base cover in response to a suspected incoming raid. This was recalled fifteen minutes later, the 'hostiles' having been taken 'off the board'. The squadron was stood down for the rest of the day and flew back to North Weald at 1800 hours, but they knew that they were to be at Manston once again by 0730 hours the next day, when goodness knew what lay in store for them.

During the day the Germans had reached the coast near Abbeville, dividing the Allied armies. Later, General Guderian's Panzer Corps took Abbeville itself.

An Allied counter-attack was planned for the 21st, with Lord Gort's command launching an attack at Arras. It was No. 151 Squadron's duty to provide air cover for the advance; this they did from 0900 hours, once they had flown to Manston and refuelled. Three sections flew at 20,000 ft over the Cambrai-Arras-Lens-Vimy district, taking the fight to the enemy. Despite an intensive search, no enemy aircraft were sighted and the offensive patrol returned without firing their guns in anger. Following the squadron's initial successes of the preceding few days, this must have seemed an anticlimax although it was soon to experience combat again.

At 1720 hours it joined No. 56 Squadron in escorting a bombing raid by three Blenheims of No. 18 Squadron accompanied by a further six of No. 82 Squadron. The bombers' target was a railway junction along the Boulogne – Etaples line. Prior to the rendezvous over the Channel, the Blenheims from No. 18 Squadron came under attack from a Spitfire from No. 610 Squadron. The remainder of the formation realized the mistake and pulled out of the attack, leaving one aircraft damaged.

Minutes later Teddy ordered Blue Section to investigate an aircraft flying below the formation. Sergeant George Atkinson attacked what turned out to be a Henschel Hs 125 of 1(H)/14Pz from 2 Pz Division. He fired a four-second burst at close range. Both Teddy and Flight Lieutenant Ives saw the enemy aircraft engulfed in flames before it plummeted to the ground. Atkinson was credited with one enemy aircraft confirmed.

With the bombing raid successfully undertaken and without further incident, the Hurricanes turned for home. Teddy recorded the events in his log book, adding details of his own aircraft's difficulties over the English Channel: 'Escort for bombers South of Boulogne – engine failed over Arras. Came back at 140 mph escorted by Squadron. 120 mph . . . engine stopped twice over Channel. Thick fog over water near South England. Landed Martlesham. No attacks.'

Teddy was a strict disciplinarian in the air and had already reprimanded his wingman, Jack Hamar, for staying too close to him when he had got into trouble and lost speed and altitude as a result of combat damage. He later gathered his pilots together and spelt out his instructions to them in no uncertain terms. The task was to guard the bombers. The only excuse for breaking was when given permission to go into combat. Even then, they were not to pursue the enemy, but to fend them off and return to their charge. 'This is an order,' he said, 'and is to be obeyed.'

However, his squadron found it impossible to leave one of their own to their fate, least of all their CO, who later wrote about what would appear to have been the events recorded in his log book on this day:

> During this escort mission, however, my Hurricane got into trouble, the engine cut out and I began to lose altitude, the air speed being reduced to 140 mph. I was not flying in my regular Hurricane but a loaned aircraft. Losing height rapidly I found the Squadron following me down giving cover while I tried to coax the engine to pick-up.

In another account, he says, 'The engine gave a couple of nasty coughs and stopped. I told my No. 2 to take over. I would look after myself. To my amazement the whole Squadron descended with me.'

Teddy was furious that the mission might be compromised and shouted over the radio: 'What's the matter with you? Obey my orders. Leave me and do your job!'

His words were to no avail and it was only when his engine spluttered back into life and with altitude regained that the Hurricanes resumed their original path. A livid Teddy summoned the pilots on landing and asked why they had ignored his orders. To a man they replied: 'I never heard any orders, sir.' Apparently the whole squadron had been struck by radio transmitter failure. Teddy later rescinded the order.

On the 22nd, with the Arras offensive having been pushed back, the squadron took off from North Weald at 0530 hours in order to make a fighter sweep off Calais and Boulogne. (During the day Boulogne would capitulate while German forces encircled Calais in preparation to besiege the city.) The formation came across five Junkers Ju 88s which were bombing a convoy 10 miles north of Cap Griz-Nez. Attacking by sections, they drove the bombers off, Teddy shooting at three. One was seen to crash into the sea during the general mêlée. By the time they arrived on the scene, however, an oil tanker had already been hit. It was still burning three days later. Following this patrol, the squadron re-fuelled at Manston.

At 1000 hours they were scrambled again, Teddy leading them on a patrol to Arras to attack a formation of dive-bombers which were harassing Allied troops. Disappointingly, the patrol was a wash-out due to adverse weather conditions. In the air once again at 1800 hours, they were ordered to escort three Ensign transporters to Merville. During their return flight a force of Junkers Ju 87s, in two formations of twelve aircraft, were spotted bombing St Omer. Teddy gave the order to attack and the squadron went in.

Diving and out-turning the enemy, the Hurricanes gradually gained the advantage, sending a number of enemy aircraft plummeting to the ground, totally destroyed. At least six fell to Teddy's guns and those of his wingman, Jack Hamar, Sergeant Atkinson and Flying Officer Milne.

The pilots' combat reports for this engagement show that they came in contact with two formations, each of a dozen or so Junkers Ju 87s, the scrap taking place between about 7,000 ft and tree-top level.

Teddy and Hamar were each officially credited with one confirmed and another unconfirmed destroyed. Teddy's log book confirms that of the twenty-four enemy aircraft encountered, six fell to the guns of the Hurricanes, although he claimed two Junkers Ju 87s destroyed and another severely damaged.

Hamar's combat report says:

While on patrol over Merville Aerodrome a bunch of Ju 87 aircraft were sighted flying north. The leader ordered Red Section to attack + we dived towards them. I lost sight of my leader + circled to select an E/A to attack. I closed on one which was diving but failed to attack before E/A dropped bombs on a village. As E/A pulled up I attacked giving a 5 second burst at 200 yards which killed rear gunner. I closed to 100yds + after a 7 second burst E/A turned on its side with smoke pouring from engine. It went into a steep dive + crashed in a field. I attacked another E/A which I gave a short burst at 200 yards + experienced no further fire from the rear. I closed to 100 yards + opened fire which tore the side of the fuse-lage + top of port wing. I was forced to break away without observing what happened to this E/A because I ran into another 5 Ju 87s. I did not see any further E/A crash but saw a parachute descending. Having turned on to gravity + having little ammu-nition left (15 rounds per gun) I returned to base. The weather was clear.

At 1430 hours on the 23rd, three sections of No. 151 Squadron rendezvoused with twelve aircraft of No. 56 Squadron to carry out an offensive patrol in the Merville district. During the patrol one aircraft of No. 56 Squadron was badly damaged in combat. Teddy's Hurricanes were not able to engage the enemy.

A further patrol was flown between Calais and Boulogne. No combat took place and the squadron returned directly to North Weald, where they were later stood down for the day.

On the following day, the 24th, they flew to Manston at 1400 hours from where, two hours later, they took off to join No. 56 Squadron on an offensive patrol around Dunkirk, Calais, Boulogne and St Omer. The patrol passed off without incident.

The same formation linked up again at 1930 hours for an offensive sweep over Cambrai, Courtrai, Lille and St Omer. The enemy failed to engage this comparatively small fighter force.

Elsewhere in northern France, bombers of No. 2 Group were despatched to bomb bridges to the rear of the German front line in order to try to slow the advance. Six Blenheims were lost.

Teddy's log book records a third sortie that day, flying from North Weald to Merville, where he dropped a message for Pilot Officer Strange, who was to return to England. Three Messerschmitt Bf 109s attacked the squadron but were fended off without causing any losses, despite their obvious speed advantage. Later, a dozen Messerschmitt Bf 110s were sighted and engaged, with Teddy recording that Pilot Officer Hamar appeared to damage badly one enemy aircraft. This remained unconfirmed, as it was not seen to crash.

On 25 May at 1330 hours the squadron took off from North Weald and flew a high-level offensive patrol with No. 56 Squadron. A Junkers Ju 88 was sighted, which Teddy chased, fired at and damaged, but could not bring down. The patrol continued as ordered and with no further enemy aircraft being sighted.

Tragically on the same day, No. 151 Squadron lost two pilots, one an experienced flight commander in the form of Flight Lieutenant Ives. The casualties came at the beginning of the combat and as a result of a midair collision with Pilot Officer Bushell during an escort to St Omer.

The squadron had taken off at 1615 hours from Manston, linking up with No. 56 Squadron and No. 24 Squadron's Blenheims on what Teddy recorded as a 'St Omer offensive patrol Dunkirk-Calais offensive'. The bombing run completed, No. 151 Squadron were on the return leg when the disaster struck.

Witnesses said that Pilot Officer Bushell appeared to pull up from below Flight Lieutenant Ives as they went into combat and the two Hurricanes collided. Bushell seemed to spin out of control into the sea, while Ives was last seen turning towards the French coast some 12 miles away.

Flight Lieutenant Ives managed to reach land, belly-landing on the beach some 12 miles south-west of Ostend. Here he met up with a former No. 151 Squadron pilot, New Zealander Pilot Officer I. J. Muirhead of No. 605 Squadron, who had baled-out after being shot down by a Messerschmitt Bf 110 while patrolling near Dunkirk.

Muirhead later wrote to No. 151 Squadron, informing them of Flight Lieutenant Ives's fate:

> He originally landed on the beach 12 miles S.W. of Ostend and I met him in Ostend after being shot down and jumping at the same place. We spent the next 2 days together dodging bombs and bullets and 'Ivy' spent a lot of his time helping the wounded (Ives had been part of the way through a medical course when, with war looming, he entered pilot training.) In fact he was everything anyone who knew him would have expected – and then some. We sailed in the *Aboukir* at about 10.00pm on Tuesday night. 'Ivy', myself and an Army officer were on top manning the gun as we expected to be bombed at any time. Eventually, however, we were torpedoed at point blank range and blown into the water. The motor boat that torpedoed us then went around machine gunning people in the water. Only 24 people out of over 500 on board were saved and I was the only officer. Please express my heartfelt sympathy and admiration for 'Ivy' to his people – he was a brick.

When this letter arrived at No. 151 Squadron it was recorded in the Squadron Diary, which concluded with the words: 'It is considered unnecessary to add to the above about the Squadron's feelings, for they are the same.'

The cold-blooded killing of Ives changed Teddy's attitude towards the Germans, who up until then he had regarded as 'rather decent chaps'.

Jack Hamar destroyed a Junkers Ju 88 some 4 miles north-east of Boulogne during a sweep on the 25th. His combat report says:

> Whilst flying as Red Two with Yellow + Blue Section on a general sweep in the Calais-Boulogne district, a Ju 88 suddenly appeared out of the clouds + passing slightly above + across our formation. The leader ordered a No 1 attack. The E/A dived for sea level and after Red 1 (Squadron Leader Donaldson) broke away I attacked. My sights were set at 80ft span 250 yds range. I used full throttle + gradually closed + opened fire at 300 yds range. The slip stream effect was noticed + keeping the sights dead on I fired two long bursts, finishing at approx 50 yards using all my ammunition. I then broke away. During the attack I noticed three large pieces drop from the port side of the E/A which may have been bombs. No other damage was noticed.

While the squadron was greatly saddened at the loss of two brave men in Bushell and Ives, their exact fates as yet unknown, the squadron's number was boosted by the return of Flying Officer Forster from secondment, while Flying Officer Blair was posted from No. 85 Squadron. Flying Officer Blair had destroyed two enemy aircraft on 10 May and was awarded the DFC, as promulgated in the *London Gazette* of 31 May 1940:

Flying Officer Kenneth Hughes Blair (39704).

This officer has shown exceptional keenness both before and during the present operations. He has engaged successfully two enemy bomber aircraft, viz., at dawn, one day in May, when he succeeded in being the first off the ground in pursuit of a Heinkel, and at dusk on the same day, when he successfully attacked another Heinkel between Arras and Vitry. He had a very narrow escape when a bomb landed within 20 yards of a room in which he was sleeping. He was badly shaken, but insisted on volunteering and taking part in a patrol over Maastricht, when he engaged two Messerschmitt Bf 109s.

CHAPTER TWELVE

Dunkirk – Doing Our Level Best

W ith the death of Flight Lieutenant Ives, No. 151 Squadron had lost not only a greatly respected pilot and a selfless hero but also, as a flight commander, a key member of the set-up. On the following day, 26 May, when it became apparent he had not been picked up by a rescue launch, Flight Lieutenant Blair was appointed as B Flight Commander.

At 1300 hours on the 26th, Teddy led the squadron in a patrol over Dunkirk and Calais. The land there was low and cut by numerous canals and drainage ditches so it seemed poor country for tank operations, which should have given the defenders some chance of holding up the German advance. Even so, the panzers swept towards the Channel ports, cutting off Boulogne, Calais, and Dunkirk. Boulogne had fallen on 22 May and Calais was captured five days later.

With the situation in France now critical, Churchill's War Cabinet gave Lord Gort (who had been appointed as the Commander of the BEF on 19 September 1939) permission to retreat the remnants of the BEF to Dunkirk ready for an evacuation by sea, the order being given by the Admiralty that evening. The quickly organized British operation, code-named Operation Dynamo, was initially designed to evacuate some 45,000 men from the beach-head using Royal Navy destroyers. In the event, the evacuation was to last nine days, resulting in the safe evacuation of a third of a million men.

In shielding the remnants of the BEF, much of the aerial combat took place either at high altitude or away from the *Luftwaffe*'s intended targets, the beaches and the rescue ships themselves. The troops only saw the aircraft that got through. Consequently, many of the men evacuated from Dunkirk believed that the RAF had abandoned them to their fate. Certainly, the bombing of troops within the confines of the beach and the ships had devastating results, but what was not widely known is that only a fraction of the *Luftwaffe* bombers ever reached their

intended targets. This was due largely to the bravery and devotion of the
RAF aircrew who were, like the army, Royal Navy, merchant navy and
civilian volunteers involved in Operation Dynamo, simply doing their
level best.

Although enemy aircraft were sighted and engaged, Teddy noted
these combats as 'unsatisfactory clashes with enemy, no results both
side'. Despite his obvious disappointment, the day's sorties would give
Blair time to settle into the squadron and his role. There was a second
patrol at 1830 hours with the same results, so the squadron returned to
North Weald where they were stood down for the day.

On 27 May, the day Belgium formally surrendered to Germany, with
the Germans advancing once more in France, the evacuation of Allied
troops across the English Channel began. The squadron flew a patrol
over Dunkirk and St Omer at 1400 hours. No enemy aircraft were seen
but they spent as much time as their fuel would allow over France. Teddy
had issued his pilots with instructions to stay over the Dunkirk area even
if they were out of ammunition; they might still prevent an attack by
their mere presence.

Once again, at 1830 hours, they patrolled from Dunkirk to Calais,
returning to North Weald with their fuel spent. During the patrols they
witnessed the reality of the evacuation: tens of thousands of troops lining
the beaches or sheltering in amongst the dunes, waiting to be ferried out
to the destroyers which lay off the long, shallow beaches. It was a very
slow business. Only a few thousand of the trapped servicemen escaped
during those first few days – if things did not change the BEF was facing
destruction.

It was learned later that day that Flying Officer Newton and Pilot
Officers Courtney and Blomeley were to return to the squadron
following their posting to other squadrons then based in France. All
three men had seen combat. David Blomeley's log book was lost due to
enemy action but he had claimed a share in the destruction of at least five
enemy aircraft while with No. 605 Squadron. With No. 605 Squadron's
records also destroyed, his gallantry went unrewarded until 1943 when
he received an immediate DFC for destroying three enemy aircraft in a
matter of a few months while flying night intruder raids with No. 604
Squadron. At the time his actual tally may have been as high as thirteen
enemy aircraft damaged or destroyed. Later, the nose of his de Havilland
Mosquito bore fifteen swastikas, which included the two more aircraft
he destroyed following the award of his DFC. Blomeley was later to win
both a Queen's Commendation and the AFC for his instructional duties
on jets. Later still, he flew the RAF's V-Bomber and took part in two
bombing raids during the Suez Crisis.

With the return of these seasoned campaigners, the squadron would
be able to fly at full strength for the first time since they had engaged the

enemy. They flew with No. 56 Squadron on a patrol to Dunkirk at 1145 hours on 28 May. A number of Messerschmitt Bf 109s were chased but all fled into cloud when faced by two squadrons of Hurricanes. At times like these Teddy must have remembered the words of the German ace Ernst Udet when he scoffed at the 'foolishness' of the British in fighting when the odds were not stacked heavily in their favour.

During the patrol Teddy engaged a Junkers Ju 88 at very low altitude. Although he did not claim it as damaged, Teddy was convinced that his bullets would have struck his target: 'I could see bullet splash water either side of Ju 88.'

A second patrol began at 1600 hours but, according to the Squadron Diary, had to be abandoned when the weather closed in. Teddy's log book noted that a number of combats did take place at high altitude during the second patrol on the 28th, as he recorded: 'The air was lousy with Germans but no satisfactory results. 29,000 ft.'

A new phase to the mass evacuation began on 29 May. A call had gone out to the owners of seaworthy shallow-draught vessels which could get close in to the troops on the beaches and either ferry them to the waiting destroyers or sail back to England with them. So a great flotilla was created and to the Royal Navy's destroyers were added fishing boats, yachts, motorboats, fire boats, tugs, pleasure steamers, cargo boats and cross-channel ferries.

During that afternoon, No. 151 Squadron was once more assigned to defend the skies over Dunkirk, being joined by the Hurricanes of No. 56 Squadron. There were several combats with Messerschmitt Bf 110s and Bf 109s at around 25,000 ft, resulting in a confirmed Messerschmitt Bf 110 being credited to Pilot Officer David Blomeley.

The squadron took off again from Manston at 1900 hours on an escort mission over the same area in support of a formation of Boulton Paul Defiants. Lacking any front-firing guns, the Defiants relied on machine-guns in a manned turret to the rear of the pilot. If the enemy mistook the Defiants for either Hurricanes or Spitfires and tried to attack them from behind, then they would face four .303 machine-guns. The Germans very quickly recognized the distinctive silhouette of the gun-turret and adopted a head-on attack, leaving the slower and less manoeuvrable Defiant practically defenceless. However, flying in a formation of Hurricanes, the Defiants might prove their worth by catching the enemy out. This tactic was rarely used and during the early phases of the Battle of Britain the Defiant squadrons suffered such high casualty rates that they would be relegated to the role of night fighter.

No. 151 Squadron's Diary recorded, in brief, the combats that followed: 'Me 109s and He 111s were engaged at 15,000 ft and a fierce fight ensued.'

Teddy and Hamar shot down a Ju 88 which was acting as a decoy for

Messerschmitt Bf 110s and around a hundred Messerschmitt Bf 109s. In his combat report, Hamar wrote:

> While flying as Red Two on a high escort patrol over Dunkirk, a Ju 88 was seen flying approximately due East at 7,000 ft. The leader (Squadron Leader Donaldson) ordered Red Section into line astern and delivered a No 1 FA [fighter attack]. The leader also ordered Yellow 1 to take over + remain above on guard. As I followed the leader into attack I saw a large formation of Me 109s high above. As the leader broke away, I saw white smoke pouring from the E/A's port engine, and it started flying crab-like. Thinking that this may be a 'ruse', I decided to attack, aiming at the port engine. I opened fire at approximately 150 yards and continued the burst until at about 20 yards. Large pieces of the port engine were seen to drop off. I did not experience any fire from the rear + E/A did not adopt any evasive action except fast dive towards cloud. I saw E/A go into cloud nearly on its side + I then rejoined Red 1.

Of the fierce dogfight, Teddy wrote in his log book only 'Fought 4 Me 110s. No result.' His combat report, however, explains the event in more detail.

> Whilst carrying out high escort duties at 21,000 ft sighted 5 Me 110s in formation flying east towards Dunkirk (escort for some bombers being dealt with by another unit).
> Ordered No. 5 attack and closed left hand fighters dived down at 45 degrees onto rear gun and fired 10 second burst ending astern. No visible effect. Broke away sharply left and climbed to cover Green Section.
> Something went wrong with 56 Squadron who were covering us (they went off in the different direction. I believe their leader had oxygen failure) and found myself alone with 4 Me 110s. I fought for about 5 minutes as hard as I knew. Me 110 out-climbed and out-turned my Hurricane at that height. Eventually one Me came up either side and above me and two stayed on my tail. There were no clouds whatsoever in the sky. I threw my aircraft all over the place and got in several bursts (inaccurately).
> There was no way out so I turned onto my back and allowed engine to stop with black smoke pouring out of the exhaust and petrol glycol etc poured out of the vents. Then I pulled the stick back and dived 23,000 ft to the sea. They thought I was hit and fortunately did not follow. The belly of the Hurricane split but no other damage. Landed with 5 gallons of petrol left.

Despite having its 'belly split', the Hurricane P3305 was evidently serviceable thanks to the supreme efforts of his ground crew, and Teddy was up flying in it the following day.

It was during this combat that the higher-flying Messerschmitt Bf 109 fighter escort shot down both Pilot Officer R. N. H. Courtney (flying P3321) and Flying Officer K.E. Newton (flying P3303) into the sea. At the time Newton was reported 'missing', while Courtney was seen in the water and picked up by the corvette HMS *Shearwater*, and taken to Ramsgate Hospital suffering from wounds to his back and right leg – he would not return to the Squadron until 18 July.

Flying Officer Newton's fate was only learned two days later when, at 1100 hours, a communication was received at North Weald confirming that he had been picked up out of the Channel by a hospital ship after baling out.

The Squadron Diary later recorded Flying Officer Newton's account of the loss of Pilot Officer Courtney. He reported that he and Courtney:

> . . . were attacked by 5 Me 109s. Plt Off Courtney did not seem to see them and was seen to go down with smoke pouring out. Fg Off Newton stated he then 'saw red' and marked and shot down the Me109 that got Plt Off Courtney. He was then shot down by the others and got away by rolling over and over as though finished. He was not followed down and sighting a hospital ship near he glided down to 3,000 ft and baled-out. After about 10 minutes in the water he was picked up by the hospital ship which was going to Dunkirk. Fg Off Newton stated that the hospital ship was bombed and machine-gunned all night in Dunkirk harbour while picking up wounded.

Both pilots were fortunate in being picked up so quickly, evidently they had been spotted parachuting from their stricken Hurricanes, otherwise their chances of survival were remote. The Germans had organized an air-sea rescue service for their pilots within weeks of the fall of France. This consisted of both high-speed motor launches and nimble float-planes, which were able to work in the Channel and pick up ditched pilots. The RAF had their own rescue launches but the infrastructure was lacking. Dowding managed, however, to obtain around a dozen Lysanders which could be used as spotters and could drop dinghies and circle the downed pilots until help arrived.

On 30 May, twelve Hurricanes of No. 151 Squadron took off from North Weald at 1400 hours to link up once again with No. 56 Squadron and carry out patrols over Dunkirk. The patrols turned out to be uneventful and they returned to North Weald, their fuel just about spent. A second patrol was mounted at 1800 hours and again resulted in no contacts with the enemy. On their return they were stood down for the day.

The *London Gazette* promulgated details of two awards made to No. 151 Squadron on 31 May. Squadron Leader Donaldson had been awarded the DSO, and Flying Officer Blair the DFC. Teddy's citation read:

> The KING has been graciously pleased to approve the under-mentioned appointments and awards in recognition of gallantry against the enemy:
>   Appointed Companion of the Distinguished Service Order:
>   Squadron Leader Edward Mortlock Donaldson (32043).
>   This officer has inspired such a fine fighting spirit in his squadron that, on the first encounter with enemy forces, nine aircraft of his squadron destroyed six enemy aircraft and a further five were believed to have been destroyed. Four or five enemy aircraft were accounted for on the following day. His high courage and his inspiring qualities of leadership have made his squadron a formidable fighting unit. He has, himself, shot down four enemy aircraft.

News of the award had reached North Weald on 20 May, the day after his Mention-in-Dispatches. The four enemy aircraft attributed to him in the citation were the two destroyed, the one damaged and one 'probable' from the Squadron's encounters with the enemy during the Battle of France on 17 and 18 May.

Between then and the promulgation of the award, Teddy had already added another two and a half more enemy aircraft to his tally. More were to follow over the next few weeks. He destroyed a further five or possibly six enemy aircraft before he completed his tour on fighters, bringing his total to ten and a half confirmed destroyed, with many more uncon-firmed or damaged.

It subsequently became apparent that, had the paperwork been more efficiently processed, as it was later in the war, Teddy would definitely have been awarded at least one DFC, like other 'ace' pilots with five or more aerial victories. Moreover, had he been dealt with fairly, he should probably have also received a bar to his DSO for his further dazzling example of courage and skilful determination in the air, together with his infectious spirit and focused influence in command, whilst contin-uing to lead No. 151 Squadron from the front during the early dark days of the Battle of Britain as well as over Dunkirk. Certainly his outstanding leadership and conspicuous bravery were to become benchmarks within the service at the time. It was a moot point with Teddy, and one which, on reflection, niggled him later, especially when in the uniformed company of his bemedalled friends and fellow heroes, including his younger brother, Arthur, who earned his DSO and two DFCs over the next couple of years.

On 31 May a Messerschmitt Bf 110 fell to his guns, although this was shared with his wingman, Pilot Officer Jack Hamar.

With the air battles over Dunkirk still raging, Churchill flew to Paris to meet the ageing Marshal August Pétain, who was a growing force in the French government. The French attitude had grown increasingly defeatist. Claiming to be willing to fight on from their colonies should Britain fall, Churchill felt the intention was actually to end the war unilaterally, as Pétain was willing to make a separate peace with Germany. Churchill and his staff warned him that surrender might mean the bombardment of French ports held by the Germans. Dejected, he flew back to London.

Meanwhile, closer to home, Wing Commander Victor 'George' Beamish AFC was informed of his posting to North Weald, where he was to take over as station commander with effect from 6 June. Beamish was, like Teddy, a natural leader of men. He had been awarded the AFC while commanding No. 64 Squadron. In mid-January 1940 he was posted to Canada to assist with the Empire Air Training Scheme but had managed to get the posting to a desk job reversed very quickly.

The squadron was at readiness at 0400 hours on 1 June; four hours later this was changed to fifteen minutes available. At 1400 hours both No. 151 and No. 111 Squadrons were ordered to make a Channel sweep around Dunkirk to maintain some cover for the remainder of the retreating BEF.

Teddy's Hurricanes arrived just in the nick of time for one ship. Teddy swooped on a Junkers Ju 88 just as it was about to launch its attack. He quickly emptied his ammunition into the weaving aircraft which he claimed, in his log book, to have damaged having stopped its engine. His wingman confirmed seeing the Junkers Ju 88 gliding into the sea.

The attack had stopped the Junkers Ju 88s in their tracks; the bombers broke off and fled. Later on in the patrol the squadron came across several Messerschmitt Bf 109s which they chased and engaged. Teddy fired at one but did not record any major damage.

They returned to Hawkinge to refuel before repeating the patrol at 1800 hours, but without any further combat taking place owing to poor visibility. Both sorties had been flown at altitudes below 3,000 ft. A third Channel sweep was to follow that day but this too was uneventful.

Late the following day, 2 June, at 1830 hours, the two squadrons were again launched to fly patrols over Dunkirk, where an air battle was fought with several Messerschmitt Bf 110s at 2005 hours. Teddy fired at a total of five enemy aircraft during the massive dogfight, destroying at least one. He recorded that two more were shot down by the squadron, while Jack Hamar got another one which was unconfirmed, and many more were thought to be badly damaged. No. 111 Squadron flew top cover for Teddy's men, and they too had a number of conclusive combats. Teddy led his Hurricanes back to North Weald to refuel.

The squadron was rested on 3 June. The aircraft and spares for No. 56's Hurricanes arrived at North Weald, which became their base from the following day. Whilst the last remnants of the BEF were being successfully evacuated from Dunkirk, news from Norway and France was not good – the withdrawal of Allied forces from Narvik had begun, and not only did German bombers strike Paris for the first time, but their advancing army also began to move south towards the French capital.

On 4 June, with Operation Dynamo at an end, the squadron was allowed to reintroduce leave, with the battle-weary pilots being granted two days off in rotation. For most of the nine-day period, they had been in the air for six hours a day, flying three, sometimes four sorties over the evacuation beaches and the Channel.

Fighter Command as a whole flew some 2,750 sorties, providing air cover for the beleaguered army. More than seven times the original number planned for in Operation Dynamo, 338,226 men in all, had been rescued, abandoning their equipment but ready to fight another day.

Meanwhile, the Blenheims of No. 2 Group, Bomber Command, flew nearly 1,000 sorties and lost fifty-seven aircraft with more damaged. Teddy's No. 151 Squadron had only flown as escort to the bombers during the latter stages of their campaign but had helped to reduce their casualty rate drastically by giving close cover while over enemy-occupied Europe.

Just two British Army divisions, the 1st Armoured Division, which was the UK's only armoured division at that time, and the 51st Highland Division, remained in France and continued to fight alongside the French army for a further fourteen days.

Hitler had hoped to finish the BEF off by using his *Luftwaffe* rather than engaging them further with land forces. The RAF, however, flew with such gallantry and determination that the Germans often fled or jetti-soned their bomb loads rather than face even numerically inferior forces. There was a certain snobbery involved in their defeat too – most claimed to have faced the legendary Spitfires, rather than admit to having been beaten off by Hawker Hurricanes. Certainly, some Hurricane squadrons were withdrawn following their service in France, Spitfire squadrons taking their place. However, No. 151 Squadron had remained in the thick of the action throughout.

During the defence of Dunkirk No. 151 Squadron had flown around 100 sorties, scoring seven victories with the loss of two pilots shot down. They had played their part in the 'miracle of Dunkirk'. Some, like

Newton and later Blomeley, were to earn the unofficial 'Dunkirk Medal', being evacuated with the troops after baling out. Others were recognized for their gallantry and leadership. But it was not about medals or personal glory, it was about saving men who would make up the nucleus of the British Army, an army that would later defeat the Axis powers in North Africa, Sicily and Italy – men who would land on the D-Day beaches on 6 June 1944, fight their way to the heart of Germany and snatch victory from what had been the jaws of defeat.

On the evening of 4 June, Churchill addressed Parliament, where he spelled out clearly, to his country and to the world, the intention of Britain to carry on the war. Prophetically, he said in his speech to the House, 'Wars are not won by evacuation but there was a victory inside this deliverance, which should be noted. It was gained by the Air Force . . .'

He went on to deliver one of his memorable wartime speeches.

Our thankfulness at the escape of our army with so many men, and the thankfulness of their loved ones, who passed through an agonizing week, must not blind us to the fact that what happened in France and Belgium is a colossal military disaster.

The French Army has been weakened, the Belgian Army has been lost and a large part of those fortified lines upon which so much faith was reposed has gone, and many valuable mining districts and factories have passed into the enemy's possession.

The whole of the Channel ports are in his hands, with all the strategic consequences that follow from that, and we must expect another blow to be struck almost immediately at us or at France.

I have myself full confidence that if all do their duty and if the best arrangements are made, as they are being made, we shall prove ourselves once again able to defend our island home, ride out the storms of war, outlive the menace of tyranny, if necessary, for years; if necessary, alone.

At any rate, that is what we are going to try to do. That is the resolve of His Majesty's Government, every man of them. That is the will of Parliament and the nation. The British Empire and the French Republic, linked together in their cause and their need, will defend to the death their native soils, aiding each other like good comrades to the utmost of their strength, even though a large tract of Europe and many old and famous States have fallen or may fall into the grip of the Gestapo and all the odious apparatus of Nazi rule.

We shall not flag nor fail. We shall go on to the end. We shall fight in France and on the seas and oceans; we shall fight with growing confidence and growing strength in the air. We shall defend our island whatever the cost may be; we shall fight on beaches, landing grounds, in fields, in streets and on the hills. We shall never surrender and even if, which I do not for the moment believe, this island or a large part of it were subjugated and starving, then our empire beyond the seas, armed and guarded by the British Fleet, will carry on the struggle until in God's good time the New World with all its power and might, sets forth to the liberation and rescue of the Old.

Ominously, at the same time as Churchill was eloquently rallying the British spirit, Italian *Duce*, Benito Mussolini, was directing his forces to plan for the invasion of Southern France. The entry of Italy into the war on the side of Germany was a blatant attempt to grab French spoils. Hitler asked Mussolini to postpone his attack until 10 June. Duly, at midnight, Italy declared war on Britain and France, and her armies moved into southern France. At the same time, the British moved against Italian forces in Libya. Both theatres eventually saw the defeat of the Italians.

CHAPTER THIRTEEN

Escort Duties

The fighter squadrons of No.11 Group, Fighter Command, operating from the south-east of England, had provided air cover
throughout the Dunkirk operation, although fuel constraints had
limited the time that patrols could spend over the beach-head area. As
the pilots of No. 151 Squadron knew all too well, this had resulted in
intensive air combats between the *Luftwaffe* and the RAF, with neither
side able to achieve permanent air superiority. Overall, the RAF lost
177 aircraft over Dunkirk, including 106 fighters, whilst the *Luftwaffe*
lost 132 aircraft of all types. Churchill's reference to 'a victory inside this
deliverance' therefore fell somewhere outside the bounds of pure truth,
but it was nevertheless a welcome rallying call for what was to come.

Like other squadrons who defended the skies over our retreating
army, No. 151 was drained and exhausted when Dunkirk was over.
There were some days which started at four or five in the morning whilst
others went on until nine or ten at night. Because the Hurricane did not
have the same speed or endurance as the Spitfire, patrols flown by the
squadron were not as protracted. However, the sting in the tail was that
this meant that the Hurricane pilots usually had the time, if needed, to
fly three or even four sorties a day. Teddy's dogmatic and uncompromising expectations of the whole squadron were unyielding. For the
younger pilots, it had been a hard 'blooding' period.

'My *Luftwaffe* is invincible. And now we turn to England. How long
will this one last – two, three weeks?' said Hermann Goering in June
1940.

Flying Officer Allen, who had recently recovered from the shrapnel
wounds he had received in France, was warmly welcomed back to North
Weald on 5 June. Meanwhile, Flight Lieutenant Loxton had been posted
in as a supernumerary squadron leader, prior to taking up an appointment to command another squadron. The Air Ministry could have found
few finer squadrons for Loxton to witness the spirit between CO, pilots
and ground crew, all of whom, under Teddy's leadership, were fired
up and keen to take the fight to the Germans.

Victor Beamish had arrived ahead of his official posting as station

101

commander. His name is largely absent from the Squadron's Diary, although he regularly flew sorties with both Nos. 56 and 151 Squadrons. Returning from a patrol over Dunkirk during the morning, he requested that Teddy should make one of A Flight's Hurricanes available for his personal use. And so Hurricane DZ – B was duly assigned to him. He would add the DSO and DFC to his growing collection of awards while commanding North Weald.

The squadron was placed initially on 30 minutes' readiness from dawn until 1300 hours, after which they were placed on fifteen minutes' readiness, this state lasting until after dusk. It was to be a day of tension. Teddy sat by the telephone in Dispersal awaiting a call from the Sector Controller, taking a break to step outside and mingle with his pilots. Ground crew and pilots alike sat or lay on the grass beside their Hawker Hurricanes, awaiting the scramble that never came. In the event no sorties were flown and the squadron was stood down until dawn the following day.

At 1000 hours on 6 June, twelve pilots of No. 151 Squadron, led by Teddy, patrolled with No. 56 Squadron from Abbeville to Amiens, flying at 10,000 ft. A few contacts were made with Bf 109s but without claiming any victories.

While on patrol near Le Treport. Teddy shot at three Me 109s during the engagement but did not notice the results due to the speed of the air battle. All the surviving aircraft refuelled at Boos near Rouen, with the exception of Flying Officer Atkinson who force-landed near Rouen, damaging his Hurricane.

At 1700 hours the squadron was scrambled to protect the aerodrome but no contacts were made and they returned to North Weald.

Teddy's log book shows a second mission on the 6th, a low-altitude sweep between Rouen and Boos, during which they intercepted twenty-seven Dornier Do 17s and clashed with Messerschmitt Bf 109s but, as Teddy wrote; 'without results'.

On 7 June the squadron flew to Manston at 1300 hours, setting off an hour later to join No. 56 Squadron on a patrol over the areas around Abbeville and Amiens. During these sorties a Heinkel He 113 was engaged but these were once again, as Teddy noted; 'unsatisfactory clashes'.

The patrol was repeated at 1845 hours, with several Heinkel He 113s attacking the rear section of No. 56 Squadron. No. 151 Squadron became involved in combat with Messerschmitt Bf 109s over Le Treport with the loss of Pilot Officer J. F. Pettigrew, wounded (flying in P3329). Teddy's log book again recorded 'unsatisfactory clashes'.

All the aircraft refuelled at Manston before returning to North Weald where they were stood down for the day.

On the following day, 8 June, Nos. 151 and 56 Squadrons escorted Nos.

21 and 82 Squadrons on a bombing mission to Amiens, taking off at 1100 hours. All did not run smoothly, with two of the Blenheims being lost to ground-based anti-aircraft fire.

Over Amiens, Pilot Officer David Blomeley's aircraft (P3315) was also hit by flak; he lost speed and altitude, and became separated from the rest of the formation. Later, French anti-aircraft guns damaged his aircraft further and he was forced to bale out. During his descent, he was shot at by French soldiers and the canopy of his parachute caught fire. Fortunately, it did not disintegrate until he was a few feet off the ground, and he sustained little more than a turned ankle as he fell in a crumpled heap.

Diving for cover as bullets whizzed around his head, he eventually managed to make his voice heard over the rounds and persuade the French to stop trying to kill him. He was then, thankfully, taken into their 'protection'. As the Germans advanced that evening, however, the French soldiers left their temporary base without first collecting him. He awoke suddenly to the sound of vehicles and, more ominously, German voices. Scrambling through an open window, Blomeley headed for a cropped field where he hid until his temporary billet had been thoroughly searched. He was then forced to make his own way to the coast, only evading capture by moving under cover of darkness and, where he could, keeping to the hedges and ditches. He was eventually evacuated from near Calais and returned to his squadron to rejoin the battle.

Blomeley's Hurricane was, Teddy noted, the squadron's only loss to anti-aircraft fire during the whole of the Battle of France and later the Battle of Britain, although Blomeley did later have a second aircraft blown onto its back by 'friendly fire' from the Dover Barrage.

On 8 June Pilot Officer Hamar took over Hurricane P3316, which his CO had flown off and on for a month or so. Since the middle of May he and Teddy had shared a number of Hurricanes, so presumably Teddy passed on his finely tuned aircraft to his wingman knowing he would fly it to the limit in defence of his leader, and bag a few enemy aircraft at the same time.

No. 151 Squadron flew another escort mission in the afternoon, taking off at 1530 hours. During the patrol the rear section of No. 56 Squadron was once again attacked by a formation of three Messerschmitt Bf 109s. The tables were very soon turned and during the ensuing air battle Teddy fought with ferocious accuracy, he destroyed two of the enemy aircraft that were on No. 56 Squadron's tail. Other members of No. 151 Squadron confirmed these claims, although in his log book Teddy noted them as being 'He 113s'.

His combat report recorded the engagement as taking place at 1800 hours and at 12,000 ft over Le Treport.

After escorting bombers we were returning when I sighted about 5 Me 109s 2,000 ft above us and flying into the sun.

I chased full throttle. They turned left away from me so I wheeled sharply right. 2 Me 109s broke away to right. I watched the 3 carefully as I guessed they would turn in behind my Squadron, which they did and I was able to turn in behind them. I was about to open fire on the lead one when a voice on the RT yelled 'LOOK OUT!

This made me momentarily stop my attack so I missed him but turned onto No. 2 Me.

I got him after a 5 sec. burst. His engine stopped dead and he rolled over but straightened out and I saw him gliding away. I zoomed up and round and then down again onto No. 3 Me 109 and after a two second burst he rolled off pouring white smoke. His engine also stopped. As I thought they were the advance of lots more I did not re-attack them.

We were running very short of fuel so I zigzag out at sea. About 1 mile out an Me (presumably one of the two who had broken away at the beginning) carried out a head on attack on me. I took no notice except to fire at him the whole time. About 100 yards ahead he turned on his back and disappeared. I do not think he was damaged.

F/Sgt Higginson of No. 56 Squadron witnessed both the Me 109s I hit. Likewise some members of my Squadron.

Although the news came through some time later, it was on 8 June that Teddy's brother, Squadron Leader J. W. Donaldson of 263 Squadron, was lost with the sinking of HMS *Glorious*.

Flying Officer Atkinson returned to No. 151 Squadron on 9 June. At 1100 hours the squadron carried out an escort of eighteen Blenheims to Abbeville and Amiens with No. 56 Squadron, landing at Manston at 1300 hours. Although German fighters were seen, they would not engage the patrols.

No. 151 Squadron's second patrol of the day began at 1700 hours; they once again linked up with No 56 Squadron to provide an escort for a formation of twenty-seven bombers of No. 2 Group. As had happened on previous occasions, this was carried out without hindrance from the *Luftwaffe*, who shadowed them. Both Squadrons returned to North Weald at 1900 hours.

A joint request from Nos. 151 and 56 Squadrons was sent by the latter's Intelligence Officer to No. 11 Group Fighter Command, requesting that Bolton Paul Defiants should be made available to patrol the rear of all fighter formations. This was endorsed by the commanding officers and all the pilots of both squadrons.

As I have said, the Defiants, which had a similar appearance to the

Hawker Hurricane, had no forward-firing guns and would fall prey to German fighters once they had been correctly identified. Their rear-firing gun turret was designed to catch out enemy fighters attacking from above and to the rear, the classic attack approach adopted by many of the German single-seater fighter pilots. It was always the role of the 'tail-end-Charlie' to look-out for the enemy making a surprise attack from above and behind, and the pilots of Nos. 56 and 151 Squadrons were all too keenly aware that men were being lost by such attacks and that rear-firing Defiants flying at the rear of their formations might provide additional defence, or at least make the Germans think twice before attacking.

Later, on 19 July, nine Boulton Paul Defiants of No. 141 Squadron were attacked over the English Channel by sixteen Messerschmitt Bf 109s. Six were shot down, the remaining three only surviving because Hurricanes from No. 111 Squadron turned up to engage the enemy and drove them off. The Defiant squadrons were subsequently withdrawn from the daylight combat role and reassigned to become night fighters.

CHAPTER FOURTEEN

Short Leave
as Paris Falls

Accroding to the Squadron Diary, Teddy began a seven-day leave on 10 June, having received an invitation to attend an investiture at Buckingham Palace, where he was to be presented with the DSO by His Majesty King George VI. The ceremony was to be held at 1030 hours the following day, 11 June. Around forty other airmen joined him on the palace forecourt, being led up a short flight of carpeted steps to join the King on a dais, where the presentations took place. To the front were the family and friends of the award-winners.

Teddy's name is absent from the record of operations carried out on the day he was meant to have started his leave. However, his log book records that he flew on the squadron's operational patrol, an offensive sortie to Le Treport, in conjunction with No. 56 Squadron. The squadron flew this patrol between 1215 hours and 1340 hours, led, according to the Squadron Diary, by Flight Lieutenant Loxton and included Flying Officer Allen, Pilot Officer Tucker, Pilot Officer Wright, Sergeant Savill and Sergeant Aslin in one flight, and Flight Lieutenant Ironside, Pilot Officer Hamar, Pilot Officer Forster, Sergeant Atkinson and, according to Teddy's log book, Squadron Leader Donaldson in the other. The Squadron Diary recorded the patrol with the words: 'No enemy aircraft were seen and the patrol returned without loss.' However, a curious contemporary annotation occurs in Teddy's logbook: 'Lost Sgt [Sergeant Atkinson] who returned later having formated on German squadron.'

Teddy later elaborated on this episode when he wrote:

During an offensive patrol to Le Treport on 10 June, Sgt [Atkinson] was found to be missing while over enemy held Continental Europe. He had not radioed for assistance and no one had observed him pealing off the formation. The Sergeant Pilot landed as the remainder of the Squadron were refuelling.

The sergeant pilot's absence had, however, been noted and Teddy summoned him to his office to explain why he had put himself at such a risk and, in so doing, exposing the rest of the squadron. He was threatened with a court martial if his account was unsatisfactory.

His explanation was remarkable. The squadron had made a sudden avoiding manoeuvre which had caught him off guard. Straightening up and re-forming, he had then noticed a problem with his fuel. Looking up from his gauges he noticed something strange about the 'Hurricane' he was formed up with. It was about 20 yards astern and flying faster than him, drawing slightly away in level flight. Suddenly he noticed it had bracing struts on its tail unit. Pulling back his Hurricane's canopy he double-checked his own tail-plain which, of course, had no strut. Easing to one side, the clear outline of a black cross appeared on the aircraft's wing – he had formed up with a *staffel* of Messerschmitt Bf 109s.

Keeping cool, he took aim at his 'leader' and pressed the gun button. The eight Browning .303 machine-guns converged on the Messerschmitt Bf 109, which blew up in mid-air. Rolling onto his back, he dived down to ground level, looking back to see if he was being followed. Luck was on his side and the *staffel* flew on, unaware of the loss of one of their number.

Although this incident might seem far fetched considering the pilot's high degree of training in aircraft recognition and the time and concentration it would have required for him to formate with the faster Messerschmitt Bf 109s, tiredness and the stresses of combat all contributed to such mistakes, and this was certainly not the only incident of its kind.

Flight Lieutenant Loxton was assigned as CO during Teddy's absence. A new pilot, Flight Lieutenant Roddick Lee 'Dickie' Smith, was posted to the squadron as the new B Flight Commander. He had previously served with the Fleet Air Arm, serving on HMS *Glorious*, and came to the Squadron from No. 12 Group Pool, Aston Down, where he had served as an instructor. He only had three hours flying time on Spitfires and Hurricanes. Smith was to fly the squadron's experimental Hurricane (L1750), fitted with two 20 mm cannons rather than machine-guns. This aircraft was heavier and slower than the rest of the Squadron's Hurricanes, hence no one wanted to fly it. Smith was to fly some 130 sorties during the Battle of Britain, mainly in the squadron's two- and four-cannon aircraft. He destroyed one enemy aircraft and claimed three more probables and two damaged.

The very next day, 11 June, as Teddy was on his way to Buckingham Palace, Churchill returned to France. Instead of Paris, which was now surrounded by German forces, he met the French Supreme War Council in Briare. Also there was Charles de Gaulle, now Under Secretary for National Defence. A heated exchange followed; the French demanded every available fighter for the French battle. Churchill refused, saying the decisive battle would come over the skies of Britain, and every fighter would be needed there. Only twenty-five fighter squadrons remained, and Air Chief Marshal Sir Hugh Dowding, Fighter Command's Commander-in-Chief, had already famously and rightly rejected the idea of sending any more fighters to France.

Further escort missions were flown that day when, starting at 1315 hours, Nos. 151 and 56 Squadrons were to escort thirty-five Blenheims to Rouen. However, as the bombers were not seen by the enemy, the fighters simply patrolled the Rouen area. They were in the air again at 1845 hours when they joined No. 56 Squadron on an offensive patrol to Le Camp-Rouen-Le Treport.

On 12 June they took off at 1320 hours to patrol with No. 56 Squadron, giving air cover to shipping in the St Valery area, where Allied troops were embarking. A second patrol in the afternoon was uneventful.

The same day, it was announced that Flight Lieutenant Lomax was promoted to the rank of Squadron Leader with effect from 1 June 1940.

Notification reached the squadron that 'no further operations will be required of them in the Rouen-Dieppe area. Training in operational flying for new pilots to be intensified in view of expected raids on SE England shortly.'

The Squadron Record book shows that the training of fresh pilots was intensified from the 12th, in readiness for the anticipated *Luftwaffe* air assault on the south-east of England. The squadron was later stood down until the 14th when, at 0430 hours, they and No. 56 Squadron were sent on an offensive patrol in the Gravelines-St Omer-Merville-St. Pol area. This was followed by sweeps between Dieppe and Treport. No enemy aircraft were seen. Once back at North Weald the squadron was stood down until 0430 hours on the following day.

Squadron orders from two days previous were rescinded: 'The orders regarding operations over France have been cancelled by the Cabinet and the Squadron is to continue patrols. The German Army is entering Paris.' Teddy later recalled that the reason his squadron was allocated so many bomber escort missions at this time was partly due to Wing Commander Basil Embry, CO of No. 107 (Blenheim) Squadron, who said: 'They always stayed close to the bombers and gave the best protection.'

It was not surprising that these views held such sway as, by May 1940, Embry had already won the AFC plus two DSOs for his tenacious and brave leadership, his second award being for the Norway campaign a month earlier. He was shot down while on a raid on St Omer on 27 May, the day before he was due to take command of RAF West Raynham. He could have handed over leadership of the mission to Squadron Leader L. R. Stokes, who was promoted to wing commander, to take over his command on the 28th.

Embry was hit by anti-aircraft guns just after releasing his bomb load. Captured by the Germans he was being marched away to a PoW camp with other captives when he saw a sign 'Embry 3 km'. Taking this as an omen he rolled down a bank and made his escape. Evading the Germans for two months and making his way towards Spain, he was captured by the Vichy French, escaped again and eventually arrived in Gibraltar after almost ten weeks on the run. After two months' sick leave, he returned to operational duties in October 1940.

Basil Embry went on to become one of the RAF's most highly decorated pilots, being one of only two to be awarded an astonishing four DSOs, and ending his career in 1956 as Air Chief Marshal Sir Basil Embry GCB KBE DSO and three Bars, DFC, AFC.

Teddy later recalled an incident that occurred during one of these close escort missions during late May.

One time I remember having to escort thirty-three Blenheim bombers on a raid to France to disperse tank concentrations.

Before we reached the coast I noticed smoke pouring from one of the bombers and I expected him to turn for home.

He appeared to ignore it and after a little while his engine stopped. Although he could not maintain height he still continued on his course.

Owing to the fact that he was getting so far behind it then became difficult for me effectively to look after both him and the other bombers. I decided he was too good a man to lose and I would look after him myself so I told my No. 2 to carry on the close escort of the remainder.

This man was still unable to maintain altitude and passed over the gun positions on the coast at a dangerously low level. Indeed, at times he was almost invisible from the bursts of AA shells. But still he continued.

We reached the first concentration of tanks; he shut off his one good engine, dived down and dropped two perfect bombs, which blew one tank into the air. He then went on to the next target and did the same thing. I knew he only carried four bombs and expected him to make for home now. But he didn't. He went down to ground level, flying like a huge crane on one engine while his rear gunner machine-gunned German infantry moving up to support the tanks.

He appeared in no hurry to start for home and it was not until he had finished all his ammunition that he started back to England.

I don't mind admitting I was scared.

Now the important part of the story lies here. On arriving back I got into contact with this pilot's Squadron Commander, Basil

Embry, intending to have him commended for his brave action.

I said I did not know his name but he would be easily recognizable as he flew with a silk stocking round his neck like a scarf.

His Commanding Officer told me 'What's the matter with you Teddy? You are losing your sense of proportion. He was simply doing the job he has to do.'

I nevertheless found that act a tremendous inspiration to me for the rest of the war.

It was another uneventful day on 14 June, although things were quite tense with the squadron placed on thirty minutes' readiness. Three of Teddy's operational pilots were being rested as of the previous day: Flying Officer Milne, Flying Officer Blair and Flying Officer Atkinson.

With David Blomeley on survivor's leave and Pilot Officer Pettigrew and Pilot Officer Courtney in hospital after earlier being reported missing, and Pilot Officer Tucker and the CO on leave, the Squadron had the following effective pilots: Squadron Leader Loxton (posted to command No. 25 Squadron with effect from 13 June 1940), Flight Lieutenant Ironside, Flying Officer Allen, Flying Officer Forster, Flight Lieutenant Smith, Pilot Officer Wright, Pilot Officer Hamar, Sergeant Atkinson, Sergeant Aslin and Sergeant Savill.

News from the continent was that German troops had entered Paris on 14 June and that General von Studnitz had led his 87th Infantry Division in a victory march through the city.

On 15 June the squadron flew from North Weald to Tangmere with No. 56 Squadron at 0630 hours and were placed at thirty minutes' readiness. A patrol of three aircraft did get off the ground to sweep the Boulogne area but nothing was seen. Teddy returned from leave on the 16th. There were no operations on the 16th or 17th, although the lull was used for some air-firing practice at Dengie Flats.

On 16 June the squadron's log recorded, 'Information received that the Squadron will not be required for French operations and the immediate future should be employed in preparing for Home Defence.'

CHAPTER FIFTEEN

Posted Missing

Having returned from home leave following his investiture at Buckingham Palace, Teddy was once again at the helm. His first mission following his return was an eventful one. At 1315 hours on 18 June his squadron took off as escort to Blenheims making a bombing raid 10 miles to the south of Cherbourg. Having seen the bombers safely to their target, the Hurricanes circled for a while and spotted three Heinkel He 111s attacking a group of ships. Teddy led the squadron by sections on No. 5 attacks. He attacked the port aircraft, forcing it to jettison its bombs, quickly followed by the other two bombers doing the same. Six Messerschmitt Bf 109s were spotted flying top cover but they failed to engage the Hurricanes.

During the air battle that followed two of the He 111s were destroyed, with Teddy's Hurricane being hit by return fire, a bullet fracturing the hydraulics system and covering the cockpit in oil. He attempted to bale out but, he later recorded: 'The destroyer which I had hoped would pick me up sank, so I remained in the air and got back to Tangmere. Hydraulics U/S.' Jack Hamar escorted his CO safely back to home shores, where he made a safe landing.

After the combat, Pilot Officer L. 'Pop' Wright and Sergeant M. R. Aslin were both posted missing. 'Pop' Wright, flying Hurricane P3313, was shot down and is buried at the Hook of Holland. Sergeant Aslin, flying Hurricane P3324, was killed during the same combat and was buried at Westende Communal Cemetery, Belgium. Both men were twenty-seven years old. Teddy recorded heavy 'friendly' anti-aircraft fire from the ships, which came perilously close to several of the Hurricanes.

At 2100 hours on 18 June Winston Churchill spoke to the nation and the world, with his now accustomed rhetoric, repeating what he had said earlier that day to the House of Commons. Teddy had gathered the officers in the mess to hear the Prime Minister's speech.

What General Weygand called the Battle of France is over. I expect that the Battle of Britain is about to begin. Upon this battle depends

111

the survival of Christian civilization. Upon it depends our own British life, and the long continuity of our institutions and our Empire. The whole fury and might of the enemy must very soon be turned on us. Hitler knows that he will have to break us in this island or lose the war.

If we can stand up to him, all Europe may be free and the life of the world may move forward into broad, sunlit uplands. But if we fail, then the whole world, including the United States, including all that we have known and cared for, will sink into the abyss of a new Dark Age made more sinister, and perhaps more protracted, by the lights of perverted science. Let us therefore brace ourselves to our duties, and so bear ourselves that, if the British Empire and its Commonwealth last for a thousand years, men will still say: 'This was their finest hour.'

His words did what he intended them to do. They inspired every man and woman in Great Britain. They also defined the job ahead, giving the forthcoming battle its name, used for the first time. Despite the accurate reporting of the calamities of the army in France and Belgium, and the losses at sea and in the air, few people believed that Hitler could win the war.

Only the day before, the French Marshal Henri Pétain had asked for an armistice as the last British Army formations in France were evacuated via Cherbourg. Churchill immediately decided that General de Gaulle should be recognized as speaking for France, not Marshal Pétain. De Gaulle escaped by plane to England, fearful that the new collaborationist government would arrest him. On the same day that Churchill made his impassioned speech to the British nation, de Gaulle addressed all of France on BBC radio: 'France is not alone!' he said, and proclaimed himself leader of the exile force of Free French. Vichy collaborators condemned him to death.

Many, including King George VI, were simply relieved at no longer having to see the country's armed forces depleted in the struggle to save France, which seemed incapable of defending herself. The morning papers focused on France, noting the 125th anniversary of the Battle of Waterloo, while *The Times* quoted from Wordsworth's sonnet 'November, 1806', written when England stood alone against Napoleon's might, awaiting the threatened invasion:

'Tis well! From this day forward we shall know
That in ourselves our safety must be sought;
That by our own right hands it must be wrought;
That we must stand unpropped, or be laid low.

Donald, John Willie (Jack) and Edward play in a pedal car in their parent's garden in Kuala Lumpur circa 1915. *(Courtesy of Kate Gregory)*

Teddy (third from left) presented to George VI and the two princes at Mildenhall, 1935. *(Teddy Donaldson archive NJT Collection)*

No 1 Squadron's Display Team 1935 (Hendon Show 1935 and later Zurich 1937). Left to right: Pilot Officer P. Hanks, Pilot Officer P. R. 'Johnnie' Walker, Pilot Officer H. E. C. 'Top' Boxer, Flying Officer E. M. 'Teddy' Donaldson.

(Teddy Donaldson archive NJT Collection)

Rare photograph of Teddy Donaldson (second from left) flying in formation as team leader of No. 1 Squadron's aerobatics team.
(Teddy Donaldson archive, NJT Collection)

Teddy Donaldson as Flight Lieutenant CO B Flight No 1 Squadron RAF while at Tangmere.
(Teddy Donaldson archive NJT Collection)

Squadron lined up in front of one of 151 Squadron's Hawker Hurricanes the day after Teddy was forced to take to his parachute over the English Channel: Flying Officer James 'Buzz' Allen, Flying Officer Tony Forster, Squadron Leader Edward 'Teddy' Donaldson, Group Captain Victor Beamish, Acting Pilot Officer Dickie Smith, Pilot Officer Jack Hamar, Pilot Officer David Blomeley, Pilot Officer Aiden Tucker and Flying Officer Richard 'Dickie' Milne. *(Teddy Donaldson archive NJT Collection)*

Teddy with his brother, John Willie (Jack) on Teddy's wedding day. Winifred's cousin Katherin Skingley acting as bridesmaid.

(Courtesy of Kate Gregory)

Teddy with his brother, John Willie (Jack) on Teddy's wedding day.

(Courtesy of Sally Rudman)

John Willie (Jack), Arthur, Teddy. Between them the three airmen brothers were awarded nine gallantry medals.
(Courtesy of Sally Rudman)

A drawing of Harry 'Broady' Broadhurst by Cuthbert Orde (1941). Broadhurst had ended Teddy's run of victories in the Brooke-Popham Air Gunnery Trophy, eventually winning three times in succession. The two were to remain firm friends.
(Teddy Donaldson archive NJT Collection)

Pilot Officer Jack Hamar DFC. Teddy knew he was safe when Hamar flew as his wingman. Hamar died performing an inverted loop-the-loop over North Weald the day his award was announced in the *London Gazette*.

Pilot Officer David Blomeley of No. 151 Squadron. Teddy met David's father at the inaugural meeting of the Stafford ATC in early 1941. Teddy and David were to remain firm friends for the rest of their lives, David and his wife Joy spending Christmas with him up until 1990. (*David Blomeley archive NJT Collection*)

Teddy's wedding car 'dressed' as a giant bed. (*Courtesy of Kate Gregory*)

Cartoon celebrating the characters on-station at North Weald circa March 1940.
(Teddy Donaldson archive NJT Collection)

Teddy, with his second wife, Estelee Holland and their 9 month old son, David, taken in August 1946 during the build-up to the record attempt.
(Teddy Donaldson archive NJT Collection)

Studio photograph of
Group Captain Teddy
Donaldson DSO, AFC,
taken in America in 1943.
(Courtesy of Kate Gregory)

Teddy (center) and his brother, Arthur, (far right) at Teddy's retirement party, RAF
Manby.   *(Teddy Donaldson archive NJT Collection)*

Teddy standing beside the Star Meteor in which he set the world air speed record. *(Teddy Donaldson archive NJT Collection)*

Teddy Donaldson looks on as one of the souped-up Derwent engines is stripped-down under the supervision of Squadron Leader A. H. Porter (crouched and wearing RAF uniform). *(Teddy Donaldson archive NJT Collection)*

Royal Aero Club Britannia Trophy plaque presented to Teddy Donaldson in 1946 in recognition of his setting a new world air speed record. Silver plaque on original black plastic base.

(Teddy Donaldson archive NJT Collection

Teddy and his third wife, the Norwegian-born Anne Sofie, formerly the wife of Teddy's friend Eric Stapleton, pictured in the garden of the Commandant's House at Manby circa 1960.
(Teddy Donaldson archive NJT Collection)

Air Commodore Teddy Donaldson as Deputy Commander, HQ British Forces Arabian Peninsula (Aden) in 1958.
(Courtesy of Julian Stapleton)

Teddy Donaldson and Julian Stapleton at his
passing-out parade, RAF Cranwell, July 1964.
(Courtesy of Julian Stapleton)

Teddy Donaldson with his cousin, Douglas
Bader, attending Julian Stapleton's passing-
out parade at RAF Cranwell, July 1964.
(Courtesy of Julian Stapleton)

Teddy inspecting a squadron of the ATC during his time as
Commander of the Air Training Corps and Combined
Cadet Forces.   *(Teddy Donaldson archive NJT Collection)*

'Three Beauties'. Hawker Hunter, Anne Sofie and Teddy's Austin Healey 100 all pictured at RAF
Chivenor 1957.

(Courtesy of Julian Stapleton)

With one of the coldest
summers on record and
problems with fuselage of
Teddy's Star crumpling and
one of the balance weights
dropping off and nearly
killing him, things didn't go
the High Speed Flight's way.
Teddy had this photo taken
and added the various
thought/speech bubbles.
(Teddy Donaldson archive
NJT Collection)

Air Commodore Teddy
Donaldson on his retirement
from RAF Staff College, Manby.
(Courtesy of the Grimsby Telegraph)

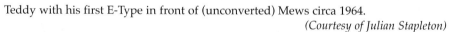

Teddy with his first E-Type in front of (unconverted) Mews circa 1964.
(Courtesy of Julian Stapleton)

'The Air Correspondent'.
Teddy Donaldson leaving
his London home at No 41
Princes Gate Mews.
(Courtesy of Julian Stapleton)

Anne Sofie and Teddy Donaldson with Julian Stapleton (Teddy Donaldson's stepson)
circa early January 1960. *(Courtesy of the Grimsby Telegraph)*

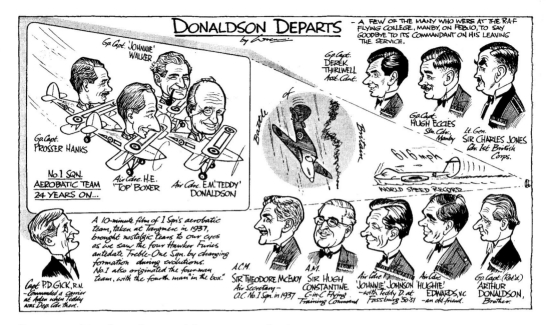

Cartoon marking the gathering of the 'great and the good' at Teddy's retirement party at RAF Manby.
(Teddy Donaldson archive NJT Collection)

Teddy's love of sailing began at Selsey. Both he and his younger brother, Arthur, were at their happiest on the sea and owned sailing boats. While working for *The Daily Telegraph*, Teddy used to take three months off during the summer, which he spent sailing, wearing his old group captain's cap while at sea.

The first man to fly at 1,000 kmph, Teddy later became a member of the Mach 2 Club, when he was one of the first passengers on Concorde, being invited to fly on one of the test-flights.

No. 151 Squadron was placed at readiness on the 19th, but no operational sorties were flown. This additional respite allowed for further training for the new pilots, while giving the ground crews time to catch up on vital maintenance. Teddy flew air tests on P3305, which had been shot up on the previous day. In the event it could not be repaired on the station so he flew it over to maintenance. The relative calm was only interrupted by a brief sortie by Teddy and Red Section at 0900 hours on 20 June to patrol Clacton. Three enemy aircraft were chased but could not be caught. There then followed seven days' rest, during which time leave was reintroduced.

France formally surrendered to Germany on 22 June when the Government signed an armistice in the Forest of Compiegne. The ceremony was conducted in the same railway carriage in which the Germans had signed their armistice in November 1918. Hitler then had it blown up so that it would never be used again.

Britain, with her paltry twenty-five squadrons of fighters against a much larger *Luftwaffe*, now stood completely alone against Nazism and Fascism. She and her Empire would remain alone and defiant for an entire year.

On 24 June Victor Beamish, the station CO at North Weald, gave Nos. 56 and 151 Squadrons a speech about the consequences of the fall of France, and praising the men for their determined efforts which had greatly contributed to the miraculous escape of the greater part of the BEF. He went on to tell them that now more than ever they needed to give their all, and that the future of Great Britain and the Empire depended on them as the next few weeks and months would decide the outcome of the war.

At 1100 hours on 27 June His Majesty King George VI visited North Weald to express his and the nation's gratitude for the station's efforts during the Battle of France. The men of No. 151 Squadron were drawn up outside their hangar and the King made a brief inspection, talking to many of the pilots as he was escorted along their ranks by Teddy. Flight Lieutenant R. H. A. 'Dickie' Lee of No. 56 Squadron was presented with the double award of the DSO and the DFC. However, for the men of No. 151 Squadron, the highlight of the royal visit was the presentation of the DFC to Flying Officer K. H. Blair.

Later that day the squadron took off on a bomber escort mission to Amiens. On the return leg from Abbeville, eighteen Messerschmitt Bf 109s pounced on the bombers, compelling Teddy to lead his Squadron to intercept the enemy. During the ensuing mêlée he damaged two Messerschmitt Bf 109s.

With the knowledge that the Germans would very soon be bringing the fight to our own shores, the ground staff at North Weald were given a taste of what to expect during a strafing attack by 'enemy fighter-bombers'.

The Hurricanes flew mock attacks on the aerodrome, allowing the gunnery commanders and other airmen to go through their drill in relative safety. The hope was that any failings in procedures would be ironed out and lives would be saved in the event of the real thing.

At 1610 hours on 28 June Teddy led Nos. 151 and 56 Squadrons on an escort mission. Six Blenheims were dispatched to photograph the Calais-Boulogne area. During the operation, six Messerschmitt Bf 109s attacked the squadron's rear section, shooting down Flying Officer K.E. Newton, who baled out and landed in the sea for the second time in a matter of weeks. Sadly, this time there was no rescue ship and he drowned before he could be picked up.

Teddy's log book (incorrectly) records these events as having occurred on 26th. He also noted that Pilot Officer Allen returned late from the sortie and that over 300 anti-aircraft guns were reported to have been firing at the patrol, the most intense fire yet experienced by the squadron.

With the previous day taken up with practice sorties, 30 June was once again a day of intense activity. No. 151 Squadron was dispatched with No. 56 at 1330 hours as escort to a formation of six Blenheim bombers, this time on a raid on Vignacourt. On the return leg six Messerschmitt Bf 109s attacked the Blenheims. No. 151 Squadron destroyed four, with another claimed as unconfirmed. The records show Wing Commander Beamish as destroying two, Flying Officer Allen one unconfirmed and Flight Lieutenant Smith another. The combats took place at 1420 hours. During the battle, Teddy (flying P3787) damaged two of the enemy fighters before he was shot down during a head-on attack and ended up in the Channel. He was posted as missing but was picked up, very luckily for him, about 12 miles off Boulogne by an RAF high-speed air-sea rescue launch which was looking for other 'downed' aircrew. Such was his resolve not to be captured, that he had swum for five hours away from the French coast, and was eventually put ashore at Ramsgate.

It is significant that on this occasion Jack Hamar did not fly as his wingman. Teddy later claimed that he had never been shot up when Hamar was covering his tail as wingman. The Squadron Diary recalls that the full line-up of pilots on this patrol was: 'Wing Commander Beamish, Squadron Leader Donaldson, Flight Lieutenant Ironside, Sergeant Atkinson, Flying Officer Forster and Pilot Officer Blomeley'.

Teddy gave a number of accounts of this combat as well as filing an official report; each version differs slightly in the exact details of the day's events.

> I had been shooting a good line to the newer pilots on the Squadron, telling them that the German pilots were not really hot; it was just their numbers that made them dangerous. I said that I looked

forward to the day when I could meet one of them alone. I'd show him!

However, deep down, he knew the Hurricane's limitations as well as its capabilities more than any other. He also knew when he was being out-foxed by the Germans.

I could always tell within a few seconds when I had an Me 109 on my tail and whether the pilot was an experienced opponent.

I would pull round into a tight turn and if he followed me, I would relax and grin, for I knew I could beat him at this game. But if he broke away and climbed fast to get into position to dive on me, I would say to myself, 'oh b—'

A high-ranking ministerial visitor was on the station that day. Teddy sat in the officers' mess wearing his best dress uniform and was about to tuck into a rare treat of a turkey lunch. Just as he was about to savour his first mouthful the order came through to take off immediately to escort six of Basil Embry's Blenheim bombers bound for German ammunition and fuel dumps in France.

As on so many occasions the outward leg of the mission passed off uneventfully. But with the bombers safely escorted to their target, and Teddy having ordered the squadron to turn for home, they suddenly came across a formation of five Messerschmitt Bf 109s, which they quickly engaged. Teddy fixed his sights on two, into which he emptied nearly all of his ammunition but without being able to observe any conclusive results. He ended the engagement only 10 ft above sea level, with the remainder of his squadron outnumbering the enemy and picking them off.

This was when Teddy came across a Messerschmitt Bf 109 that was unusually keen to take him on. With little ammunition remaining, Teddy had climbed above the combat, ready to form up with his squadron as they disengaged and then return to base. His lone Hurricane was seen circling 'on top' by five Messerschmitts, one of which came down out of the sky to attack him. This aircraft is believed to have been flown by *Hauptmann* Herbert Ihlefeld of 1/JG2, who had singled out Teddy's Hurricane. Later Teddy was told that Ihlefeld's transmissions were over-heard as he said: 'Watch me get this one. I'll give you an object lesson in dealing with a Hurricane.'

Teddy had only a few rounds left when the Bf 109 jumped him. Unaware of this at first, the German remained cautious of letting the Hurricane get onto his tail. Teddy got a few rounds off but then his guns fell silent.

The German pilot soon realized that this Hurricane was not going to be the 'easy meat' that he had first thought. Teddy threw his Hurricane about, keeping it out of Ihlefeld's gun-sight for a full fifteen minutes, twisting and yawing, frantically throwing the much slower Hurricane into tight turns, trying every trick in the book, and many of those not in the book, to shake him off. Teddy tried three times to unnerve his would be assailant with collision-course attacks, the Bf 109's bullets and cannon-fire spraying the sky around his Hurricane as he flashed by. Teddy could see all around him the ripples of smoke and intense yellow and red lights whizzing past his aircraft as he fought to lose his enemy. As he did so the German pilot was heard to concede: 'I've got a tough one here!'

Again Teddy saw the opportunity to use his favourite attack. With the Bf 109 speeding towards him, Teddy set himself on a head-on collision course. This normally scared even the most determined adversary. As they hurtled ever closer, the Messerschmitt remained true, pumping cannon shells into the helpless Hurricane. Teddy felt the terrific judder as shells drummed into the wing and fuselage. With a collision speed well in excess of 600 mph, the two fighters wheeled a second away from disaster.

An explosion ripped through the fuselage below Teddy's feet as half the floor disappeared. More damage had occurred elsewhere, the oil tank being blown out of the leading edge of the wing while the petrol tanks were ruptured and had burst into flames.

The air was heavy with the choking fumes of high-octane fuel. Suddenly Teddy was engulfed in a sheet of flames. Gloves alights, he thrashed around trying to pull the pin from his Sutton harness and to release the oxygen and radio connections. As he desperately tried to push the hood back, the flames dispersed.

Looking over at the wings, Donaldson could see that the flames appeared to have gone out, yet to his astonishment, the aluminium skin of the starboard wing was melting before his eyes, exposing the under-lying structure, which glowed white hot, burning in a blow-lamp type flame.

Teddy later said: 'It is at these times you do the stupidest things without realizing it, but recall them later. I sat there shouting "Help! Help!" Naturally, not a soul could hear me.'

With his crippled Hurricane streaming flames and white smoke at around 1,000 ft, the Messerschmitt Bf 109 continued to attack before peeling off. Teddy trimmed the aircraft into a 100 mph glide, crossing the coast near Boulogne. He had two choices; he could bale out and hope his parachute was not damaged; or he could try to crash the Hurricane into the sea and hope to escape losing consciousness as a result of a heavy impact and inflate his Mae West.

Decision made, he climbed onto the port wing root, away from the flames. He looked down and saw the choppy English Channel below. It looked cold and unforgiving. Maybe he was too low for his parachute to deploy properly. He changed his mind; a crash in the comparative safety of the Hurricane cockpit now looked more survivable. But as he attempted to climb back, the rush of air threw him clear.

Tumbling through the air from about 800 ft, Teddy desperately grabbed at the ripcord. He was very low. He pulled and waited. The wait was nerve-racking. The canopy would either deploy or he would hit the sea. With a 'bang' and a jerk on his shoulders, the canopy opened almost immediately but only after what seemed like a lifetime, filling the space above him and blocking out the enemy fighters way above. His own crippled aircraft veered away, off down towards the bottom of the Channel.

With the cold waters looming below, Teddy felt for the valve to the Mae West, which he endeavoured to inflate. He fumbled, blowing air through the rubber tube. The parachute harness cut deeply into him as he descended, forcing air out of the Mae West, only allowing him partially to inflate the bulge behind his neck. He plunged into the water like a torpedo, only the drag of the canopy preventing him sinking further. Luckily for him the strong winds got under the silk and dragged him back to the surface. With the prevailing wind slowly pulling him back towards the French Coast at a rate of about 5 knots, he turned the metal release box and struck it hard, freeing himself from the parachute. His desire to get back to his squadron remained greater than his instinct to reach dry land, and so with what little energy he had left, he began to swim away from the shore and relative safety. This was a dilemma often discussed in the mess and Teddy remained true to his armchair argument that their job was to fight on at all costs and therefore they should try to avoid capture.

The shock of the cold cut through him. His waterlogged clothes now began to weigh him down and, after a little while, he found himself fighting against hypothermia, which threatened to finish him off.

After what had seemed like a lifetime, it hit Teddy that he was not making a great deal of progress, hampered by the Mae West and unable to put in a full swimming stroke. The fate of Flight Lieutenant Ives and Flying Officer Newton was uppermost in his mind and he was now preparing for what might happen to himself. Then, out of the blue, with his own fate still very much in the balance, he saw a high-speed launch coming towards him from the direction of Boulogne harbour. Fearing the worst, he felt for the lanyard around his neck and followed it down to the grip of his service revolver. However, his luck was in. The rescue launch was British and had been looking for the crew of a torpedo-bomber lost mine-laying the previous day. Hauled on board and wrapped in towels, he took some shelter as the launch turned and sped towards England. One of the crew took his uniform and threw it over the exhaust to dry. Unfortunately, when he returned to collect what had been his best dress uniform, it was blackened and useless.

After landing at Margate, Teddy thanked the launch crew and took their details to ensure that they received a commendation. He managed to hitch a lift back to North Weald, arriving in time to find the mess mourning his demise. His name had been wiped off the duty boards and his successor as squadron leader, 'Tin Ribs' Ironside had already been chalked-up. Teddy later claimed he strode in as Ironside was sewing on an extra 'ring', and said drily: 'Not just yet, son!'

Having escaped bullets and cannon shell, nearly been burnt to death and then fallen nearly 800 ft before his Irvin parachute deployed only a few feet above the water; and having elected to release his parachute and take his chances to swim rather than being dragged to the French shore and captivity; and furthermore, having forgone any thoughts of survivor's leave, or even a post-ditching medical, Teddy immediately resumed his command. One can only imagine his thoughts when his application for compensation for his dress uniform was declined with the words that he was 'foolish to wear his best uniform on operations'.

He later said in rather restrained terms; 'It was not exactly the sort of treatment appreciated by men who never knew whether they would return from a mission.'

In 1980 Teddy recalled some further details of this incident in an article he wrote for *The Daily Telegraph*,

My squadron was ordered to escort Basil Embry to destroy a large enemy fuel dump in France. We did not particularly like this assignment because Basil, absolutely fearless himself, took so long with positive identification of the target dump, for the Germans had so many dummies.

Basil was not about to waste bombs on dummies so round and round he went with his Blenheim bombers being shot at from the ground while we were continuously attacked by Messerschmitts from above. But we did not leave him and this kept the Messerschmitts from attacking the bombers.

Eventually, flying home from this, Basil's squadron was jumped by Messerschmitts low over the sea and a terrific battle started. It was then that a particularly threatening Messerschmitt arrived and went straight for me. We fought for fifteen minutes ending up with head-on attacks on each other. Usually Messerschmitts did not like this, for a Hurricane could turn more sharply, so it usually made off, which it could do so at 60 mph faster than a Hurricane.

In this case, on about the fourth head-on attack, shells and bullets started to strike my poor aircraft. The first shell knocked my oil tank clean out of the leading edge of the wing, so I knew the engine could not run much longer. Then the petrol tank blew up and my clothes caught fire and I became hot but still the bastard continued to shoot. My gloves were burning and my goggles 'frizzled' up but I took neither off – luckily!

I undid my straps and climbed on the wing, for the Hurricane was flying very slowly and I could actually see the burning wing bending upwards. Then I realised with alarm that I was only 800 ft off the sea. I though this too low for a safe bale-out but at this time I fell off and it took me seconds to locate the pull ring, which I must have pulled, for, as I was about to hit the water, my parachute opened. I disappeared to the full extent of the cords and the wind got under the parachute and lifted me like a missile to the surface and started pulling me at about 5 knots towards the French coast. Boulogne was 2 miles away, so I got rid of it at once, but then again shells started coming over, even when my head was under the water. It certainly hurt my ears.

The Germans had been shooting at pilots in the sea at that time but my squadron flew over me as long as their fuel lasted. They were not going to let the Germans near me.

Teddy received a message from Air Vice-Marshal Keith Park, AOC No. 11 Group, congratulating the squadron on a most successful combat, during which they had claimed five enemy aircraft destroyed. He added that he 'hoped that the Squadron Leader had not had his ardour dampened and that he will soon have an opportunity of putting his opponent in the sea!'

The AOC, a New Zealander from Auckland, was greatly respected by his squadron commanders, having been a highly decorated fighter pilot in the First World War. Keith Park knew what he was talking about as he knew the physical and mental hardships of warfare through his personal experience, having endured months of squalour in the trenches at Gallipoli in 1915 as an artillery battery NCO. After gaining a commission and joining the Royal Horse and Field Artillery, his battery was shipped to France to take part in the Battle of the Somme, where he was blown off his horse by a German shell. Wounded, he was evacuated back to Britain and graded 'unfit for active service', which technically meant that he was unfit to ride a horse. After a brief spell recuperating, he joined the Royal Flying Corps in December 1916. By the end of war, his final tally of aircraft claims was five destroyed and fourteen 'out of control'. Having also been shot down twice during this period, he empathized with Teddy's predicament. He retired in 1946 as Air Chief Marshal Sir Keith Park GCB KBE MC and Bar DFC.

Typically, Teddy analysed his own experiences and filed a report for his CO, Victor Beamish. He made a number of key observations: that Mae Wests should not be inflated during the descent; that attempting to use the valve in the water resulted in the Mae West deflating further and that it was better to remove it, then inflate it using the valve; and that many enemy aircraft that were seen to catch fire and then 'go out' might actually be burning in a similar way to Teddy's Hurricane.

The following day, 1 July, Teddy and Victor Beamish were photographed in front of one of the squadron's Hawker Hurricanes, along with the pilots of No. 151 Squadron. Teddy, sporting a neatly trimmed handle bar moustache, was captured in typically defiant mood, sharing a joke with his men despite his near-death experience of the previous day. The photograph was syndicated to a number of news-papers. One used the headline: 'They gave the Nazi flyers a Hurri caning.' The full line-up caught on camera that day were: Flying Officer Charles Atkinson, Flying Officer James 'Buzz' Allen, Flying Officer Tony Forster, Squadron Leader Edward 'Teddy' Donaldson, Group Captain Victor Beamish, Acting Pilot Officer Dickie Smith, Pilot Officer Jack Hamar, Pilot Officer David Blomeley, Pilot Officer Aiden Tucker and Flying Officer Richard 'Dickie' Milne

Overall, the air operations over France and the Low Countries had cost the RAF 1,029 aircraft, including 432 Hurricanes and Spitfires. However, German losses for the same period ran to over 1,250, the greater proportion of which fell to the guns of the RAF's Fighter Command.

Churchill said of this phase of the campaign: 'there was a victory inside this deliverance which should be noted. It was gained by the Royal Air Force.'

CHAPTER SIXTEEN

Prelude to the 'The Battle'

The odds were still heavily stacked against the RAF as the *Luftwaffe* was quickly replacing its losses and taking over airfields in the captured countries. In Britain the time was spent putting as many new fighters and trained pilots into service as possible, to guard against the attack everyone knew was coming. The lull as the German forces consolidated their position was vital to the British armed forces, as it allowed them time to prepare. By the beginning of July 1940, the RAF had built up its strength to 640 fighters, but the *Luftwaffe* had 2,600 bombers and fighters. The stage was set. In the skies above south-east England, the future of Britain was about to be decided.

With many of No. 151 Squadron's pilots battle-weary and nearing the end of their tour of operations or incapacitated through wounds, it was important that the pilot's replacements be brought up to operational fitness and ready to take their places. Five new pilots arrived at North Weald on 1 July: Midshipman Owen Maurice Wightman (killed in action on 4 February 1941 during convoy protection operations off HMS *Ark Royal*), Sub Lieutenant Henry William Beggs (killed in action with the loss of HMS *Avenger* on 15 November 1942), Pilot Officer L. G. Hunt, Pilot Officer John William Edward Alexander and Sergeant McIntosh (killed in action with No. 605 Squadron on 13 September 1940).

Teddy led the new men in a gruelling programme of flying practice over the next eight days, including formation flying, practice attacks and scrambles. These few quiet days were to prove vital and allowed the men to get used to the characteristics of the Hurricane, and to the ethos of their squadron. The stories of the Battle of France and the Battle of Britain are littered with accounts of brave men who arrived at operational squadrons with only a couple of hours' practice on fighters, and who had their first combat training while actually in action. Of course, many never lived to tell the tale!

On the next day the first plans for the invasion of Great Britain were put into action following the *Luftwaffe* operational order to deny the Channel to British shipping and to gain control of the skies.

Towards the end of this rest period, Flying Officer Charles F. Atkinson, his tour of operations having expired, was posted away as an instructor on 8 July.

The squadron's role for the next few weeks included a number of offensive sweeps and convoy patrols as the *Luftwaffe* forced the RAF into mounting resource-sapping standing patrols. Later research has shown that many of these Channel convoys were unnecessary as their cargoes could just as easily have been transported across the country by rail.

On 9 July No. 151 Squadron was once again in a major combat. A Flight, accompanied by Wing Commander Victor Beamish, encountered a formation of around 100 enemy aircraft, recorded to be a mixture of Messerschmitt Bf 109s, Messerschmitt Bf 110s, Junkers Ju 88s, and Heinkel He 111s, flying over the Thames Estuary and heading for a nearby convoy. The formation was forced to break up by a determined attack led by Beamish, during which Milne destroyed a Messerschmitt Bf 109E, Midshipman Wightman a Messerschmitt Bf 109, and Beamish damaged a Messerschmitt Bf 110 off Margate, while Flying Officer Forster and Pilot Officer Hamar shared a Messerschmitt Bf 110, the combats all taking place near Margate at 1610 hours. The Squadron Diary recorded that Flight Lieutenant Ironside's cockpit hood was damaged by a cannon shell and he was wounded by splinters. Midshipman Wightman, who had only joined the squadron the previous day, was hit and forced to bale out into the cold waters of the Thames Estuary. He was picked up by a trawler and taken to Sheerness, from where he made his way back to North Weald that evening. It was a tough introduction to air operations. All the action took place between 8,000 and 1,000 ft and was centred on an area about 20 miles north-east of Margate.

Jack Hamar's combat report reads:

At 1430 hours on 9.7.40 A Flight 151 Squadron was ordered to patrol a large convoy about 5 miles off the coast just north of the Thames Estuary. I was flying as Red 2 in the formation. At 15.40 hours a large number of E/A in several waves were sighted flying N.W. at about 10,000 ft. It was impossible to attack the first wave, which consisted of Heinkel 111 bombers, because of the large number of escorting fighters which were very near to us. Red 1 therefore ordered line astern + attacked the nearest formation of fighters which consisted of 12 Me110s. No. 1 F.A. [fighter attack] was used + after Red 1 had broken away, I attacked the rear

Me 110. I closed to 150 yards. + gave it a 5 second burst. I saw my
bullets tear into the fuselage + wings of the E/A which staggered
badly. I then had to break away quickly as the air seemed just full
of E/A.

I then saw bombs bursting near the convoy which I approached
at full throttle, I chased 1 section of 3 E/A away from the northern
end of the convoy but failed to get in a position to open fire, I then
continued to patrol the convoy for about 15 minutes as the air had
by that time cleared of E/A. No ship in the convoy appeared to
have been hit by bombs.

I then returned to base as fuel was running low.

The daring assault by a handful of Hurricanes forced the enemy into
smaller echelons, only one of which eventually found the convoy and
none of which managed to bomb the vessels successfully. Jack Hamar's
Messerschmitt Bf 110 was confirmed by Midshipman Wightman.

Pilot Officer Anthony Forster fought in the same combat, sharing in
the destruction of a Messerschmitt Bf 110.

After patrolling convoy off Thames for an hour E/A were spotted
to the East flying West. No. 1 attack delivered on escorting Me 110s
which were forming defensive circle in line astern. I carried out
quarter attack on Me 110 and saw bullets hitting it and on closing
up could see the machine was riddled with bullet holes. 1 Bf 110
was seen by F/O Milne breaking away with white smoke
streaming from it. After breaking away from the dog-fight, I
patrolled convoy but there was no sight of enemy bombers. There
was no apparent damage to any ships in the convoy.

Ironside's Hurricane was hit by enemy fire and limped back to base
where he made a crash-landing. Teddy followed the flight of the
damaged Hurricane as it approached and, realizing that it was in
trouble, raced to the pilot's aid. He recalled the incident many years later
with his customary self-mocking modesty.

My senior Flight Commander, Flight Lieutenant Ironside, known
throughout the Squadron as 'Tin Ribs', was coming in badly shot
up. I grabbed an axe from the fire tender and yelled at him that I
was going to cut him out of the wrecked Hurricane, which by this
time was leaking aviation fuel all over the place. Perched on the
wing, my first blow, I am ashamed to say, went straight through
the canopy where it had buckled due to enemy fire, and seriously
injured Tin Ribs in the shoulder. He had to spend a week or two in
hospital to recover.

Ironside was sent to St Margaret's, Epping, wounded by shell splinters, possibly also receiving minor additional injuries during his rescue. He did not return to combat during the Battle of Britain.

Whether Teddy had actually caused Ironside any injury is debatable but his actions in climbing onto a crashed Hurricane which was spilling aviation fuel to rescue of a friend, despite being physically and mentally drained from his own role in the earlier combats, was typical of the man. He, of all people knew that in an instant the aircraft could have exploded or turned into an inferno, and that even the act of cutting Ironside out of the wreckage with the axe was liable to create a spark which could have spelt the end for both men.

This courageous act appears to have gone unrecorded and unrecognized by the authorities, probably because the station CO, Victor Beamish, was still in the air at the time of the incident and therefore not a witness to the daring rescue. Similar incidents elsewhere were to result in the award of the GM, BEM, King's Commendation for Bravery, or Mention-in-Dispatches, depending on the perceived level of risk involved. As Teddy saw it, however, he was simply helping to save the life of one of his men.

CHAPTER SEVENTEEN

Britain Alone –
To Hell and Back

I n order to invade Britain, the Germans had to have control in the air
over the English Channel, otherwise the RAF and the Royal Navy
would have been able to destroy their invasion force before it
reached England's shores. The *Luftwaffe*'s command of the air was
therefore vital to any plan for an invasion fleet to cross the Channel
successfully, and to prevent British sea or air forces from interfering
with the operation.

In this preliminary stage of its attack on Britain, the *Luftwaffe* was to
probe the British defences – looking for weaknesses before a major
assault could be launched to exploit them – as well as to draw the RAF
into combat and wear down its strength. Shipping convoys in the
Channel and England's southern ports were to become the initial targets
although the Germans also suspected the importance of the British radar
masts on the south coast.

Interestingly, the German navy, army and air force each had their own
plans and ideas as to how and where the invasion should be launched.
There seems to have been little co-operation and, despite the impressive
build-up of barges and other equipment in French and Belgian ports, the
actual detailed planning for the operation, code-named 'Sealion', was
never really thrashed out. All, it appeared, depended on the success of
the *Luftwaffe* before an invasion could to be taken seriously.

The date chosen later by the Air Ministry as marking the first day of
what would be officially known as the Battle of Britain was 10 July 1940,
although most squadron records agree that the general air campaign was
little different from that of the previous few days. Teddy's log book
indicates that No. 151 Squadron had flown several fighter interceptions
between the 8th and the 10th, including the very eventful one over the
Thames Estuary on 9 July, although most of the other patrols ended in
the enemy either turning back or out-running the much slower Hawker
Hurricanes.

On 12 July, the squadron took part first in an offensive sweep and later in a convoy patrol, protecting Convoy 'Booty' some 20 miles east of Orfordness, during which a Do 17 was destroyed. Later on, a further battle developed when three Dornier Do 17s were encountered. Wing Commander Beamish flying as No. 2 to Teddy Donaldson shot down one of these but his aircraft sustained damage from return fire. Flying Officer Milne shared another during the same engagement.

Teddy's Hurricane was hit by heavy cross-fire as he made his attack on a Do 17. His rudder control was shot away, and at least one round had entered his engine, resulting in an oil leak which covered him and the cockpit. With the careful use of his throttle, he was able to guide his crippled aircraft back to Martlesham, the engine giving in just as he made his landing. He touched down with a flat tyre and damaged wheel, both having been hit by another bullet.

Sadly, Flying Officer James Henry Leslie Allen was less fortunate and was lost during this patrol, his aircraft (P2375) having been hit by return fire from a Dornier Do17 of II/KG2 at about 0945 hours. He was last seen falling out of the sky with a dead engine, gliding 20 miles off the coast at Orfordness. Sergeant Hewett circled the spot where Allen's Hurricane ploughed into the water but nothing was seen beyond a patch of oil and a few fragments of debris.

Flying Officer Allen, a New Zealander, had served with the squadron since February 1939 and was greatly respected by all ranks. He had been briefly seconded to No. 87 Squadron during the Battle of France, returning to No. 151 is in early June. Allen's body was never found, but he is remembered on Panel 5 of the Runnymede Memorial. He was the squadron's first fatality during the Battle of Britain.

On 13 July No. 151 Squadron was put on thirty minutes' stand by. A patrol was flown over Manston and an investigation, quickly recalled, was made of a suspected raid. At 1415 hours a formation of Dornier Do 17s was seen heading for Convoy 'Pilot'. At North Weald Nos 56 and 151 Squadrons were scrambled, breaking up the attack but without claiming any enemy aircraft damaged or destroyed.

At 1500 hours on the following day the squadron was scrambled to intercept a raid over Dover at between 10,000 and 12,000 ft. In the air for less than half an hour, they came across a formation of some forty Messerschmitt Bf 109s and Bf 110s. Teddy latched onto a Bf 109 which was about to shoot down Flying Officer Forster, sending the would-be attacker down in flames. Meanwhile Pilot Officer Hamar destroyed the other Bf 109 on Forster's tail, while Flight Lieutenant Smith got a probable Bf 109 with his cannon-firing Hurricane. The remainder of the enemy would not engage and fled back over the Channel.

The action is taken up by Hamar's combat report:

At 1500 hours on the 14.7.40 the squadron was ordered off from Rochford to intercept E/As south of Dover. At approximately 1520 hours, when the Sqn was almost over Dover a bunch of Me 109s were sighted about 5,000 ft above our formation. I was flying Red 2 in the formation. As it looked as though the E/A were about to attack us Milne leader ordered our defensive line astern tactics. As we turned sharply to port, 2 Me 109s were seen diving to attack the last aircraft in our formation. Milne leader attacked the leading Me 109 + I the second. I turned inside the E/A which had pulled up into a steep left hand climbing turn. I closed rapidly + opened fire at about 250 yards with a 45 degree deflection shot. The E/A seemed to falter + straighten out into a dive. I placed myself dead astern at about 50 yards + opened fire closing to almost no distance. I saw a large explosion just in front of the pilot and a large amount of white smoke poured from the E/A which was by this time climbing steeply. I was then forced to break away due to fire from the rear + lost sight of the E/A + therefore did not see it crash. This action was also seen by Flying Officer Forster of 151 Sqn.

I fired two bursts of about six seconds each at E/A. By this time I had little ammunition left + could see no further E/A. I returned to base to refuel +rearm.

Teddy's own combat report was timed at 1515 hours and records one Messerschmitt Bf 109 confirmed destroyed north of Dover at 12,000 ft.

Ordered to Dover to intercept large number of enemy a/c. We found them alright but they were about 5,000 ft above us, so I climbed with my squadron to get at them. F/O Forster's aircraft was not refuelled when we took off but was just catching us up when I saw 2 Me 109s detach themselves from the main mass and come down on him. He did very well because before I could get round to him the leading Me had fired about a 4 sec burst at him and not scored one hit. He did this by kicking on rudder throwing the Me's shots out to the side. I had to go into attack the leading Me 109 in front of the second Me 109 because I thought F/O Forster was critical. I hit him with a full deflection shot. He flicked onto his back with a smoke and muck pouring out of him but I did not stop firing. I gave him about a 10 sec burst whilst he floated up side down from about 15 yards. He went straight in with smoke pouring out. This was confirmed by W/C Beamish and Midshipman Wightman. Luckily for me, and exactly as we had planned, P/O Hamar my No. 2 shot the other Me 109 down in flames as it started onto me.

I continued to patrol Dover but as I had about a dozen attacks by

Spitfires and Hurricanes made on me (they did not fire) and there
were no e/a in sight I returned to base to rearm and refuel.
   This is a change as the last three times in action I have been shot
down.

The Squadron Diary for 14 July recorded the arrival of three
Commonwealth pilots to the Squadron from No. 2 FTS at Brize Norton.
They were Pilot Officers Robert W.G. Beley (a Canadian), Irving 'Black'
Stanley Smith (a New Zealander) and John L.W. Ellacombe (British, but
born in Northern Rhodesia, where his father had formed a health service
in Livingstone, and recruited in Cape Town). Pilot training was already
being shortened at the beginning of the Battle of Britain, and the latter
two had not even flown a Hurricane prior to their arrival on the
squadron. Needless to say, Teddy quickly ensured they had instruction
on the station's Miles Master and were then given hours on Hurricanes
before they were even considered for operational service. Pilot Officers
Smith and Ellacombe later won two DFCs each and went on to have
successful careers, reaching group captain and air commodore rank
respectively. As a wing commander, 'Black' Smith led the famous raid
on Amiens Prison on 18 February 1944.
   Pilot Officer John Ellacombe recalled that the Hurricane . . .

   was a stable aeroplane. Quite easy to land once you got the sort of
   feel for it. You had to land in your semi-stall position otherwise you
   would start bouncing, but once you learnt all that, it was a
   delightful aeroplane to fly, stable, and you could pull a very tight
   turn, and we were taught all that, and we were told [by Teddy] that
   we could out-turn the Messerschmitt 109, as long as you saw him
   coming. The good thing about the Hurricane, it had a big mirror
   above the cockpit, so if you looked at that when you were looking
   around you would, with luck, not get somebody on your tail.

It should, perhaps be noted that 14 July was the date given by Air Chief
Marshal Newall for Dowding's retirement from the Service. This date
had later been moved to the end of October, which coincided with the
end of the period regarded by the Air Ministry as marking the Battle of
Britain.
   Little overall enemy activity was seen on 15 July, partly due to adverse
weather conditions. At 1015 hours, an interception was flown against a
Dornier Do 215 flying a reconnaissance sortie over a convoy in the Dover
area. The enemy aircraft was chased away but could not be engaged as
it disappeared into thick clouds. During the day, three more new pilots
arrived from Operational Training Unit (OTU): Pilot Officer K.B.L.
Debenham, Sergeant L. Davies and Sergeant G.T. Clarke.

On 16 July, Hitler issued his War Directive No. 16, which detailed advance planning for the invasion of the United Kingdom. Intended only for his commanders-in-chief, it was forwarded by Goering to his air fleet commanders via the Enigma coding machines. Thanks to Polish resistance workers, the British had secured an Enigma machine and so the contents of the Directive, and therefore the German's plans for the invasion of Britain, were soon known by Churchill and the War Cabinet.

The assault was codenamed *Seelöwe* ('sealion'). Hitler decreed:

As England, in spite of her hopeless military position, has so far shown herself unwilling to come to any compromise, I have decided to begin preparations for, and if necessary, to carry out the invasion of England.

This operation is dictated by the necessity to eliminate Great Britain as a base from which the war against Germany can be fought. If necessary the island will be occupied. I therefore issue the following orders:

1)   The landing operation must be a surprise crossing on a broad front extending approximately from Ramsgate to a point west of the Isle of Wight. The preparations must be concluded by the middle of August.

2)   The following preparations must be undertaken to make a landing in England possible:

   a)   The English Air Force must be eliminated to such an extent that it will be incapable of putting up any substantial opposition to the invasion troops . . .

Three days later, in a speech in the Reichstag, Adolph Hitler issued what he described as 'a final appeal to common sense', calling for Britain to sue for peace.

At North Weald, 16 July was a quiet day, due to low cloud and heavy rain. Shipping patrols were flown on the 17th and 18th, as well as on the 20th, 21st, 22nd, and 23rd, but all these turned out to be uneventful. On 18 July Pilot Officer Courtney returned to the squadron following his recovery from wounds received in combat on 29 May.

The squadron moved from North Weald to the more advanced RAF Station at Rochford on 19 July, and on the following day Midshipman Wightman of the Fleet Air Arm was posted away to No. 760 Squadron. Sadly he was killed on 30 June 1941 while flying a convoy operation from HMS *Ark Royal* with No. 807 Squadron. Acting Sub-Lieutenant Wightman is buried in North Front Cemetery, Gibraltar.

News reached the squadron on 23 July of the richly deserved award of the DFC to Pilot Officer Jack Hamar. Sadly, he was never to receive the award in person nor ever put the ribbon up. There was no spare medal ribbon to hand and therefore he was unable to sew the small but distinctive blue and white diagonally-striped decoration onto his uniform; and within twenty-four hours of the news of the award he was dead, killed in a tragic accident like his uncle, a First World War pilot before him.

On 24 July the squadron was to fly a few local sorties, while the new pilots continued on their training programme. Early in the morning information reached the Sector Controller about an unidentified aircraft heading for the mainland. No. 151 Squadron's Green Section was ordered to take off and investigate. Teddy and Jack Hamar were accompanied by Sergeant Atkinson. Within minutes of their being scrambled the threat had gone and at 0404 hours the patrol was ordered to return to base.

Over the previous few weeks Teddy and Hamar had developed a routine whereby, as they came in to land, they would separate, one going left and the other right, each performing an upward loop, almost in symmetry, before coming in to land. As they turned back for base on this occasion they had been up for only a couple of minutes and had not built up sufficient altitude or airspeed to put the Hawker Hurricane through such a manoeuvre. Teddy and Sergeant Atkinson could only look on in horror as Jack (in P3316), with his canopy still back from the take-off moments earlier, creating extra drag, broke away at 120 knots and began to throw his aircraft into the usual inverted upward roll. Teddy shouted a warning over the intercom but it was in vain. As he did so the aircraft juddered on the brink of a stall approaching the top of the loop. Suddenly the engine cut and it plunged, inverted, to the ground, crashing in from about 500 ft. Teddy was down beside the crippled aircraft within minutes but there was nothing that could be done.

There was no time to grieve for the loss of his friend – Teddy was scrambled less than two hours later, taking off over the wreckage of Jack's Hurricane. He was deeply affected by the loss, however, and was never again able to achieve the same combat successes, although he fought on as bravely as ever. He and Jack had claimed their last enemy aircraft together on 14 July, just four days into the Battle of Britain.

The squadron diary recorded the official line:

Jack Hamar brought down three confirmed enemy aircraft and six others probably destroyed; it is particularly tragic that his death should occur as a result of an accident. Green Section was taking off on a patrol when Pilot Officer Hamar's aircraft was seen to dive into the ground.

Of his friend, Teddy wrote on 25 November 1989:

> Jack Hamar was my Number Two. Now as CO I had to navigate as
> well as lead attacks. He can only do this if he has a good No. 2 who
> he can completely rely on. A CO knows no one can creep up behind
> him as long as his No. 2 is in that place. I knew Jack would be there.
> If he were shot down, the last thing Jack would do would be to tell
> me on the radio he had 'had it'.
> Looking after me was a very hazardous task. Jack did it loyally
> and even so shot down 6½ enemy aircraft, the half was for a bomber
> I had damaged and might have returned to its base. He blew it out
> of the sky in flames.
> I made nine forced landings; Hamar was resting on these days. I
> was never shot down with Hamar as my No. 2. Jack and I were
> extremely close; I loved the fellow. From mid-July we slept the
> nights in the dug-outs on the airfield at North Weald.
> There were eight pilots on camp beds at the beginning. By the
> 24th of July, only Jack and I were left. On the night of the 23rd, Jack
> sat on the end of my bed and said 'Sir, I think you and I will live
> through this. We have been to hell and back together and are still
> alive.'
> I said, 'For God's sake, don't say that. It's bad luck.'
> The next morning the weather was appalling. I got an urgent call
> from the AOC Keith Park. He said 'the weather is awful but I have
> an unidentified aircraft circling Ipswich at 10,000 ft, I don't like it.
> As the weather is so bad I must ask if you can go after him.'
> I said to Jack 'what about it?' he said, 'Let's get the bugger, Sir.'
> The AOC said 'Thanks a lot', so off we went.
> The visibility was about a quarter of a mile. The danger at North
> Weald was the international radio masts. These went up several
> hundred feet and whilst the controllers could get pilots back to the
> field, to avoid the mast you had to see them in time.
> No sooner than we were airborne with wheels up, than Group
> identified the aircraft circling Felixstowe as 'friendly'.
> We turned round and, flying slowly at 120 mph and some 60 ft
> above the ground, I waited for North Weald to reappear, which it
> did within a few minutes.
> I signalled Jack to break. To my horror he broke upwards and
> commenced an upward right-handed roll. At that speed it simply
> was not possible. I called out 'Don't! Don't!' It was too late; he
> stalled and hit the ground upside down.

As station commander, it was Wing Commander Victor Beamish, not
Teddy, who wrote to Jack's parents:

It is with the deepest sympathy and regret that I write concerning
the death of your son. He was one of the bravest of our officers,
beloved and respected by all – I can say no more.

Three days ago he had been awarded the Distinguished Flying
Cross – a signal honour which he knew of before his death.

May I again convey my very deepest sympathy on a sad loss to
us all.

The fact that Jack had been informed of his award may have contributed
to his death – but we will never know. It did, however, get the squadron
into trouble with the Air Ministry which might have changed the award
to a posthumous Mention-in-Dispatches, which was then the only award
other than the Victoria Cross which could have been awarded posthumously.

Jack's award appeared in the *London Gazette* of 30 July.

Pilot Officer Jack Royston Hamar (70898) – since deceased.

This officer has participated in all operational and most of the
patrol flights undertaken by his squadron. He has shown coolness
and courage of a high order, and has personally destroyed six
enemy aircraft.

The same Gazette included the announcement of the award of the DFC
to Forster, whose life Donaldson and Hamar had saved a few days
earlier:

Flying Officer Anthony Douglas Forster (90290), Auxiliary Air
Force.

This officer has displayed great courage and devotion to duty in
participating in all patrols recently undertaken by his squadron,
during which he has destroyed at least two enemy aircraft.
Previously he has been engaged in intensive flying operations in
France, where he destroyed four enemy aircraft.

The tragedy of Jack Hamar's death, performing aerobatics over North
Weald may well have had repercussions on Teddy's military career.
Certainly in later years he appeared, on occasions, to have been overlooked for well-deserved promotion. With his notable record of combat
victories, gained more than frequently against overwhelming odds, he
should unquestionably have been rewarded with a second gallantry
decoration. His station commander, Victor Beamish, who always kept
his personal Hurricane outside the control tower in case he should see a
raid coming, and who frequently flew with No. 151 Squadron, would
have been aware of Teddy's pugnacious and dynamic leadership in the

air as well as his combat victories, and it was his duty to make recommendations for such awards. To be fair, he may, of course, have put Teddy forward for a second gallantry award which may, in turn, have been rejected by a higher authority. Once again, we will never know as Beamish was killed later in the war, posted as 'missing' whilst on operations on 28 March 1942. By the time of his death, soon after taking over command of his second fighter station at Kenley, he had claimed eleven enemy aircraft destroyed and won two DSOs and a DFC to add to his AFC.

After the war, Teddy was once asked why he was not awarded more gallantry decorations. As only he knew what heroics he had performed, his reply probably hid an inner truth. Nevertheless, he was unassuming and succinct: 'It was not about winning medals but winning freedom. Anyway, as CO, one can hardly recommend oneself!'

It should be remembered that Teddy was a crack shot and twice winner of the RAF's Brooke-Popham Trophy. His log book and combat reports record numerous occasions when he got clear shots at the enemy but made no claim on those occasions when he could detect no conclusive result from his hits. Many other pilots, under similar circumstances, claimed the aircraft as 'damaged', but not Teddy, who was more interested in making what he considered to be an accurate record of the state of the enemy rather than accruing a personal tally.

However, history should record that he was a very brave Hurricane pilot who led his squadron on numerous combat missions over enemy-occupied territory and the English Channel. He flew throughout the Battle of France and the British Army's evacuation from Dunkirk as well as both before and during the early stages of the Battle of Britain. He frequently completed several sorties in a single day, and his inspirational leadership, example and material contribution to the successes gained were all of the highest order.

Furthermore, he was a CO who remained in the thick of it throughout his squadron's period in operations against the enemy, remaining eager to get at them, despite the risks and the growing casualties. He knew that being a fighter pilot was a young man's game. Even at twenty-five or twenty-six a pilot's reactions might be too slow, and many squadron commanders were amongst the first casualties, including the CO of No. 74 Squadron, Squadron Leader White, considered to be one of the best air-to-air shots in the RAF. He was shot down by a relatively slow Henschel 126 reconnaissance plane while on his first sortie. Teddy, self-effacing as ever, put his survival down to luck and to his wingman, Jack Hamar, but once involved in the mêlée of combat it was largely a case of every man for himself. His supreme skills as a pilot and marksman saw him through against often overwhelming odds. Even when his aircraft was caught in cross-fire or during one-on-one combat, he invariably managed to break with the engagement and make for safety, confirming that it was he who was making the play and not his opponent. Even when his Hurricane was damaged he was able to choose the moment that the air battle was over and to retreat for repairs, ready to take on the enemy again another day.

CHAPTER EIGHTEEN

Aftermath and Reflection

Station morale must have been low on the morning of 25 July as the previous day's events hit home. To lose a pilot was bad enough but to lose one who had been so well liked and respected across the two squadrons at North Weald, and in the manner Jack had died on the runway, must have been doubly so.

Teddy is said to have sobbed at the sight of his decapitated wingman and to have to be assisted away by Victor Beamish, who told him he thought he had had enough. Beamish immediately sent a message off to the Air Ministry requesting that Teddy be rested. He had flown on most of the squadron's missions, leading from the front as the top scorer. He had put himself into dangerous positions when he could so easily have let his subordinates take a greater share of the risk – but that was not his style.

The squadron diary recorded that No. 151 Squadron maintained its usual convoy escort patrols on 25, 26, 27, and 28 July, but without any contact with the enemy. On the 26th Teddy flew on an uneventful convoy patrol and was scrambled again later that day to defend the aerodrome from an enemy attack which did not materialize, much to his annoyance. He landed without having fired his guns.

Flight Lieutenant Ironside and Pilot Officer Smith flew to Knighton, Radnorshire on the 26th to attend Jack Hamar's funeral, but they failed to find the landing ground and had to return. Floral tributes were sent and Teddy marked the sad occasion in his own way.

Pilot Officer J. B. Ramsey reported for flying duties from No. 7 OTU on 29 July. The squadron was using Rochford alternately with No. 56 Squadron, with both 151 and 56 participating in shipping patrols, flying down the coast as far as Dover. The enemy were encountered in the Harwich area at about 1715 hours, with Flying Officer K. H. Blair claiming an unconfirmed Messerschmitt Bf 110, while Pilot Officer D. H. Blomeley and Sergeant G. Atkinson both claimed a Bf 110 damaged.

During the day, Squadron Leader J. A. G. Gordon arrived for flying duties with No. 151 Squadron. He would spend the next few days shadowing Teddy gaining valuable operational knowledge in preparation for taking over command of the squadron.

During one of the Squadron's regular convoy patrols, Flying Officer Whittingham's and Flying Officer Milne's Hurricanes were hit by fire from Messerschmitt Bf 110s off Orfordness and they were forced to make emergency landings at Martlesham[1] and Rochford[2] respectively. Milne had damaged a Bf 110 but was hit by return fire.

The squadron flew a convoy patrol from Rochford on 30 July; these missions continued into the first five days in August but without any contacts.

A simple ceremony took place in the officer's mess on 4 August, when the officers and pilots of No. 151 Squadron presented Teddy with a finely modelled brass Hawker Hurricane, hand-painted in the squadron's camouflage colours and with the letter code DZ W and Serial No P3940 – his personal Hawker Hurricane. The base bore a silver plaque on which was engraved:

> To Squadron Leader E. M. Donaldson DSO
> From the Pilots of 151 Squadron August 4th 1940.

On 5 August Teddy took up his new posting at Sealand for staff pilot duties, Squadron Leader Gordon taking over command of No. 151 Squadron on the same day. Teddy's departure almost exactly coincided with the date generally considered to be the end of the first phase of the Battle of Britain, when the *Luftwaffe* largely concentrated on attacks on convoys in the English Channel and the Thames Estuary.

The Squadron Diary marked his departure with the following words: 'During his command the squadron destroyed 29 enemy aircraft and damaged 22 others. This high toll of enemy aircraft for so few losses is a testimonial to the efficiency of the squadron and to the fine example of its CO.'

Teddy's gunnery skills were still as sharp as they had been when he won the Brooke-Popham Trophy two years in a row in the early 1930s. His personal tally stood at ten and a half confirmed kills with a further eight unconfirmed. Furthermore, as I have said, he never claimed as damaged or destroyed any of the many aircraft he noted in his log book as having received accurate fire at close range without results.

Teddy later wrote that his group commander, Air Vice-Marshal Keith Park, had recently told him that he 'was sorry to have to work the squadron so hard and give it more than its fair share of the harder jobs, but we were "battle hardened" and he knew he could rely on us to fully do out duty. He ordered us to do three sweeps a week over France to fight the *Luftwaffe*.'

There had been a terrible price to pay. Teddy had lost many men, all of whom he considered friends. Each death had hit him hard, none more so than that of his wingman. Leadership in times of war was often a terrible burden. Many years later Teddy recalled some of the difficulties that he faced on a daily basis.

> If I thought it was a rest a man needed, I'd give him a fortnight's leave. If I felt the war had really got to him, I'd move him on. I didn't have to do that many times. There was one chap who told me one morning, 'I think I'd better stay down today because I've got double vision.' He was obviously fatigued; we all were though we didn't use that word for it then. I looked at him and his eyes really were pointing in different directions. I said, 'Look, the Germans don't know you've got double vision so you'd better come with us. The Germans will see twelve Hurricanes, not eleven with one extra chap who can't see straight'. Someone said, 'You're a shit, sir. But I saw him not long ago.'

Before leaving, Teddy recommended Maxwell Milne for the DFC. It was approved and later promulgated in the *London Gazette* of 30 August 1940.

> Flying Officer Maxwell Milne (40129).
> Flying Officer Milne has personally destroyed seven enemy aircraft, and seriously damaged a number of others. He has led his section throughout with skill and courage, and has set an example to other members of the squadron.

A quarter of a century later, Teddy, who had by then become Air Correspondent of *The Daily Telegraph*, was invited by the Editor to write the paper's lead article on the twenty-fifth anniversary of the Battle of Britain, 15 September 1965. His journalistic piece, typically modest, was simply entitled 'One Man's Battle of Britain'. Reflecting on this brief but frantic period of his life, he revealed from whom he drew his strength as well as some surprising emotions. He wrote:

> Twenty-five years ago Britain stood alone and in peril. Meticulously trained, highly efficient and well-equipped, the overwhelming might of Germany's military forces could not move across the English Channel for a successful invasion of Britain without air superiority. To win this the Royal Air Force had to be destroyed.
> I was one of the Few who were the RAF. I cannot, however, claim to have contributed much to winning the Battle of Britain.
> Twenty-five years later, I am ashamed to relate that when I relinquished command of the famous No. 151 Fighter Squadron in

August 1940, on promotion to Wing Commander, I was convinced that we were beaten, that we had lost the battle.

I was fantastically tired and utterly depressed. My squadron had been in heavy fighting since May without a break. I left, I thought, a very depleted and thoroughly beaten fighting unit.

How wrong I was. For this tremendous fighting unit, with a new commander, rallied, went on fighting and finally came out on top of the so-far-unbeaten *Luftwaffe*.

During these months of fighting I had personally lost nine Hurricanes under me, as a cavalry officer might put it referring to the horses killed from under him in battle. I was perhaps more famous for my defeats than my victories and my squadron was described as 'unlucky' when casualties were discussed. A long swim in the Channel did not help my own morale.

In those days we had no limited tours of duty, such as were rigidly enforced later. We went on flying until we were either maimed or killed – or promoted.

Looking back, I hope I can be excused for being depressed. For I was always on the receiving end of the *Luftwaffe*'s fury. Flying a Hurricane, which was 50 mph slower than my adversary, I had to be brave; simply because I could not run away. Perhaps more important, I could not attack; simply because I could not catch my foe (unless, of course, he wanted to be caught).

But the enemy had to come to Britain to fight and we were always waiting for him. He was grossly over-confident and did not bother over-much when fighting the inferior Hurricane. This was his downfall.

My experience was no better and no worse than any other pilot in the Battle of Britain. We envied the Spitfire pilots; at least they could catch their foe, whereas the Hurricane pilot had to wait to be attacked and then fight like hell.

During those months I fired over 200,000 bullets in anger. I can only claim one Messerschmitt 109 shot down over England. Even though my score was not high, I hope I scared at least some of my opposite numbers in the German Air Force. They certainly scared me at times.

What made pilots go on and on? I do not think a single pilot would disagree with me when I say that it was Winston Churchill who most of all inspired us to fight and to continue fighting.

After a bad day we would be having a weary and depressing beer before trying to get some sleep. It must be remembered that in the latter stages of the Battle of Britain we were bombed at night too. Then out of the radio loudspeakers would come the voice of this great Briton saying: 'We will fight, we will never surrender.'

The next day, feeling as if we had had a 'shot' of dope in the arm, we would go back into the fray as new men, determined never to be beaten. This is the effect Churchill had on us.

All days were the same. We never got out of our flying suits from dawn to dusk. Sometimes we flew at night as well. All of us made several sorties a day. Some, of course, were false alarms, but every flight had its tension; one never knew if one would come back. Even relaxing in my bath late at night I would lie wondering if it would be my last soak in warm refreshing water.

We lived beside our aircraft at the dispersal points – waiting. Then over the loudspeakers would come the order 'Scramble 151 Squadron.' At that there would be the mad rush. Mechanics would have the planes' engines started by the time we reached them. Climb in, open the throttle, roar across the airfield, the squadron following as best it could, pilots still tying on their straps. As we climbed we took up our fighting formation.

Then it was a matter of steering the course ordered to the height ordered until the next message was received. 'Bandits approaching you from the south, same altitude.' Then silence. Then 'Bandits 100 plus.' Then one's eyes got like organ stops with staring until every plane was placed. You had to sort out friend from foe before engaging the enemy.

Then followed the mad pulling and pushing of the control column as you manoeuvred for attack. Then press the firing button and feel the terrific deceleration as eight guns coughed up 9,600 bullets a minute.

Then the rapid break-away as tracer bullets passed overhead from a Messerschmitt on your tail. Dodge like hell. Shake him off – but quick, don't let him get an easy shot. Then climb to look for more enemies.

Finally, with fuel gauges looking sad and ammunition finished, you would hear the incredibly calm voice of the controller giving you a bearing to base.

That was the Battle of Britain to all of us. History has recorded the facts. We did not know we were making history. We were fighting for our lives and the lovely green fields that lay below.

As we saw them then from the scarred surface of North Weald aerodrome on the outskirts of beautiful Epping Forest, north-east of London, the personalities of the Battle of Britain were:

Winston Churchill, whom we worshipped and who inspired us beyond belief.

'Stuffy' Dowding, our Commander-in-Chief. We respected him as a good commander but did not know him intimately as he was too busy to visit us often. But he endeared himself to us by turning a blind eye when pilots helped themselves to a little aviation spirit to drive to London and let their hair down.

Keith Park, our Group Commander, dedicated to winning the Battle and conducting it without fear or favour in the most ruthless manner. We liked him as a good man who often flew a Hurricane in those dark days.

Victor Beamish, our Station Commander, a real fighting Irishman who inspired us by fighting with us and drinking with us but always found the time to look after our every need.

I remember well when Beamish said to me one day, 'Get your squadron together. I want to talk to them.' The day before there had been some trouble at Lympne where mechanics had run for cover when refuelling and rearming our Hurricanes because of a fierce attack by German fighters.

'This was bad, the machines must be got back into the air without delay, it must never happen again. I know 151 Squadron and I know it well,' said Beamish. 'I know they will not run. But, by God, if they do, I will personally shoot the first man to do so with my own pistol.' And he would have done so.

We remember also the widows of the pilots killed. I had a dozen or so on my hands at one time. We had to get the RAF Benevolent Fund to help them temporarily as they missed their husbands' pay, which had stopped somewhat suddenly.

Finally, we remember our opponents. We never hated the *Luftwaffe* and I never saw a coward German. We knew they were killing our countrymen, but we thought of them as men obeying orders and doing their duty. We had the same orders and the same duty when we struck back at Germany later on.

Footnote 1
Seven miles to the east-north-east of Ipswich lies Martlesham Heath. The aerodrome was established in 1916 and the following year was taken over by the RFC for air testing. The inter-war years saw a new generation of the RAF's fighters and bombers, including the Supermarine Spitfire.+

On 1 September, with the need for Fighter Command stations to protect London, the Aircraft and Armament Experimental Establishment moved to Boscombe Down, Wiltshire.

During the spring of 1940 Hawker Hurricanes from Nos. 56 and 151 Squadrons both operated from North Weald, alternating with fighter squadrons from Debden.

Footnote 2
Rochford aerodrome was opened in 1914 for Home Defence, with operations being flown against German Zeppelin airships and Gotha bombers targeting

London. Having returned to farmland following the Armistice, Rochford was re-commissioned in 1933 with the Southern Corporation purchasing the land for an airport. The municipal aerodrome opened in September 1935, with a local flying club and later the RAFVR and the Auxiliary Air Force flying out of Rochford. The RAF selected the aerodrome as a satellite. In November 1939 No. 54 Squadron arrived, the squadron sharing the airfield with No 74 Squadron during the Battle of Britain, the two alternating with Hornchurch. On 18 June 1940 the nearby radar station at Canewden, two miles to the north was bombed.

CHAPTER NINETEEN

Chief Flying Instructor

Teddy was posted as the Chief Flying Instructor of the Advanced Training Squadron, No. 5 FTS at Sealand, near Chester, on 5 August 1940. During his first two months, he flew Spitfires, Fairey Battles and Miles Masters, giving his charges a keen insight into his combat experience and with it the confidence to face the overwhelming numbers of enemy aircraft time and time again.

On 17 August, in response to Fighter Command's insatiable demand for replacement pilots, fighter OTU courses, like those run at Sealand, were shortened. So, for the remainder of 1940, which included the later phases of the Battle of Britain, pupils were passed out of OTUs with as little as ten to twenty hours on Spitfires or Hurricanes.

Desperate to guarantee his pupils the very best chance of survival, Teddy threw himself into his work. Many of his pupils were in service before the end of the Battle of Britain, making the difference between victory and defeat. Among those brought up to operational readiness by Teddy was Pilot Officer 'Smithy' Duncan-Smith (later Group Captain W. G. G. Duncan Smith DSO and Bar DFC and two Bars) who subsequently wrote:

> Squadron Leader Teddy Donaldson, the CO, gave us invaluable help and advice on how to deal with enemy fighters and with the tactics to be used against enemy bombers. He did not spare himself in flying and showing us in practice what he preached on the ground. Teddy Donaldson was one of the most exceptional fighter pilots in the RAF. One of the best shots, too; he had led his Squadron, 151, brilliantly in the early fighting in France and at Dunkirk. His recent tactical operational experience and excellence in air gunnery helped enormously to condition us for the job of air fighting and he took infinite care in developing our aptitude as pilots. He considered the Germans mediocre and ineffectual, once they had lost their formation leader. He impressed on us that anyone flying a Spitfire or Hurricane was the equal of five Germans in their Me 109s. 'Just go after them

142

and rivet their backsides to the armour plate,' he said with his infectious laugh.

Teddy's experience of combat was often of the enemy fleeing unless they had the advantages of numbers and height. He even remarked in his log book that the enemy were 'yellow' because they refused to engage the slower Hurricanes.

In his now famous speech to the House of Commons on 20 August, Winston Churchill was clearly moved by the contribution which the pilots of Fighter Command had already made in the defence of the home-land, in which the 28-year-old Squadron Leader Donaldson had so recently played a leading and active combat role. The Prime Minister's words, whilst cleverly instilling much-needed pride in the middle of the RAF's most famous battle, also rang a deeply appreciative chord on behalf of the nation. In it, his familiar voice boomed:

> The gratitude of every home in our island, in our Empire and indeed throughout the world, except in the abodes of the guilty, goes out to the British airmen who, undaunted by the odds, un-wearied in their constant challenge and mortal danger, are turning the tide of world war by their prowess and by their devotion. Never in the field of human conflict was so much owed by so many to so few.

Having already made his mark on many of the pilots who were to play a crucial role in the later phases of the Battle of Britain, Teddy continued taking instructional flights through October. From November he was taking flying tests, sixty pupils in all, assessing what type of aircraft best suited them – fighters or bombers – as the air battle to prevent a German invasion had by now been won and the RAF was turning to the offensive.

Teddy had already received the DSO and a Mention in Dispatches for his first few day of operational flying with No. 151 Squadron; he received a second 'MiD' in the New Year's Honours List of 1941. This may have come as recognition of his contribution in bringing the new generation of pilots up to operational readiness in time to make the difference in the great air battle over Britain during the latter part of 1940. Next to Teddy's name in the Honours List came that of his brother John Willie whose 'MiD' was made posthumously. Had he lived, his gallantry and leader-ship during his squadron's second tour of operations in Norway might well have earned a Bar to his DSO or a DFC, however, the War Department did not like the negative publicity of dead heroes and so only the Victoria Cross or the 'MiD' could be awarded posthumously; sadly John Willie only received the latter.

In his spare time Teddy helped with fund-raising, making personal appearances in the north of England, the Midlands and North Wales. He attended fêtes, fund-raising events, coffee mornings and dinner-dances, and did anything he was asked to do in order to help raise money and morale. In February 1941 the newly formed Air Training Corps (ATC) needed speakers and Teddy made himself available, covering hundreds of miles giving talks and making personal appearances, including one in the Borough Hall, Stafford. Among the audience that night, along with the founder members of No. 395 Squadron of the ATC, were the parents of David Blomeley, one of Teddy's pilot officers during the Battle of France as well as during the early days of the Battle of Britain. Mr Harry Blomeley, a local headmaster, introduced himself after the lecture, the meeting being reported in the local press. David remained a life-long friend of his former CO; in later years he and his wife, Joy, sister of the legendary 'Bob' Braham, spent many Christmases with Teddy.

It is worth recording that Group Captain John Randall Daniel 'Bob' Braham was the RAF's top-scoring ace flying twin-engined fighter aircraft during the war. Having destroyed twenty-nine enemy aircraft, probably destroyed another and damaged six more, he was fifth in the list of all the top-scoring British and Commonwealth fighter pilots. After winning three DSOs, three DFCs, the Belgian Order of the Crown with Palm and the Belgian Croix de Guerre 1940 with Palm, he became the most highly decorated fighter pilot in both the RAF and the Commonwealth air forces in the Second World War. With his post-war awards of an Air Force Cross and the Canadian Forces Decoration, he was then thought to be the most highly decorated British Serviceman.

In February 1941, Teddy learned that his brother, Arthur, had been given command of John 'Willie's' former Squadron, 263, then flying the new Westland Whirlwinds out of St Eval in Cornwall. Later that year Arthur would hit the headlines leading a low-level raid on Morlaix Airfield, winning the DFC for this and numerous other airfield and anti-shipping attacks. The award was announced in August of that year.

Meanwhile, Teddy's brilliant and inspirational flying training at Sealand, particularly during the latter phases of the Battle of Britain, as well as his earlier tutoring of RAF gunnery instructors, did not go un-recognized. The award of his well-deserved AFC was eventually announced in the *London Gazette* of 30 September 1941.

CHAPTER TWENTY

A 'Limey' in America

With the ever increasing strain in relations between Japan and America, the United States Army Air Force (USAAF) needed hundreds of new fully trained pilots to help strengthen their ranks should war break out.

During the spring of 1941 General Arnold, Chief of Staff, United States Army Air Corp (USAAC), later to become USAAF, asked the RAF to provide experienced fighter pilots and air gunners to help train American pilots and aircrew, and, more importantly, a new generation of instructors who would take the strain following these stop-gap measures.

The Air Ministry forwarded a list of suitable pilot gunnery instructors on which Teddy, with ten and a half kills and eight probables – all within a combat period of just three months – figured high. No doubt his two victories in the Brooke-Popham Trophy and high-profile aerobatics displays at Hendon and Zurich helped in the selection process. His experience in training the immediate pre-war generation of RAF gunnery instructors was, however, the decisive factor.

When Teddy was told of his posting as a fixed gunnery and pursuit-tactics advisor to the USAAC he initially resisted the move. The timing could not have been worse as his wife 'Freddy', as Winifred was known, had just given birth to their second daughter, Sarah Louise, who was born on 6 June 1941. He would have to leave Freddy and their two young daughters alone in England for at least the next six months.

When the importance of the posting was more fully explained, and the fact that 'General Arnold has asked for you personally,' he relented and 'resigned' his commission, travelling as a civilian due to America's neutrality.

The instructors were sent to America via Canada, a journey which involved running the gauntlet of German U-boats. Much to Teddy's dismay he and a veteran air gunner were to sail in a slow-moving merchant cruiser armed with 6-inch guns. Things got worse halfway across the Atlantic when the captain gathered the crew on deck and announced: 'I have splendid news for you. I have just received a coded message stating that the *Scharnhorst* has slipped out and is heading into the Atlantic. My orders are to leave the convoy and to intercept her and stop her playing havoc with the Allied shipping.'

To a man the ship's crew let out a deafening cheer. Teddy and his fellow passenger were much happier facing the enemy in the air and were not so enthusiastic. Teddy could not help but think of his brother's fate on HMS *Glorious* just over a year earlier.

As luck would have it the *Scharnhorst* did not appear within striking range and, after a nerve-racking twenty-four hours, the captain announced: 'I have some disappointing news for you. I have just received orders to rejoin the convoy and proceed on our way.'

Two voices cheered nearly as loudly as the whole ship's company had the previous day – the two RAF instructors at the back of the group.

Following an uneventful voyage the two men journeyed to Washington, and on 1 July Teddy reported to the US War Department for further orders. He was assigned, 'in an entirely advisory capacity', to the Staff of General Weaver USAAF, GOC South East Coast Training Centre, Maxwell Field, Montgomery, Alabama. It was a seven-hour flight to his new base. Here he remained for a brief spell, only adding three hours' flying time to his log book. On 10 August, he proceeded to Randolph Field, San Antonio, Texas by car, on attachment to General Brant, GOC Gulf Coast Training Centre, his log book records flights to and from nearby airbases at Victoria and Duncan Field during the following months but no training or instructional flights.

The two RAF men were at first resented wherever they went. Teddy reported to one air base where the Colonel rebuffed him, saying, 'Look here, I don't like Limeys and now I have seen you I like 'em less. I'm told you are here to advise. If I want any advice from you I'll ask for it; otherwise son, just don't offer any.'

His hostility continued and so Teddy decided to take some leave and drove to Washington. Calling at the address of one of the few American officers who had befriended him, he rang the bell. The door opened to reveal a scantily clad woman standing on the threshold. Eyes on stalks Teddy excused himself. 'Oh, I say, I'm terribly sorry. I thought this was General—'s apartment.'

He turned swiftly away and began to leave, only to be called back. 'Hey there, Teddy Donaldson, where the hell do you think you are going? Come right back here!' He needed little further encouragement and, joining the party, thought to himself: 'If this is life in war-time Washington, I think it is going to agree with me!'

When asked how he was doing, Teddy would reply; 'Oh, absolutely splendidly, sir.' But he was brought down to earth with a jolt when he met up with General Arnold at one of the less raunchy parties. Arnold glared at him, asking sharply: 'What the devil are you doing here?'

After Teddy had explained his situation at some length, General Arnold said; 'You just get the hell out of here and get back to base as fast as you can and get on with the job I gave you. When you get there you will find a new commanding officer.'

It suddenly struck Teddy that his mission was of the highest importance. True to Arnold's word, he found the new station commander to be highly receptive and was able to work more effectively.

In early October, he drove by private car to the West Coast Training Centre, Moffet Field, California, beginning a five-day lecture programme under General Yount. At the end of this period, he was ordered to Luke Field Advanced Pursuit School, flying over 120 hours as an instructor during the following six weeks.

The local press ran a feature on Teddy's posting under a photograph of Donaldson and the camp commandant, Lieutenant- Colonel Ennis C. Whitehead:

RAF Hero Visits Luke to Deliver Series of Lectures.

One of the War's newly-crowned heroes, Wing Commander Edward M. Donaldson of the Royal Air Force, arrived at Luke Field this week where he will deliver a series of informal lectures on combat tactics before Luke Field Officers and Aviation Cadets in British training schools of this area.

Wing Commander Donaldson, who has personally sent twenty Nazi airplanes earthward never to rise again, came to the United States early in July, and will spend a year here acquainting U.S. Air Corps authorities with the practical problems in actual warfare.

Regarding his adventures in the skies above the English Channel, and over France, Germany and Belgium, the dapper, red moustached Wing Commander who is only thirty years old, related to Air Corps officials that, on five different occasions, he and his plane had been shot down by Nazi fighters.

The most dramatic of these instances, he said, was the time that he went down in flames above the Channel. 'For five hours I swam around in that bloody cold water before a motorboat commander finally picked me up.' During the Dunkirk evacuation, Donaldson spent a total of seventy-three hours in the air helping to cover departing troop ships.

An acknowledged authority on the pursuit type of battle, Donaldson was one of the instructors of the original American Eagle Squadron, composed entirely of American pilots. Of them he says, 'They're fine men – all of them. They'll go a terribly long way.'

Pilot training in England, the Wing Commander reports, continues periodically after commissions are granted. After the initial training period, pilots are assigned to combat service for six months, after which they return to school for an additional six months instruction. 'This way it is possible to keep RAF pilots familiar with the very latest aeronautical advances,' Donaldson said.

Regarding American-built airplanes, the Wing Commander said that while there were but a few US planes in England before he left, the late models he has seen since arriving in this country are superb.

Donaldson's English rank of Wing Commander is equivalent in America to the office of Lieutenant-Colonel.

In speaking to this man from troubled England about America he referred to it as God's Country, but with a far away look in his eye and set face he said, 'I must go back soon.'

At the beginning of December Teddy returned to Maxwell Field where, his log book notes, he was under the command of General Weaver. Here he flew over ninety hours of gunnery instruction before heading to Washington on 20 December to attend an important meeting at the Army Department. A posting to the West Coast training Centre at Phoenix, Arizona, followed; he arrived on New Year's Day 1942. There was to be no let-up in the intensity of his workload, and over the next three weeks he was to cram in a further sixty-six hours flying time as a gunnery instructor.

On 21 January, Teddy moved to Elgin Field Gunnery Ranges, Florida, lecturing and giving instructional flights before another trip to Washington to attend conferences in the War and Navy Departments.

The war had by this time taken another turn. At 0800 hours on Sunday, 7 December 1941, the Second World War entered a new phase when the American fleet was decimated during the sneak Japanese attack on Pearl Harbor. Suddenly the whole nation was awakened to the need for trained fighting forces. Soon their pilots would face well-trained and blooded German and Japanese fighter pilots. If they were to have any hope of survival, they needed to be ready.

A particularly aggressive anti-British colleague asked General Arnold why an Englishman was training 'our boys'. Arnold replied in no uncertain terms how important Teddy's work was in America's rearmament plan: 'It would take me twenty years to produce a Teddy Donaldson and I haven't even got 20 minutes.'

Teddy was to revolutionize the US training system over the next years, writing their new text book, *Notes in Air Gunnery and Air*

Fighting, of which 7,500 copies were eventually printed, each of which had to be signed for, as their contents remained top secret.

In February 1942 his young family ran the gauntlet of the U-boats and sailed to America. Freddy and their elder daughter, Susan, known as Sue, spent most of their time on the deck, almost waiting for the torpedoes to hit, while Sarah, then only nine months old, lay in her carrycot in their cabin, ready to be snatched should the worst happen.

Once in America, Freddy settled in with the children at the Banana River Naval Base in Florida, now Cape Canaveral. Here the children were looked after by a nanny and, as Sarah put it, 'presented clean and tidy to our parents when it was convenient'.

It was at about this time, just as Freddy and the girls were able to join Teddy, that he was once more stolen away from them. He was ordered to make a three-month tour of the American training centres, submitting a report on each. His brief stated: 'These reports should cover briefly your activities, special conditions encountered which may affect out training programme, either favourably or unfavourably, and such recommendations as you may have.'

He recommenced gunnery instruction at Phoenix, Arizona, on 9 February, returning to Elgin, Florida, a fortnight later, flying a total of eighty hours of gunnery instruction during the month. March continued in much the same way, with a transfer to Gulf Coast Training Centre, Randolph Field, Texas, on 10 March, followed by a move to Matagorda Island Gunnery School, off the coast of Texas, three days later. At the end of the month, he was once more making regular instructional flights at Maxwell Field, driving to another War Department conference on 20 April, followed by a return to Randolph Field, and later to Interceptor Command School, Orlando, Florida, flying gunnery instruction, as his log book notes 'still attached to Flying Training Command'.

He gave a series of gunnery training demonstrations for the commanding general of the Gulf Coast and his staff at Matagorda Island from 18 May. Then he flew a number of instructional interceptor missions before attending another War Department conference in Washington on 15 June. After a ten day tour of airbases, he returned once more to gunnery instruction. Then he began an 'examination and report on a new synthetic gunnery trainer for Commanding General Gulf Coast Training Command'.

He was commissioned to make monthly visits to the airbases under his supervision, flying regular tours through to the end of the year. His arrival at a new airbase was generally heralded by his breathtaking aerobatics display over the aerodrome in his P-40. He would do three slow rolls at 50 ft followed by a loop with a roll out, after which he would land and meet the officers and men before getting down to observing the

courses. This was not pure bravado. His displays broke the ice and made
his job all the easier in that he, quite rightly, earned the recruits' immediate respect. There was no time to build respect; he needed it from day
one. Unusually, his exploits were fully sanctioned by the 'brass', as
General Arnold had explained to him that the P-40 had gained an
unfounded reputation for being a death-trap if thrown about too much.
Teddy's job was to reassure the new pilots as to how much it could take,
and in this he dutifully obliged, with hair-raising aplomb. His death-
defying aerobatics displays were known throughout the service.

Teddy later recalled that for a spell during his time in America he
shaved his trade-mark moustache off. While on one of his many tours
of American air-bases, he was approached by a USAAF Colonel, who
said, 'Are you in the RAF'.

'Yes.'

'Do you know a little guy called Teddy Donaldson?'

'Oh yes, the RAF think a hell of a lot of him.'

'You know what I saw that great little guy do once down at Lake
Charles Air Base? He flew through a hangar upside down.'

Teddy managed to keep a straight face as he said: 'I do hope the
doors were opened at the other end.'

The reply came with all seriousness: 'Yes, it was arranged for him.'

Teddy swore he had never heard of Lake Charles, never mind been
there, but such was his reputation. His stunning exhibitions of low
flying continued. His antics left the pilots breathless but the authorities
were less impressed and he was reported.

General Peabody, commanding the School of Applied Tactics, had
him grounded temporarily and banned further shows, allocating
Donaldson a twin-engined passenger plane which had a maximum
speed of 120 mph. This, for Teddy, was like stepping back to his days
on trainers, and a move he bitterly resented.

Within a week, however, he was asked to test fly a P-47 Thunderbolt,
fitted with experimental rockets. Flying to attack his target, Teddy
came in low to avoid detection. One of the rockets fell from its tube
onto the ground, exploding and throwing the aircraft onto its back.
Teddy struggled to regain control of the badly damaged Thunderbolt,
limping back to base before setting it down in an almost textbook
landing, much to the astonishment of all who witnessed his exploits.

Teddy's role included assisting in establishing new gunnery schools
and assessing existing establishments. One of his reports was on Luke
Field, Phoenix, Arizona. This he described as 'impossibly bad,' going
on to say:

> The whole aim of teaching a fighter pilot is that when he is fully
> trained he will be able to go into combat and destroy, with gun

fire, enemy aircraft. If he cannot hit what he aims at he might as well stay on the ground.

There is no other aim in the training of a fighter pilot than just that. It is therefore up to the Training School concerned to bear this fact in mind and all the teaching of the school should revolve round gunnery, gunnery and more gunnery.

This report, on the whole, is most adverse. I strongly criticize the conduct of the officers in charge of the Gunnery Course.

Explaining in detail the flaws in the course, despite the quality of the equipment and staff, he made suggestions as to how improvements could reasonably be made and instructors' talents better used. The instructors were keen and competent but Teddy found they were using techniques even they did not approve of. This was compounded by the use of three conflicting training manuals, the most recent of which had not even reached the base yet.

While the ground-to-ground gunnery was good, this hardly helped in combat; it was the air-to-air gunnery that counted and here Teddy found that 'this course makes it mathematically impossible to hit the target by the method taught. All the air firing I watched for two days produced virgin targets.'

The pupils were not given any corrective guidance during the air-to-air firing as the instructors did not have a good enough view of the impacts to correct errors.

He rounded off with the damning indictment: 'Not even the elementary fundamental mathematics of aerial gunnery are understood. The course prescribed by them is a futile waste of time, money and personnel.'

These comments resulted in immediate action. A new CO was appointed at Luke Field, along with a new Director of Training and Director of Gunnery.

Rarely has one man's impact been so keenly felt, and with Teddy's secondment drawing to an end the Americans requested a six month extension. Just as his work had helped prepare many of the British and Commonwealth pilots who fought in the spring and summer of 1940, so his skills were to help build the core of the American gunnery instructors and fighter pool.

Lieutenant-Colonel G. W. Mundy wrote to the British Ambassador in Washington requesting that Teddy be allowed to stay in America for a further six months:

His assistance in organizing the Air Corps Gunnery School has been invaluable. At his suggestion the course of instruction has been changed, giving much better results. He has personally trained each instructor in the new system of firing.

He has given several lectures which have not only been interesting but have served to bring the war a little closer to the pilots here.

Last but not least is the respect and friendly feeling that he, by his personality and action, has created for our ally, Great Britain.

Granted an extension to his tour, Teddy got down to his job with renewed vigour.

It was clear that the existing training camps could no longer cope with the numbers of pilots required to defeat the Axis powers. Teddy was involved in the establishment of four new air gunnery schools, one of which was at Yuma Army Base Advanced Flying School. Here the Director of Training, Captain B. M. Goldwater (later Senator and presidential candidate Barry Goldwater) welcomed Teddy as a friend from the very outset: 'Listen, you guys, this man, Teddy Donaldson, knows what he is talking about. I know, because I have talked to him . . . Your life depends on whether you listen to him or not. My orders to you are "Listen."'

The very first graduating class from Yuma, Class 43-C, produced a commemorative magazine in which a picture of Teddy appeared climbing into his P-40. It was taken by Captain Goldwater and was dedicated to Teddy: 'His assistance and knowledge helped so much in making this one of the world's finest gunnery schools. The flying exhibitions in his P-40 will never be forgotten.'

During his tour of American training establishments Teddy had teamed up with an RAF bomber pilot who had nearly a hundred operations under his belt. The two worked well together. Flying together in Teddy's passenger aircraft, they produced a rapid turnover – they dropped in on bases, gave their lectures and were quickly off to the next base.

On one occasion they got chatting to a couple of WAC officers who needed to get to San Francisco. Ever the gentleman, Teddy offered to take them at least a part of their way in his 'crate'. Naturally, he took in the scenery and flew the two at hedge-hopping height. Suddenly the windscreen appeared to explode and Teddy was showered with Perspex and covered in blood. His co-pilot grabbed the controls as Teddy was temporarily dazed by the blow: 'I think I had better climb,' he said calmly.

They landed as soon as they could and replaced the windscreen. Their cover story was that they were flying near to the ground to avoid low cloud. The discovery of several feet of high-tension electrical cabling wrapped around one of the engines did not help matters but Teddy got away without a reprimand.

The two men met up again in Phoenix, and Teddy ended up

offering his friend a lift in his single-seat P-40. The flight was made with Teddy saving space by leaving his parachute behind and by having his 6 ft tall friend sit on the pilot's seat with his legs apart, Teddy sitting on top. Two hundred and eighty miles and three-quarters of an hour later, Teddy landed at Yuma where he was greeted by an astounded base colonel. He took off from the air base the following day, the Colonel seeing him off from the control tower – otherwise he would have had to throw the book at him.

Teddy led a charmed life as a pilot. His P-40 did, however, eventually give up the ghost, halfway through a display. Teddy was flying at 20 ft, inverted of course, when there was a huge bang and he found himself splattered with oil, the engine having blown apart. Somehow, he managed to roll, turn and land. He later admitted that this was perhaps his greatest ever display of flying skills.

Once he had landed, Teddy saw he extent of the damage; sections of cowling were pierced and the engine shot. He was given a new plane and he set off for Orlando. However, he was just about to experience his third accident in a very short space of time. The weather soon closed in and a massive thunderstorm erupted ahead of him: 'The weather was ghastly . . . Huge thunderstorms, black as hell and clouds down to the ground, and I had to refuel to get around it as my machine was stripped down and minus the main gas tank. I had 300 miles to go.'

As he approached Tallahassee he looked out for a landmark on the coast which would lead him to base. The noise from the engine began to get louder until it began screaming. The propeller governor had gone, and even with little power the revs were terrible. Teddy knew the engine would blow at any second. He reduced power even further but this only resulted in a drop in airspeed. He recalled: 'It was raining heavily and so I heaved back the hood to see if I could get a better view but the rain was blinding. I got lower and lower. I was over thick jungle. A clearing ahead, quick with the wheels . . . bloody stupid thing to do on reflection.'

In 8,000 hours and thirty years of flying, Teddy was only responsible for one crash, and this was it. Next second there was a bang and out of the corner of my eye I saw a wheel flying off backwards and to the side.

'I knew it would not be long now before the crash and God I was not disappointed.'

The port wing was sliced off by a tree as the plane hurled through the canopy at 110 mph. Teddy was thrown about, still strapped in. 'Next I was hit in the face with a load of mud and the floor of the plane disappeared. Then a terrific bump and all went deadly quiet. I rubbed my eyes . . . I was alive. I don't know how, but I was still alive.'

With his head still spinning and his body aching all over, Teddy checked for fire; there was none. Before he had time to worry about rescue, the sound of voices filled the air. It was a jungle training exercise and the officer was at first hostile, believing Teddy had been buzzing them. They had been living off parachute drops for the previous six weeks and were in no mood for games. Once he had explained the situation a signal was sent and arrangements made for transport back to an air base.

A new phase in Teddy's career began on 10 August 1942 when he proceeded by car from Maxwell Field to Randolph Field, on attachment to General Brant. This posting lasted until October when he was transferred to the West Coast Training Centre, Moffett Field, California, driving himself by private car from the Gulf of Mexico to the Pacific Coast.

The *Orlando Morning Sentinel* for Tuesday 22 September 1942 carried the following feature on Teddy which is of interest because it gives an indication of his sporting interests at this time. The title of the article read: 'Misses "Rugger," Darts, Likes American Baseball, Golf, Says English Ace at Base,' and goes on to say:

> I enjoy your football and baseball so much. . . . But I do miss 'rugger and darts,' declared Group Captain E. M. Donaldson of the Royal Air Force in Orlando yesterday in commenting on the American sports scene.
>
> Group Captain Donaldson, who gives lectures at the Fairgrounds unit of the AAFSAT, reported that he was not such a tremendous cricket enthusiast as many Englishmen, and so perhaps would not be completely typical of British sentiment in this respect. He called on Flight Sergeant Harry Bielby, another member of the RAF contingent, who said he missed cricket and English football tremendously in the States.

In the interview, Teddy then went on to express his fondness for Rugby and explained the rules, and how they were at variance to those of the game of American Football.

> What I most enjoy at your American games, besides the actual play is the remarkable enthusiasm of the crowds, the way they shout and cheer, and the barracking of the players and officials during the contest. 'Razzing,' I believe you call it over here.

Speaking of the 'gentleman's game', which the Donaldson boys had once so enjoyed while at Selsey, Teddy was quoted as saying:

Cricket, to me, gets a bit monotonous. There is twice as much
action and excitement in your American baseball.

As for baseball, I have seldom seen it played in England, and
then mostly by girls. But back home the young men go in
strongly for field hockey.

I find that golf is just about the same in America, (Donaldson
went on), except that the grass turf on your courses is not as fine
as we have back home. And you use a slightly larger ball, which
cuts down the length of my drives. In England I could drive 250
yards when everything was right, but in Florida the best I can do
is about 220 yards. Your rules in America are easier on the player,
as in England you can't touch the ball until it is in the hole. My
game has improved in the States, so that now and then I can
shoot an 81 or 83.

Of all sports both Teddy and his brother Arthur were to continue
playing golf after the War, playing in the company of Douglas Bader
and others.

Both Group Captain Donaldson and Sergeant Bielby affirmed
that they sadly missed their games of darts. 'Not the kind of dart
throwing game you have here in the States, but a really scientific
game of skill, requiring the best control of eye and wrist
movement. We don't hurt the darts with a throw from over
the shoulder, but with a quick snap along the line of the eye to
the board, which is divided into numbered sections,' as the
Group Captain related.

Donaldson said every 'pub' in England had its darts game, and
the sport is taken so seriously that in peace times championship
teams tour the country playing matches with the local experts.
The best players have their own darts specially made for them,
and handle them with great care, he added.

The RAF ace is fond of American ten-pin bowling, which is not
ordinarily known in England on professional alleys, and plans to
introduce the game at home after the war.

On 6 October Donaldson began a brief lecture tour under the orders of
Major General Barton Kyle Yount. Five days later he was ordered to
Luke Field Advanced Pursuit School. Teddy's log book records him
taking instructors up on daily gunnery flights in an AT-6, an advanced
training aircraft, until 15 November when he returned to Maxwell
Field. Teddy later reckoned that he crossed America fifty times during
his mission with the USAAF. His record of morale raising aerobatics,
combined with his flying hours as an instructor and his development

of both gunnery school, courses and the USAAF's new instruction manual, might well have earned Donaldson a Bar to his AFC had he been operating with the RAF. There was, however, to be no official recognition of Teddy's outstanding service in America from the Air Ministry beyond advancement in rank commensurate with his period of service.

CHAPTER TWENTY-ONE

From Captain
to Colonel

Promotion to the rank of acting group captain came on 28 December 1942, at the same time as his appointment as RAF Advisor to the United States Army Air Force Board of Generals.

Being a group captain in America had its unforeseen drawbacks among the lower echelons, as many within the military had only heard of the rank of captain and Teddy was occasionally treated as a junior officer. Consequently he took to using the American title Colonel, his USAAF equivalent rank. General Taylor, appreciating Teddy's dilemma, always made Teddy's passes out in the name of Colonel Donaldson.

November 1942 had seen Teddy based at the Flying Command School, Orlando, Florida, inspecting and advising a number of gunnery schools in the vicinity. This posting should have given him the opportunity to spend more time with his young family. However, his roving eye had already led to a liaison with a US Army nurse called Estellee Holland with whom he was to have a child. Estellee's parents lived in Yuma, Arizona and it was there that the two had met. Freddy filed for divorce in Florida citing mental cruelty. The divorce was finalized on 6 July 1944, his youngest daughter Sarah's third birthday.

Freddy hastily made the hazardous return journey across the Atlantic, initially living with their two children in a dilapidated old farmhouse in Norfolk. There was no electricity or running water and the family relied on bicycles for transport. Later, she met and married Flight Lieutenant Michael John O'Bryen Nicholls, and the family settled at The Chalet, Shawbury, near Shrewsbury. They married in 1945, although years later there was some controversy as to whether the American divorce had been legal. This culminated in a court case which found the divorce to have been valid but not without first putting Freddy through the ordeal of a 'media circus' which portrayed her as trying to damage the reputation of a war hero. Apart from the odd birthday and Christmas present, Teddy had limited contact with his daughters, taking them out only a handful of times once he returned to Britain. His contact was to be even less frequent in later years. Sarah recalled an invitation, which her father made during a rare lunch meeting, for her and her new husband, Ray Howell, just after their wedding day. The meal, the only one she shared with her father as an adult, was at the Mermaiden in Half Moon Street, just off Piccadilly. Teddy got on well with Ray, and he invited the couple to spend the weekend with him on his yacht. However, as a mere woman, Sarah found herself banned from the wheel and instead served in the role of honorary yacht-maid, cooking the breakfasts and cleaning the heads.

Teddy's relationship with Estellee might not have developed as it did had Teddy's secondment ended when his first extension of tour ran out on 1 January 1943. However, with the establishment of the headquarters of the Army Air Force School of Applied Tactics in Orlando, its commandant, Colonel Willis R. Taylor, requested Teddy's services and wrote to the Commandant General of the Army Air Force in Washington asking for his tour to be extended for a further eight months.

> Due to his long experience as a fighter pilot in active theatres and due to his exceptional ability as a teacher Wing Commander Donaldson is vitally important to the work of the school.
>
> At the present time this school is developing, for approval, a training directive for use by all fighter units in basic fundamentals of employment of fighter aircraft in combat.
>
> Without the advice of this officer it would be practically impossible to produce a satisfactory answer to this problem.

Having gained the extension, Colonel Taylor submitted a further request for Teddy to be promoted to the rank of group captain; 'commensurate with the importance of his duties at this school'. His appraisal of Teddy's work was expressed in no uncertain terms.

> His work has been of inestimable value in the development of air tactics and fighter operational training methods.
>
> He has worked hard and long in a job that has no great glory attached to it, but is nevertheless tremendously important to our combined effort.

He was much in demand, as Flying Training Command was also asking the RAF for him to be retained to work with the development of their gunnery training schools.

He was back serving at the Army Air Force Advanced Flying School, Yuma, in early February; a letter home from one of his pupils there testified to the impression left on all who witnessed his brilliant flying displays. His breathtaking aerobatics were designed to win the instant respect of those under his tuition. On 5 February Lieutenant John B. Eddy (later killed in action with 327th Fighter Squadron) wrote to his parents:

> Today we had a flying exhibition given us by Wing Commander Donaldson of the RAF. He is a little dapper Englishman, about as big as me, but can he ever fly.
>
> He has shot down 22 Germans and has been shot down 9 times himself. In all that time he has never been hurt the slightest bit. Only once has he been injured in a plane, and that time he broke his nose on the canopy while reaching for a control.
>
> He would start a loop 20 ft off the ground and finish it at the same altitude, which takes remarkable judgement.

Yet another testament to Teddy's skill and courage were the many morale boosting flying displays he performed around the country, a description of one of which appeared in The *Panama American* of Tuesday 23 February under the heading of 'R.A.F. Pilot Thrills Scout Jamboree With Aerial Acrobatics in Aircobra':

> One of the most spectacular air shows ever put on here took place yesterday on the closing day of the Boy Scout Jamboree at Gamboa when Group Captain Terence Donaldson of the RAF put a P-39 through all its paces over the Gamboa athletic field.
>
> Donaldson, whose rank corresponds to that of an American Colonel, barrel rolled the Aircobra, looped it inside and out, put it into a steep climb and ended by swooping low over the field where 275 Scouts, Cubs and Sea Scouts stood at attention in a 'V' for Victory formation.

Throughout 1943 Teddy maintained his incredibly high work rate, travelling around the USA working both with Fighter Training Command and the School of Applied Tactics. His impromptu aerobatics and powerful lectures inspired thousands of pilots and airmen, making him a celebrity in many states. His appearances were frequently covered in the local press, earning the RAF considerable kudos.

The vagaries of promotion and quotas never failed to confuse and frustrate many RAF officers during the course of their careers. The situation seemed to be even more confusing in wartime, with the award of acting ranks, temporary ranks and war service ranks as well as substantive rank. So it was with Teddy. Already an acting group captain, he was, on 28 June 1943, made up to the substantive rank of wing commander. This was, he was told, in recognition of his valuable contribution towards the war effort.

Teddy continued to give every course his best efforts and this was reflected in the excellence achieved by his pupils as well as in the glowing testimonials of his commanding officers.

Brigadier-General Russel E. Randall, commandant of the XXVI Fighter Command said, 'As a result of his enthusiasm, conduct and pleasing personality he instilled into this command new vigour and heightened morale and contributed greatly to the furtherance of the war effort.'

This opinion was endorsed by Major-General H.R. Harmon, commanding the VI Air Force, Brigadier Hume Peabody moreover, Colonel Ralph A. Snavely, CO of the IVth Fighter Command who wrote, 'The information he gave us is of inestimable value to the young pilots soon to see action. His tactics are sound and his points on gunnery, if heeded by our pilots, may well mean the difference between success and failure to some of them when combat comes along.'

These words were well founded and the improvements were indeed impressive. One group commander in the III Air Support Command, Birmingham, Alabama, wrote simply, 'Gunnery scores have increased at least 20 per cent as a result of Group Captain Donaldson's visit.'

When the first class had passed out from Yuma Army Base Advanced Flying School, Teddy was invited to pen a few inspiring words on the pilot's completion of the programme. These were published in the course book.

There is no other reason for a fighter pilot's existence than he can shoot accurately and destroy the enemy. By this standard, class 43-E was the most murderous bunch of pilots ever produced. I'm so sorry for the Japanese and the Germans.

Congratulations Instructors, you must be the best of the finest in the world to produce the best gunnery scores ever achieved by any nation.

E. M. Donaldson
Group Captain, RAF.

CHAPTER TWENTY-TWO

A Signal Honour

In October 1943 Teddy returned briefly to the UK, flying via Montreal, Newfoundland, and on to Northern Ireland before travelling to London to report to Air Vice-Marshal E. S. Goodwin, Director-General of Training (Air), on 9 October. The following day was spent at the Air Ministry before reporting to the Polish Wing at Northolt on a six-week tour of operations in order to bring his combat skills up to scratch and to gain experience on new types of aircraft. It was important too for Teddy to get an idea of the changes in combat tactics since 1940. In those days he had flown with just nine Hurricanes, which were sometimes up against a hundred plus German fighters and bombers, most of which could out-run them. By 1943 the RAF and USAAF fighters had the upper hand.

Teddy's first operation came on 14 October, the following two days seeing him getting in some firing practice at Sutton Bridge. Six days later he was flying Spitfires and a captured FW 190 with the Advanced Fighter Development Unit, returning to operations, escorting B17 bombers on daylight raids from 23 October.

Flying the Supermarine Spitfire on offensive sweeps with the RAF's Polish Wing from Northolt, Teddy was a part of a massive formation of fighters escorting American bombers. While they flew alongside the bombers there was hardly ever an enemy aircraft to be seen. It was only once the bombers reached beyond the range of the UK-based fighter cover that the *Luftwaffe* would strike. He later admitted that when he did see a Focke Wolfe he fired 126 cannon shells without touching it. 'I did everything I knew to do, and still I missed him. I'm a disgrace. Me – a gunnery instructor!'

Teddy's second stint in America was brief; time to travel from coast to coast checking the progress of the gunnery schools and to sort out his domestic affairs. During his time in America, the RAF had asked Teddy to find out about the jet-engine trials there. So his first taste of jet flight would be in a rather unofficial capacity. The American project was still secret, although the original designs were given to the American engineers by the British, unable to develop fully Whittle's invention under wartime conditions. An opportunity arose when he was asked to survey

161

an area around Muroc Lake, Nevada for suitable gunnery ranges. The jet plane tests were also being carried out in this area.

Using a piece of headed paper from the School of Applied Tactics, the ever-resourceful Teddy typed himself an introductory letter:

> To whom it may concern. Please allow Group Captain Donaldson every facility to test out the jet project. We are very interested to hear his views on the aircraft and its possible future use in combat.
>
> (Signed)
> E. M. Donaldson

He said something about the letter being needed for later usage and retrieved it before anyone had time to study the signature. And so it was that the base CO gave him the full tour and he gained instruction on the jet. Flying the jet proved a little disappointing as it was inferior in performance to many piston-engined aircraft already in service.

Temporarily based at the AAF Overseas Replacement Depot at Greensboro, Teddy continued on his assignment. It was here, on her home-base, that Teddy was to marry Lieutenant Estellee Holland. Not long afterwards, the couple were involved in a sailing accident on the Indiana River, when the sailboat Teddy had purchased capsized due to a sudden gust. Estellee and a friend, Colonel Stark, were left clinging to the up-turned hull, while Teddy swam two miles for help. The local press later covered the story, reporting Teddy's heroics and their eventual rescue by members of a crash boat from the US Navy Boat Facility, Titusville, Florida.

This was to be Teddy's last adventure in America. Having helped train literally hundreds of fighter pilots and their instructors, Teddy's mission to America came to an end in early 1944 and he said goodbye to his many American friends and sailed back to the UK.

Since 1942 there had been a steady stream of Servicemen and women heading for Great Britain. Teddy's new wife, Estellee, was to join him in England, serving as an army nurse.

Rather belatedly, on 15 September 1948, and in recognition of his service in the United States, Teddy was awarded the American Legion of Merit (Grade: Officer). The award was pinned on Teddy's uniform by Colonel J. B. Ackerman, Acting Air Attaché at a special ceremony held at the American Embassy in London: 'For exceptionally meritorious conduct in the performance of outstanding services.' His citation, signed by President Harry Truman, reads:

> Group Captain Donaldson, Royal Air Force, performed exception-ally meritorious service with the Army Air Force Flying Training

Command in the United States from 7 December 1941 to October 1944. Group Captain Donaldson rendered valuable assistance to the Flying Training Command by his instruction in aerial gunnery procedures and training methods for student fighter pilots. At a critical period he devised texts and training aids and developed techniques that formed a basis of instruction in fighter pilots training throughout the Flying Training Command. Through his efforts, the training methods at the Army Air Force School of Applied Tactics were greatly advanced and training facilitated. The results of his work were reflected in the excellent performance of American fighter pilots in combat.

Under rules prescribed by an Act of Congress, the Legion of Merit was established by President Franklin D. Roosevelt in 1942, and required the President's approval. It is a military decoration of the United States armed forces that is awarded for exceptionally meritorious conduct in the performance of outstanding services and achievements.

The award was promulgated in the *London Gazette* of 15 February 1949, thus permitting Teddy 'unrestricted permission' to wear the American award.

As the Legion of Merit had only recently been created, and was the first American decoration awarded to military and political figures of foreign governments, this was a signal honour. Significantly, Teddy remains one of only a handful of British military officers to have received this decoration, and is in some very distinguished company, other notable recipients having been:

Air Chief Marshal Sir Harry Broadhurst GCB KBE DSO and Bar DFC and Bar AFC, who was appointed an Officer of the Legion of Merit in 1943, when he was then the RAF's youngest air vice-marshal, for his outstanding leadership as Commander of the Western Desert Air Force, composed of American and British units, throughout the Tunisian campaign. Whilst he was Teddy's greatest rival in the pre-war air gunnery contests, 'Broady' also became a lifelong friend.

Lieutenant-Colonel David Niven, British wartime commando and post-war Hollywood actor, who was made a Legionnaire of the Legion of Merit in 1945 for his part as a liaison officer between the British Second Army and the First United States Army before, during and after the 1944 Normandy landings, in which he took part. The decoration was presented to him when he returned to Hollywood after the war by General Dwight D. Eisenhower.

Air Commodore Sir Frank Whittle OM KBE CB FRS, who was
made a Commander of the Order of Merit in 1946 for his
pioneering work in the development of the jet engine. In 1976
he settled in the United States, where he became a member of
the Faculty of the Naval Academy, Annapolis, Maryland. He
died in America in 1996, aged 89, and was regarded as possibly
the greatest aero-engineer of the century.

Air Vice-Marshal J. E. 'Johnnie' Johnson CB CBE DSO and two
Bars, DFC and Bar, who won his Legion of Merit (Officer), as
well as the US Air Medal, in 1950, during the early part of the
Korean War whilst serving as a wing commander with the US
Air Force flying the F-80 Shooting Star against the superior
Soviet-made MiG-15 jet fighters.

General Sir Peter de la Billière KCB KBE DSO MC and Bar, who
was appointed a Chief Commander of the Legion of Merit at
the successful conclusion of the 1990 Gulf War in which, as a
lieutenant-general, he was Commander-in-Chief of the British
forces and second-in-command of the coalition forces under
General Norman Schwarzkopf.

Air Chief Marshal Sir Glenn Torpy KCB CBE DSO, who was
awarded the Legion of Merit (Officer), as an Air Vice-Marshal,
for his part as the UK Air Contingent Commander in the 2003
coalition operation Iraqi Freedom. In April 2006, he became
Chief of the Air Staff and professional Head of the Royal Air
Force.

CHAPTER TWENTY-THREE

'Friendly' Fire

Back in the UK ready for the build-up to the D-Day operations, Teddy served in the Fighter Control Unit, 2nd Tactical Air Force. The RAF fighter squadrons were to control the skies over the English Channel, protecting the vulnerable invasion convoy from *Luftwaffe* bombing and strafing attacks. Once ashore the success of the counter-invasion of Normandy depended on close co-operation between ground forces and their air support.

Within days of the Allies forging a bridgehead, Wing Commander 'Johnnie' Johnson of the 2nd Tactical Air Force had landed a squadron of his Canadian Wing on the first temporary airstrip in Normandy, enabling the RAF to provide close air support for the advancing Allied forces.

With the foothold in Normandy established, the Allies pushed inland to fight the battles for Caen and the Falaise Gap. Johnnie Johnson's wing supported the armies with strafing attacks and by taking on the enemy's fighters. Johnson's last and thirty-eighth combat victory of the war came on 27 September in the skies over the battle for the Falaise Gap. He shot down a Focke Wolfe 190 that day, but his aircraft sustained damage (his first during the entire war) when it was struck by a single cannon shell. Teddy was pleased to have the RAF's top-scoring ace to serve as his wing leader a few years later during the height of the Cold War.

Unusually for Teddy, he was forced to fight his campaign from an operations room rather than in the cockpit of a fighter, leading a wing. Consequently, he did not qualify for the France and Germany Clasp to his Aircrew Europe Star, despite his involvement in the tactical side of the operations.

A few months into the campaign, he was sent on a course at the Empire Central Flying School, to study tactics. He was more advanced in his knowledge than many of his tutors, and he quickly became bored. Time had moved on and the RAF had too, with new high-fliers in the limelight. Teddy would have to win his spurs all over again but in a new role, as he was now, at thirty-two, deemed too old to fly as a fighter leader.

On his first day on the new course, Teddy was invited to tea with the Station Commander. It was, however, not a social visit. He was told in no uncertain terms that he was not going to get any special treatment because of who he was, nor would he be permitted to use the advantage of his rank. He was not the only pilot in this position; there were three Americans, all aces blooded in the Pacific War, who simply left the course in a fit of pique. Knowing that they would damage their chances of promotion, Teddy headed them off in London. They complained: 'Damn it, we're grown men with combat experience. We aren't going to be treated like a lot of kids by those stuck-up air force men.'

Teddy tried to calm them, reminding them of his own position; all had either trained under him or under instructors he had taught. Eventually he managed to convince them to return to complete the course, if only for the sake of their careers.

As a part of the course all the pilots had to complete five operational sorties, at least one in each of Fighter, Bomber and Coastal Commands. Naturally, Teddy took the Fighter Command sorties in his stride. The bomber missions were not such a picnic, however. Teddy travelled to Lincolnshire to fly on his first bombing mission. Sitting in the briefing room, the pilots and navigators discovered that the raid's designated target was deep in the Ruhr and would involve a minimum of eight hours flying over enemy-held territory. Teddy soon realized that being a sitting duck in a Lancaster, without even a machine-gun in his hand for defence, did not suit his temperament. He much preferred sitting in the cockpit of a fighter, able to see the battle unfold and to control his own fate.

While the other crews headed off for a meal and a rest before take-off, Teddy grabbed a drink to help steady his pre-flight nerves. His luck was in, as within an hour of the scheduled take-off time fog came down over the airfield and the operation was cancelled. He was invited to stay on a few days to sit in on another mission but he did not like the idea of hanging around awaiting an uncertain fate over occupied Europe and politely declined, saying he needed to get back to the course.

The Coastal Command operation was to be flown in a Lockheed Ventura from a base in Northern Ireland, with a senior flying tutor piloting. Teddy was joined by one of the American pilots. Neither felt happy with the closing weather conditions as the flight developed. Huddled in the back of the aircraft, the American turned to Teddy and said: 'To think I survived all those damned Zeros to be killed by a Limey.'

'Even the seagulls aren't flying,' added Teddy.

An hour or so into the flight, one of the engines began to splutter. At this point Teddy's American pal became even more jittery and was all for taking to his Irvin parachute declaring: 'I'm not flying with this damn lunatic; he's pulled the radio plug out.'

Teddy calmed him and encouraged him to join him in the cockpit. Teddy stood behind the pilot's seat while the American strapped himself into the co-pilot's seat; maybe they thought they would feel better about the outcome of the mission if they had greater control over the actual flying. Looking at the calculations it was apparent to both that they ought to have sighted land. Teddy suggested they go below the clouds and aim for the Irish coast. Eventually the coastline appeared and they pulled up to a safer altitude, but still low enough to pick out landmarks. Teddy still was not happy. He scanned the countryside until he could see a stretch of road ahead. He saw something wrong but could not put his finger on why. Suddenly it hit him: 'You bloody idiot, we're over France!'

He had caught sight of the vehicles below – they were driving on the right-hand side of the road. Luckily they were still within the reoccupied zone; nevertheless, their unscheduled flight attracted British and American flak, the puffs of smoke coming too close for comfort.

Heading for the deck they spotted a landing ground and the tutor put the Ventura down. The next few hours were spent scrounging enough fuel for the return journey by siphoning it from damaged aircraft lying around the airfield.

Teddy had a certain reputation, and on their return he was hauled up before the commandant, who accused him of setting the whole thing up in order to try to visit his new wife Estellee, who was then a lieutenant nurse serving in an evacuation unit stationed in the Cherbourg peninsula. On this occasion Teddy was innocent and his account was backed up by all concerned.

The pupils were granted a week's leave towards the end of their course. Teddy decided he would visit Estellee, the couple having not long been married. Following the briefest of honeymoons, both had returned to duty. Donaldson went to his commandant and put his case, requesting the loan of a Spitfire. Having already failed to put him on a charge for the Ventura incident, the commandant was not impressed and his request was denied out off hand. Teddy had a word with his brother Arthur, then commanding a fighter station in Norfolk. 'Of course, I'll let you have one of the latest models,' was the response.

Teddy flew at tree-top height for most of the journey but still managed to collect a few bullet and flak holes from 'friendly' fire, something he had to explain away to a less than amused Arthur on his return. The clipped-winged Spitfire looked a little too like the Messerschmitt Bf 109 and the gunners, who hardly ever saw an enemy aircraft, had become a little trigger-happy.

Flying from landing-ground to landing-ground Teddy asked after his wife's unit. Eventually he found her working near an airstrip just 6 miles from the front line. As fortune would have it, the base commander had been one of Teddy's pupils back in the USA and gave over his quarters to the reunited couple.

With only three days left of his leave, Teddy was able to wangle an extension in his inimitable fashion. The Americans had just begun fitting a new British gun-sight linked up to the aircraft throttle control for range finding. A letter was typed and signed by his former pupil, now a general, requesting that Teddy stay on to explain the new device to the American pilots. The request was approved and Teddy bought more time with his new bride.

Having experienced ground attacks while stationed at Vitry in May 1940, Teddy was surprised to see the Americans lining their aircraft up in neat rows. All suggestions that the aircraft be moved to make more difficult targets for a ground strafe were rebuffed. It was explained to him that the *Luftwaffe* was believed to be virtually non-existent at this point in the war and the advice was ignored. Days later the airfield was bombed and many of the American Mustangs were damaged or destroyed. The bomb-craters would take two days to fill and so the Americans declared the base temporarily closed, the pilots being granted two days leave. Teddy said he could manage to take off in between the craters but was refused permission to try as this would mean the Americans had to follow suit. He was in a 'win-win' situation and 'reluctantly' agreed to stay on as long as he was given a letter explaining that he was grounded due to the airstrip being closed due to war damage.

On his return to England, several days late, he appeared before the commandant, who demanded an explanation.

'I've been to France to see my wife, sir.'

'How did you get there?' the commandant demanded.

'By Spitfire,' Teddy replied, unable to hide his amusement.

'What!'

Teddy had his story already worked out and went on to explain to an open-mouthed commandant that he had been asked to give a number of lectures to fighter pilots of the USAAF. The explanatory letters requesting the lectures and praising him for them filled any gaps in his neatly woven excuse. While rats might have been smelt, there was absolutely nothing the commandant could do about it, and Teddy breezed out of the office to resume the course.

As a part of the finale, the pupils were expected to perform in an aerobatics competition. The contest was hot from the very beginning. Teddy looked on as the bar was raised by each successive display. At the top of the heap was Teddy's American friend, who put in a magnificent performance with rolls and loops at an amazing 200 ft. Let loose with an aeroplane and a licence to perform aerobatics, however, Teddy was in heaven. With a quip and a smile he climbed into the cockpit and proceeded to slow roll and loop just above hangar level, stealing the competition as only he could.

CHAPTER TWENTY-FOUR

The Jet Age

The end of his course at the Empire Central Flying School heralded a new posting. Teddy need not have worried about his course rating, as the Commander-in-Chief of Fighter Command, Air Marshal Sir Roderic Hill KCB MC AFC and Bar, already had a new and exciting role for him. Evidently there were problems at RAF Colerne and Teddy was ordered 'to go there at once as we've had some difficulties on the station and morale is all to hell. Your job is to pull the station together'.

Colerne was to become the RAF's first operational jet station and, while Teddy had not fought in jets, he had gained some flying time in America and would soon master the British Meteor.

He arrived at Colerne in December 1944. While the jet squadrons were yet to be deployed, two night-intruder squadrons were flying regular missions 120 miles into Germany. Eager to support his crews, Teddy ensured that he was there to meet each of the airmen on their return, debriefing them personally where possible.

Life was rarely quiet at Colerne. With its long airstrip, it was often used by pilots nursing damaged aircraft that could not make their home bases. At 800 ft above sea-level it was often open when other stations were fog-bound, and it regularly received lost aircraft from other stations.

Eventually, the Gloster Meteors arrived for active service with Nos 74 and 245 Squadrons. In order to prevent them from being mistaken for the German's Messerschmitt 262, the British jets were painted white. This was a similar measure to the painting of 'invasion stripes' on all RAF aircraft in advance of D-Day.

The Meteor had already begun to make its name chasing and destroying the German V1 flying bombs. Tactical training for fighter combat and ground strikes was yet to be devised. Teddy would play and important role in their evolution.

Naturally, he had been quick to fly the Meteor and put it through its paces, pushing the aircraft to its limits and developing combat tactics based on its handling profile.

At this time an incident occurred which was typical of Teddy and which could so easily have cost him either his life or his career. It involved a First World War pilot called Joe Offord who was approaching retirement age. He served on the station's administrative staff and often drank in the company of his much younger station commander. Joe had told Teddy on a number of occasions how much he would love to fly in a jet plane before his RAF days were done, and how, if anyone could pull it off, it was Teddy. This dream seemed impossible; the only jet in service at the time was the single-seat Meteor. Eventually, Teddy relented and, secretly ditching his parachute in dispersal, walked out to his Meteor, where Joe was already hiding. He told Joe to climb in and sit on the seat with his legs spread apart so Teddy could sit in the pilot's seat between his knees. Teddy had, of course, done this before, but never in a jet fighter. Once airborne Teddy allowed his passenger to put his arms around him and take the controls – and so Joe achieved his dream of 'flying' a jet.

On landing Teddy taxied off the runway and jumped out as quickly as he could, ushering Joe away from the Meteor before anyone could get sight of him. As he disappeared into the darkness Teddy whispered as loud as he dared: 'Don't breathe a word of this to anyone, otherwise I'll be court-martialled.'

A few days later, he was horrified to hear Offord talking about the flight in the RAF Club. 'Oh yes I did, at Colerne; Teddy Donaldson took me up,' he blurted, unable to contain his delight.

'But the Meteor is a single-seater,' the reply from one of Joe's audience in disbelief.

'He sat between my knees,' Joe responded.

'Rubbish!'

When a staggered Teddy was asked the truth of the matter he gave Joe a withering look and simply replied; 'It's not possible.'

Joe knew not to respond. The matter was closed.

Teddy was to see out the rest of the war commanding the jet station, marking Empire Day on 12 March 1945 with a flying display of Meteors, enjoyed by, among others, the men of the Royal Observer Corps. For Teddy this was a personal 'thank you' to the men of the Corps, now with their 'Royal' title, who had been instrumental in the defeat of the *Luftwaffe* in the summer of 1940. With the loss of many of the radar stations due to bombing, the RAF were reliant of enemy raiders being plotted with the aid of hundreds of spotters of the Observer Corps. The RAF would not have been able to maintain standing patrols to defend these shores and so the Corps' intelligence was to prove vital. Teddy later received the personal thanks of their commandant, Air Commodore Finlay Crerar CBE.

With members of the press viewing from the station's control tower, Teddy could not help giving them a 'buzz' as he swooped and dived at speeds ranging from 200 mph to something well over twice this speed. His display was reported in the local press.

> Mainly for the benefit for the photographers, the Group Captain flew up and down in front of the control tower at a sedate 200 mph. Flying at 10–15 ft from the ground, he gave us the novel experience of looking down on his Meteor as it flashed by a few feet away.
>
> He then demonstrated just what the Meteor could do in the way of speed and repeated his tactics at velocities approaching 500 mph.
>
> His final demonstration consisted of flying towards us at top speed a few feet above the aerodrome surface. The speck that was his Meteor grew very rapidly bigger and was flying directly towards the base of the tower on which we were perched. When a collision seemed inevitable he lifted his machine almost imperceptibly and the Meteor crashed over our heads with a stunning crescendo of sound leaving in its wake a group of shaken spectators. His pull-out speed is unquotable but we had a close up of the vapour phenomena for a fraction of a second . . . The Japanese can thank their ancestors that the wrath of this, our first in the new era of fighting airplanes, was never released against them.

With the cessation of hostilities, Colerne was handed over to Maintenance Command in October 1945. Teddy's time there had brought him quite literally up to speed with modern air warfare and would ensure an illustrious post-war career, where so many others would fall by the wayside, out of sorts with peace-time flying.

Among those to have sent their compliments to him for a job well done was his AOC at No. 10 (Fighter) Group, Air Commodore A. V. Harvey CBE, who wrote to him on 27 April 1945, before he moved on to another posting:

> My Dear Teddy,
>
> Before leaving the Group I feel I must drop you a note to thank you for the way you have resuscitated Colerne, and made the Station a really live one in the few months you have been there.
>
> You have done a magnificent job in raising the morale of all personnel and getting the 'jet' business on a sound footing.
>
> Please accept my sincere thanks for this and I should like to take this opportunity of wishing you the best of luck in your career and I hope you will meet with further success.

The air commodore, always known as Vere Harvey, became a distinguished MP after the war, receiving first a knighthood, amusingly becoming Sir Vere ('severe') and later, after serving as Chairman of the Conservatives' 1922 Committee, a life peerage as Lord Harvey of Prestbury.

Late in 1945, Teddy was appointed to command RAF Millfield, the rocket-firing OCU in Northumberland, developing rocket-ground attacks. Here he trained pilots in close ground-support tactics. Once again Teddy was in the forefront of the development of combat tactics, helping to maximize aircrew efficiency on the firing ranges, to give them the edge in combat.

CHAPTER TWENTY-FIVE

High Speed Flight

The piston engine had ruled the air for over forty years since the days of the Wright brothers' first powered manned flight at Kittyhawk on 17 December 1903.

It was Orville, the younger of the two, who first piloted the 'Flyer', taking the aircraft up and achieving an average speed of 30 mph into a 25 mph headwind. The first air-speed record was not set until 1909 when a Frenchman called Paul Tissandier topped the Wright brothers' first recorded flight by a mere 4 mph, but did so over a measured course and under the scrutiny of the Fédération Aéronautique Internationale (FAI). The FAI is the world air sports federation, and was founded in 1905 with the aim of furthering aeronautical and astronautical activities worldwide.

Records were set at race meetings across Europe and America, and by the outbreak of the First World War the record had been raised to 126.67 mph. The British fighters during the war, the Royal Aircraft Factory SE5 and the Sopwith Dolphin, managed to achieve speeds of up to only about 130 mph. By 1920, however, the record had been raised to 171.05 mph. Over the next two decades a succession of duels took place, first between individual pilots, then between manufacturers and finally between air-force-sponsored aircraft, in contests such as the Pulitzer, the Thompson and the Schneider Trophies, the Gordon Bennett Cup and the Coupe Deutsch. The race to break the 200, 300 and 400 mph barriers was led by the French, quickly followed by the Americans, the British, the Italians and the Germans.

It was a Messerschmitt Bf 109R flown by *Flugkapitän* Fritz Wendel that set the last pre-war record at 469.22 mph. This record, set on 26 April 1939, was unofficially broken first by the Focke-Wulf Fw 190, a version of which achieved speeds in excess of 472 mph, and secondly by the American Mustang P-51M which flew at 491 mph. The piston engine was, however, reaching its limits, as the efficiency of the propeller diminished rapidly at speeds in excess of 500 mph.

The new generation of aircraft were to be powered by jet engines. Dr Hans von Ohain and Frank Whittle (Air Commodore Sir Frank Whittle

OM KBE CB FRS) are recognized as the co-inventors of jet propulsion. Each was working separately and knew nothing of the other's work. Although Whittle started first, the German-born von Ohain was the first to design and run a self-contained jet engine, the Heinkel-Strahltriebwerk 1 (IIeS 1), the name meaning 'Heinkel Jet Engine 1'.

An updated version of this engine, the Heinkel HeS 3b, was the first to power an all-jet aircraft. This was the Heinkel He 178 which first flew on 27 August 1939 and achieved a speed of 435 mph. The flight was, of course, top secret.

The first British jet-powered aircraft, the Gloster E.28/39 or Gloster Whittle, also nicknamed 'the Squirt', took to the air for the first time on 15 May 1941. Whittle's engine gave the Squirt, on its very first flight, a speed almost as fast as the then current Spitfire (around 338 mph); the E.28/39 later achieved 466 mph.

However, it was the Germans, with their Messerschmitt Me 262, who first brought the jet-engined fighter into operational service and with it heralded a new age of warfare. The RAF, with its twin turbo-jet Meteor, was not far behind. British jet engines had been sent to America during the war where they were developed independently. As with so many other British inventions the development resources were lacking under wartime conditions, leaving the Americans to steal a march in the post-war era.

It was in April 1946 that the Air Ministry decided to make an advance on the air-speed record, which was already held by Great Britain's Group Captain Hugh J. 'Willie' Wilson AFC, the Commandant of the Empire Test Pilots' School at Cranfield, with a speed of 606 mph, set at Herne Bay on 7 November 1945. Group Captain Wilson's record, established within a few months of the end of the war with Japan, had ensured that Britain held all three world speed records; on land; on water and in the air. All had been achieved using Rolls-Royce power-plants.

Significantly, Group Captain Wilson's record was the first set with an aircraft using jet engines and the first air-speed record over 600 mph. His Gloster Meteor F. Mk IV, christened *Britannia*, was powered by twin River Class Derwent V engines as opposed to the usual Mk Is. Each engine provided around 3,500 lb of thrust, nearly double that of the Derwent I.

Wilson had been Chief Test Pilot at the Royal Aircraft Establishment at Farnborough during the war, testing the two prototype Gloster Whittle E.28/39s, and later converting No. 616 Squadron onto the Gloster Meteor. Although the press had interviewed him, the lack of any problems or newsworthy events led to his efforts, and those of his fellow pilot Eric Greenwood, the Chief Test Pilot of the Gloster Aircraft Company, being almost overlooked. In the event, the press made their own drama by announcing that Greenwood was the new record holder. A review of the figures, however put Greenwood's average speed as 603.125 mph, with Wilson taking the record with a 606.38 mph average speed over four runs. Perhaps the unluckiest of men was Squadron Leader P. Stanbury DFC, who had pushed the Meteor to 603 mph at Moreton Valance on 19 October 1945. His achievement was not recognized as it was not under FAI controlled conditions.

It was well known that the Americans were preparing to mount an attack on Wilson's record with their Lockheed P-80 Shooting Star, which was still being trialled and might be ready to fly at any time. The British de Havilland Company was experimenting with their own jet fighter too, although the revolutionary new swept-wing aircraft was still untested and so British hopes rested with the Meteor.

The gamble was that the airframe of the Gloster Meteor F Mark IV, designed by George Carter, could just about withstand a speed of 630 mph before it risked disintegrating. If this speed was reached, then it was thought that the Americans would not be able to better it by more than 5 mph – the margin required for a new record to be recognized – without pushing the Shooting Star beyond its considered 'safe' margin.

The record attempt was made at the suggestion of Air Marshal Sir Alec Coryton of the Ministry of Supply. A meeting was held at the Air Ministry at 1500 hours on Thursday, 25 April 1946, during which the framework for the record attempt was established. Air Vice-Marshal J. N. Boothman was in the chair.

Initial preparations had to be made under strict secrecy. If the Americans got wind of the British tactics, they might press ahead with their own programme and snatch the record. Should this happen then there would be no hope of reclaiming it until a completely new airframe was designed, and that might take several years. The chips were down; there was no time to lose.

The RAF were to be supplied with four super-powered Rolls Royce Derwent V centrifugal-flow turbojet engines fitted with Nimonic alloy 90 turbine blades designed by Dr Stanley G. Hooker (later Sir Stanley Hooker), Chief Engineer at Rover's Barnoldswick factory in West Yorkshire. Each engine had to be deregulated to allow it to run at 18,200 rpm with a tail-pipe temperature 250 degrees C more than the usual 600 degrees C. These engines produced 4,200 lb of thrust but only had a serviceable life of eighteen minutes at full-throttle! This was reduced to just thirteen minutes as a safety measure. In short, a pilot would have twenty-six minutes flying time to set a world record, after which their power plants were little more than scrap metal. Furthermore, to set a new record, the pilot needed to exceed the existing record consistently over four timed runs over a straight 3 km course, with only the average speed counting, not the maximum.

The record attempt was set for 1 August. The engines would be ready for bench-testing by July, taking another month to be fitted into the airframes. The two Meteor IVs with their special configurations were christened the Star Meteors.

The Air Ministry's Air-speed Record Committee had originally insisted that command of the High Speed Flight should go to an air commodore. A shortlist was put together but no candidate stood out and so it was suggested that they should open the command to group captains. Among the names submitted was that of Group Captain E. M. Donaldson DSO AFC.

As a former front-line squadron commander, fighter ace and aerobatics team leader who had turned instructor, Teddy appeared to have all the right credentials. But he was much, much more than the sum of the parts – not only a meticulous and charismatic leader but also a man who led from the front and shared the risks of his fellow pilots at all times, even during the darkest hours when survival seemed unlikely.

Recently appointed to command the night-fighter training school at East Moor, near York, Teddy, his American wife Estellee, and their six-month old son David, were just settling in to their new lives in the north of England when a call came through from the Air Officer Commanding-in-Chief (AOC-in-C), Fighter Command, Air Marshal Sir James Robb, who wanted to see him 'forthwith'.

Teddy wondered which of his more recent transgressions had caught up with him. Would it be a charge of low flying over a populated area or unauthorized aerobatics?

Stepping into Robb's office, the ever resourceful Teddy went through the catalogue of excuses he had previously formulated and decided he would gauge the Air Marshal's mood and alter his story accordingly.

'What do you think of your new appointment?' asked Robb.

'Fine, sir.'

'Well,' Sir James said, 'we have been discussing the details of the High Speed Flight for days now and we have decided that you are the man to run it.'

Teddy's jaw dropped, then he regained his voice. 'I'm sorry, sir, but what the hell are you talking about?' he exclaimed.

While this was not exactly the response Teddy would normally give to a superior officer, he was caught totally off guard. This was the very first he had heard about any High Speed Flight, never mind his 'posting'.

Sir James remained composed and continued: 'You are to organise and run the whole thing; decide on the place, time, crews and what you need. Everything is up to you. Keep me informed . . . That's all Teddy.' Salutes were exchanged and the conversation was over.

Teddy soon realized that this was not just a matter of putting a few more miles an hour onto a record which was, after all, already held by a British pilot. It was about showing the whole world that Great Britain was still a superpower and that she could compete on the same terms as the Americans and Russians. He also knew that the RAF really did not have the airframe to take the record to the next level.

One of the first things he did, after breaking the news to Estellee, was to arrange a meeting with Air Vice-Marshal J. N. Boothman. The winner of the Schneider Trophy in 1931, Boothman was now Assistant Chief of Air Staff (Technical Requirements). He was aware of the problems the High Speed Flight might face and explained that far from being able to give Teddy the answers he sought, they were looking to him to solve those problems. He explained:

> We are solidly up against compressibility. This task of yours is completely experimental. It raises all sorts of problems. We have to have the answers. It's up to you to provide them.
>
> Your aircraft will have 3 ft 6 in chopped off the wings, larger engines, larger air intakes, no dive brakes, no flaps to reduce landing speed, no radio and most of the tanks removed.
>
> We are cutting the wings shorter to lessen the drag and increase the safety factor. We have been worried, I don't mind telling you, about the structural strength. Shortening the wings should help considerably.

Teddy thought to himself; 'This is a killer plane.'

'We are giving you two whacking great engines,' Boothman enthused, 'more powerful than any that have ever been put into a plane. You'll have all the power you can use but the aircraft's drag, due to compression, is going to limit your speed.'

Before Teddy had the opportunity to ask any questions, Boothman closed the conversation with a firm, 'Now go to it!'

In simple terms, compressibility refers to the shock waves ahead of the aircraft at speed. When an aircraft flies it pushes forward a wall of air which, in effect, warns the air in front of the aircraft's impending arrival, and so it parts to allow it to pass through.

When approaching the speed of sound the air cannot be pushed away quickly enough; it is compressed and this hinders forward motion. During earlier High Speed Flights these compression waves were measured some 18 ft ahead of the aircraft. Their presence created a rough ride for the pilot and flying even faster would threaten the integrity of the airframe and might well destroy the Stars.

Teddy was not simply dropped into a team of pilots, technicians, engineers, mechanics, fitters, and course markers (those responsible for marking and controlling the 3 km course accurately to within 3 cm per kilometre). As Sir James had explained, he would have to put together the whole operation from scratch, and in double-quick time.

Appointed in May, he had a matter of a few weeks not only to pick the men but also to form them into a winning team. The race was on and the High Speed Flight was officially formed on 14 June. In all, there were over thirty-five men, each handpicked. Two, Corporal Donald Knight and Leading Aircraftman Leonard Hall, even postponed their release from the RAF to work on the project.

The war had produced many great pilots and Fighter Command was as blessed as any. A list of fifty of the very best from all Commands was submitted to Teddy. Many of the names were well known to him, others required further investigation. He decided he wanted two men who were poles apart. One would be like himself, a daredevil who would let nothing, including his own personal safety, stand in the way of the record; the other should be a steady, reliable type.

Teddy always took the hands-on approach and so began a tour of RAF stations as he worked through the dossier. He met the pilots and talked to them about their careers and their thoughts on test flying the Meteor IV. He talked too with the pilots' COs as well as with their friends and colleagues, and studied every aspect of their service records until he was satisfied he had the right men for the job.

In the end he selected Bill Waterton and Neville Duke. They were to prove him 100 per cent right and continued to have record-breaking careers of their own beyond the summer of 1946.

A Canadian, Squadron Leader Bill Waterton was twenty-nine years old. He came to Britain in 1939 to enlist in the RAF, and had flown with Fighter Command, Ferry Command and Fighter Command's Meteorological Flight. He had gained flying time on a wide variety of aircraft types, including the new Meteor, while with Fighter Command's Air Fighting Development Unit at Wittering. He was also the recipient of the AFC for gallantry in this role, and came with the highest recommendations as a test pilot from the Central Fighter Establishment.

Flight Lieutenant Neville Duke was a tall, rugged, thin-faced man, who had flown with Fighter Command since 1941 and had ended the war with twenty-eight enemy aircraft to his credit. He had been awarded the DSO, along with the DFC and two Bars. A former CO of the crack No. 145 Fighter Squadron, Neville had recently flown as a test pilot at Farnborough.

With the pilots and the rest of the High Speed Flight drawn together, the practice flights began. The Derwent Vs were not ready initially and so the early weeks of the Flight were spent using three standard or 'hack' Meteors. These they would take up to 20,000 ft before power-diving them down to sea level, flying along the record course. The actual record-breaking flights themselves had to be made in level flight and no higher than 1,000 ft above sea level, so although the hacks could put up a good speed in a dive, this was not an indication of their best speed under record-breaking conditions.

The runs began on 1 July with flights well within the Meteor IV's normal limits. For security and safety reasons, much of the testing, especially of the two Star aircraft once they were ready, was to be carried out at sea away from the eyes of holidaymakers. When Wilson had set his record in 1945, about fifty people had witnessed it from the nearby cliff tops. By contrast it has been estimated that a million holidaymakers made their way to the south coast to follow the exploits of Donaldson, Waterton and Duke over those summer months.

On 12 July Boothman visited the flight and took one of the hacks up; he recorded a speed of 610 mph during his third run over the marked course. When he landed he stepped over to Donaldson and his team, saying, 'It's damned easy, isn't it? Nothing like flying the old racing seaplane.'

Although Boothman's words were aimed as much at the media as the men of the High Speed Flight, confidence was high that the Stars could take the record. However, the press got wind that the Meteor IV airframe was not designed to withstand world-record speeds. They started being very 'un-British' and at a press conference began asking Teddy questions about safety factors. Rather than go into details about a catastrophic failure, Teddy focused instead on engine cut-out: 'If both engines fail at 600 mph it is possible for this aircraft to climb up to 12,500 ft and to then glide for more than 30 miles and it can fly at 300 mph on one engine.'

Speaking about the High Speed Flights he added: 'My orders are to get the world record – and that is what we are going to do. I will not be satisfied with anything less than 623 miles per hour. It is very impor-tant for the British aircraft industry that we keep the record from our American friends.'

The significance of getting to 623 mph was that, if achieved, this would be the first time anyone had flown at over the highly prestigious 1,000 Kmph mark.

After the press interview, a visitor called on Teddy. He had got through security using the 'old pals act', having previously served as a wing commander. It turned out that he was from Teddy's insurance company. His high-risk job, it transpired, made his policy null and void!

The upshot of the meeting was that he was given the option of drastically increasing his payments or accepting a full refund. Despite having a wife and young son, Teddy accepted the latter course. This rather cold act by his insurance company might have been too much for some but Teddy just took it in his stride; he had a job to do.

Teddy realized that once the pilots took off they were very much on their own. He wrote to the Air Ministry:

> Once the pilot takes off we have no control over him whatsoever. There is nothing I can do on the course he may take during the sixteen minutes he is away. The whole procedure which I have trained will work like clockwork; it must. If it does not there is nothing I can do to alter it on the day.
>
> The Fighter Command High Speed Flight will definitely get the record.
>
> Give me the engines and the airframes; the rest of the set-up cannot go wrong. I have not given the matter of the choice of pilot any serious thought.

This last statement was not quite true. He had already decided that he would break the record although he would not place any barriers in the way of either of the other two pilots. As he later explained it to a friend; 'I figured it out like this. If I am not selfish and allow someone else to fly for the record, I might be considered to be lacking sufficient guts to do it myself. If I do it myself I might be considered selfish. But I would rather be considered selfish than lacking in guts.'

The scientists and engineers agreed that the record could only be broken by the Star under certain climatic conditions. Critically, they had calculated that an optimum air temperature of 30 degrees C was needed to succeed. Every extra degree of heat raised the speed of sound by 1 mph and therefore pushed the point where the aircraft faced compressibility back by the same amount. Therefore, the warmer the day the faster the Star would go. Conversely, the higher the temperature the less efficient the engines would be. Equally important, they needed 'clean' air, that is to say no moving pockets of air or eddies along the flight path.

The record attempt would be made between 1 August and 6 September, a period when meteorological records showed that on average the daytime temperature for Great Britain reached the magic 30 degrees C (about 86 degrees F) twenty-eight days out of forty-six. This would give plenty of time to do any fine tuning and to go for the record only when pilots and machines were perfectly harmonized.

Teddy and Wing Commander McGregor had studied the RAF's meteorological record going back fifty years, searching for suitable locations around Britain's coast, paying particular attention to summer temperatures as well as wind forces and direction. Ideally they wanted a hot, still day with little breeze and light cloud. The location that Teddy chose was Littlehampton, between Bognor Regis and Worthing, and only a few miles away from his mother's house at Selsey. They would use Fighter Command's station at nearby Tangmere as their air base, and Teddy rented a nearby house for Estellee and their son David, allowing him to spend time with his family between test flights. The assembled team did not realize it, but 1946 was to see the coldest summer ever recorded.

CHAPTER TWENTY-SIX

Saved by an Engineer

Throughout August the three pilots put the Meteors through their paces, learning their handling faults. Flying the hacks, they familiarized themselves with the approach run and the course so that they knew exactly when to speed up for the times runs.

Teddy later recalled the handling of the adapted Meteors and his feelings about the forthcoming record attempt:

> The controls were solid and the aircraft shook horribly. I was fearful of the time when the big engines arrived.

Finally the Derwent V power-plants arrived from the test-beds where they had been put through their paces. Teddy's designated aircraft, E549, was the first to have its engines fitted on 11–12 August, the second aircraft, E550 being worked on the following day.

Flying on the edge, the build-up to the record attempt nearly ended in tragedy on more than one occasion. Both Bill Waterton and Neville Duke had close calls, Duke when his port engine was badly damaged at 580 mph. Fortunately, both men were able to shut down the engines before they totally disintegrated and took the wing off.

Post-flight technical investigations revealed that tiny mandrel heads from the 'blind rivets' on the wings had sheared off and found their way into the engine compressor. Part of the compressor had broken lose and smashed the turbine blades. A new seal was invented that prevented further problems and this was introduced into the production model. Even so, the problem of rivets popping could not be overcome. Teddy was later to reveal that hundreds of rivets lost their heads on each of the record attempts.

The dangers of flying the Star became apparent to Teddy during his very first flight on 14 August when one of the engines failed during take-off, although he had little difficulty in wrestling the controls, turning the aircraft around and landing on one engine. The flight lasted only two minutes; an inauspicious start to the record breaking campaign.

The Star had a number of unusual flying characteristics. The team

183

discovered that once the throttles were tight against the stops, it was a two-handed job to maintain them in this position. The controls became solid, while the whole aircraft shook violently. It was not a pleasant experience, especially for someone aware of the potentials of the airframe to disintegrate in a split second. The aircraft, it should be remembered, had no ejector-seat (the first 'live' ejection from an aircraft only took place in July, 1946) and, lacking pressurized suits, no one could survive an accident at high speed.

Because of the dangers of compressibility and the extreme temperatures reached in the leading edges of the aircraft due to air friction, the Star could not fly with a standard Meteor canopy. This had to be replaced by one largely composed of steel with a small Perspex area for the pilot to look through. Apart from hampering take-off, landing and general navigation, the restricted visibility meant that the pilots were unable to see the movement of the wings and would have little advanced warning of any failure before it became catastrophic. Teddy joked wryly:

> This was a damned good thing. It prevented me from seeing out sideways and watching those wings flapping about with compressibility shakes to a terrifying degree.

Teddy recalled that a viewing of the latest film footage of the American High Speed Flights revealed their use of special flying suits and helmets. Teddy and his team would generally fly in shirtsleeves and without protective headgear. Even then, compressibility made the cockpit unbearably hot.

There were only two Stars and three pilots. Teddy had made his mind up as to who should get a crack at the record; he wanted two pilots who were poles apart to maximize their chances.

The logical answer therefore was that Bill Waterton should have the second seat. Naturally, Neville Duke was disappointed when he was told, on 13 August, that he would have to take the reserve seat.

Teddy had set a speed of 626 mph at 3,000 feet on 14 August, in only his second run in the Star. 'This,' Teddy reported, 'was the lowest altitude that I could avoid the bumps.'

During the daily press briefing, Teddy said that, weather permitting, the team would make an attempt on the record the following day. In the event the Stars would remain in their hangars and the only one flying over the next few days was to be in the hacks.

On 19 August the press reported that the weather forecast for the next 48 hours was for temperatures around 80 degrees F or about 27 degrees C. One newspaper rather optimistically led with the line that speeds of 643 mph might be achieved if this were the case.

With only a short flying life, the Derwent Vs had to be used sparingly and it wasn't until 23 August that Teddy was able to take E549 into the air again, reaching a speed of 619 mph for two minutes at 1,000 feet, the altitude at which all record attempts had to be made to conform with the official speed record regulations.

Teddy decided that it was now or never and it was announced that a record attempt would be made the following day 'sometime after 11.00 am'. He would take the gamble and give it all he had.

After a pre-record attempt test flight, the technical officer, Squadron Leader A. H. Porter, gave the Star the once over while it sat overnight in the hangar. He noticed some crinkling in the fuselage skin aft of the mainplane. Porter decided to make an internal examination even though this meant a four hour long process.

What Squadron Leader Porter found astonished all of the experts and saved Teddy's life. There was a mass of twisting and buckling in the spar and ribs of the fiselage. A section of nine feet long had collapsed inwards, unseen from the outside. If the jet had been flown at high speed it would have disintegrated and Teddy would have been killed.

All record attempts had to be put on hold until the structural problems could be rectified. Meanwhile, Teddy had to face the press to explain the 'refit'. He had express orders not to reveal the true nature of the fault, something for which he received a good deal of criticism from the media.

Originally, it was hoped that the aircraft could be repaired overnight but this proved too ambitious. The two Star jets were flown back to the Gloster factory for repairs. The weather remained too bad for a record attempt so the engineers felt less pressure to deliver to an unrealistic time-scale. Further tests resulted in strengthening to the spars and ribs – the modified Stars were ready to fly. Back to Tangmere, the aircraft were checked over by Teddy's team and re-polished to perfection with beeswax. This allowed the jets to cut through the air with less drag. The Star's air brakes were locked closed and made more stream-lined with filler. While this reduced drag, it meant that the pilots would have difficulty in losing speed, taking wide circuits around Tangmere before they could land.

August came and went and Teddy was getting anxious. He told Bill Waterton that he wanted the Star tested at full throttle, something that had only ever been done before on the test beds. Bill agreed but wanted to fly at 20,000 ft rather than under 1,000 ft, which was what his CO was asking. Teddy explained that the whole aircraft would behave differently under the lower air pressures of high altitude flight and the record attempt had to be set at less than 1,000 ft. Any data gathered from a flight at 20,000 ft would therefore be useless and would only waste precious minutes of the Derwent's short life at full-throttle.

Teddy later recalled the handling of the adapted Meteor and his feelings about the forthcoming record attempt: 'The controls were solid and the aircraft shook horribly. I was fearful of the time when the big engines arrived.'

During the record attempts the cockpit temperature rose dramatically. Instead of a perspex hood, which would weaken with the rise in temperature, the Stars had a steel hood with toughened perspex panels. Teddy explained: 'I said jokingly at the time that this was done to prevent me from seeing the wings which developed a frightening shake caused by "compressibility".'

When it came to low-altitude flying on the test runs, he had to consider the needs of the engineers and design team. He needed to have film footage should anything go wrong. They had only reached this point because of being able to study the results of previous aircraft losses and had engineered around past problems; they were part of an evolution of manned flight and their failure might allow others to succeed later. On the other hand, a dead pilot and wreckage spread over tens of miles of seabed would be a brave man's life recklessly cut short for nothing. Teddy would share the same risks as Waterton. He needed to know that the latter was on side. He told him: 'You are a volunteer for this job, as we all are, so presumably you have the right to decline. All I can do is to refer the matter to the Air Ministry and it is up to them.'

He knew that it was natural for Bill to be cautious; this was, after all, the reason why Teddy had selected him. However, in Teddy's judgement, this was the only way forward. For a while it seemed that Waterton would have to surrender his seat to the more adventurous Duke.

Teddy later reflected on the build-up to the record attempt: 'My God, it was a frightful and frightening experience. There were times when I thought perhaps, after all, Waterton might have been right. I flew them at nought feet at full throttle and both aircraft landed badly buckled internally and I was almost "bent" myself.'

CHAPTER TWENTY-SEVEN

The Fastest Man Alive

After weeks of cool weather the temperature finally began to rise, although the forecasters warned Teddy that the increase would be both modest and short-lived.

On 7 September the weather seemed calm. It was raining but slightly warmer than it had been for what seemed like an age. However, the temperature remained at a moderate 14 degrees C (under 60 degrees F), far less than the optimum 30 C. With no hope of higher temperatures to come, it looked as though it was going to be now or never for the High Speed Flight. With Neville Duke in Brussels that day, on his way to show the Meteor's paces at an international air rally at Ghent followed by another air display at Prague, Czechoslovakia, it was left to Teddy and Bill Waterton to have a crack at the record.

When interviewed by the press in August, Teddy had explained why his team had to break the record for Great Britain. 'We want to keep the record. It's important for British goods; they have got to be the best – and they are the best. This time next year we shall put the record up a lot more than we shall next month. Every day we are finding out new things.'

It was time. Teddy gave the order to go just before 1800 hours. Many of the reporters had left the course and were to miss the record attempts, much to their editors' annoyance.

Two Mosquito night fighters were ordered to take off to patrol the flight path at 1,000 ft to ensure that the record attempt did not breech the FAI regulations.

Wing Commander A.A. McGregor's team had marked out the course Teddy and the others were to fly. There was a 9 mile run-in to the measured course between Rustington and Kingston Gorse, where the nine mile run-out began.

The course would be flown four times at a maximum altitude of 999 ft over the entire course and at 246 ft during the officially timed section to remain within the FAI rules and set a new record.

Air-sea rescue launches were sent out to patrol the course. This, Teddy maintained, was little more than a token, as a failure at 600 mph would

be fatal. There were no parachutes or ejector seats. Teddy would fly at
sea level and he knew that hitting the water at anything over 30 mph
might not be survivable.

If the Meteor hit a seagull at these speeds it was also likely to prove
fatal, and not just for the gull. In fact many dead birds were discovered
along the course, killed by the shock wave ahead of the aircraft. Teddy
and his pilots were lucky to survive these potential disasters.

Teddy's jet, Meteor IV, EE549, was towed to the end of the runway.
The tanks were topped up with fuel; none was to be wasted on taxiing.
Teddy's own commentary on the next few minutes was as follows:

> Okay this is it. Climb in; strap myself in; am in shirtsleeves rolled
> up and have no helmet as there is no radio. Start the engines. They
> start instantly. Chocks away. Open throttles to the position of
> normal full power. Lets go the brakes [sic]. That terrific push in the
> back and we are accelerating down the runway. We are in the air
> at 1,000 yards and have got about 280 mph on the clock by the end
> of the runway. I keep her low, flying due west in the same direc-
> tion as take-off. Somewhere just south of Chichester start a turn to
> the left, straightening out just over Pagham Harbour, flying due
> east at just less than 1,000 ft. Start to lose height.
>
> I have to be just as close as I dare to the water to get the best speed.
> Soon I was at ten feet above the sea with 600 mph on the speedo.
> Nine miles to run. Full throttle.
>
> Ye Gods what a mess! The plane shakes like hell. Blurring vision.
> Controls solid. Centre of lift shot back. Two hands on the stick and
> pull for all you bloody well can to keep her nose up.
>
> Lined up with the buoys already and wooooooooooossssh
> through the measured course marked at each end with the barrage
> balloons.
>
> Throttle straight back; control resumed; get off the sea quick.
> Christ, what a picnic. A right turn with a constant 4½ G force; then
> left turn with 4½ G round towards Brighton and on to a westerly
> heading.
>
> Down to sea level in the mist and rain. Shake, shake, shake,
> through the course with both arms pulling with all their might.
> Course complete. Jam throttles.
>
> Throttles closed; turn right, and do the whole damned thing
> again both ways.
>
> Finally through the course for the last time. Keep throttles shut;
> 600 mph plus to get rid of. I could have climbed to 10,000 ft with
> that speed without the engines. But I am not allowed by the regu-
> lations to break the 1,000 ft mark. Back to Tangmere in a minute.
> Round the airfield to lose speed, no airbrakes or flaps to help

slowing down. After several circuits I have lost sufficient speed to lower the wheels and land. I am wringing wet with sweat. Am surprised to see the rain has not removed any paint from the machine.

The Times later wrote:

The Group Captain's control of the Meteor throughout the four runs was magnificent. Although he was subjected to fairly severe 'bumps' he kept the machine steadily on its course, turned accurately in stately arcs at each end of the 20 mile stretch and over the marked course remained unerringly on a level keel.

Thirteen minutes after take-off Teddy's fly-pasts were completed and he landed back at Tangmere. With him back on the ground, Bill Waterton went up and made a total of five timed runs in his Star Meteor (EE550). He caught one of the 'bumps', a violent upward air current off the mouth of the River Arun. His aircraft had developed a pull to the left and he had to fly the whole record attempt correcting the trim by using both hands on the control column, propping his left shoulder tightly against the cockpit to try to keep the Star on a straight and level course. Twenty minutes later and his attack on the record was completed. Both men would have to sit it out and wait for the timings to be analysed. It took six hours for the officials to check and double-check the figures. The data came from two camera huts stationed at either end of the 3 mile run. The cine cameras were synchronized by landline from the National Physical Laboratory 50 miles away at Teddington.

At 0200 hours, in the cinema at Tangmere, Air Marshal Sir James Robb announced the results of the attempt to the team and press:

After all these days and weeks of anxious waiting I have got the figures. I congratulate Group Captain Donaldson and Squadron Leader Waterton on their efforts.

These figures are subject to confirmation later. I do not propose to go into details. The record has been beaten, that is the main thing.

Sportingly, Bill Waterton raced over to Teddy shaking him warmly by the hand and congratulating him on the new record.

Over the measured course the two men had managed to increase the record by the required 5 mph. Teddy had averaged 616 mph, while Waterton had achieved 614 mph. Had Bill's run been made first, he would have taken the record, as Teddy would have had to achieve 619 mph to advance it by the required 5 mph (if the first record-breaking speed were registered.) But what was important was not who broke the record, but that Teddy's team had done its job. However, Teddy wanted to go further, he wanted to push to the 630 mph which he knew he could achieve – the record had been set at 17 degrees below the optimum temperature, which meant another 17 mph could be added to the new record.

The rules of the FAI allowed seven days between setting a new record and officially filing the documents. The Royal Aero Club held onto the official papers until the very last minute, hoping that The High Speed Flight might have the opportunity to push the record even higher. It was hoped that a second attempt could be made on 11 September when weather conditions initially looked more promising. Teddy took one of the hacks up over the course but found the air was too bumpy, while temperatures still did not improve.

During these trials, Teddy was involved in an incident which could have proved fatal. He later recalled that, once again, he owed his life to his engineering officer, Squadron Leader George Porter, and one of the aircraft mechanics. But it was not a high-speed air accident but merely a silly mistake on the ground.

On 15 September he was standing in front of the Meteor making some adjustment when Porter suddenly saw that he was being dragged into the starboard engine intake. Teddy either did not hear the shouts or was unable to act. In an instant, and without thinking of the possible dangers, Porter threw himself across the jet and rugby-tackled Teddy to the ground, keeping a tight grip while the engine was shut down and Teddy was pulled to safety, badly bruised and a bit shaken. In truth, he came close to disaster on several occasions.

The team waited for warmer weather to make further attempts, Teddy calculated that they could reach 626 mph. On one day, 23 September, with the temperature coming closer to their target, the High Speed Flight made a total of twenty-nine runs between 0700 hours and 1500 hours. Teddy made fifteen flights, during one of which his Meteor slewed momentarily out of control when the mass balance snapped free of its housing inside the rudder.

According to the *News Chronicle*, which reported that this incident occurred on 24 September, Teddy lost the mass balance off his aircraft's rudder due to vibration while travelling at over 600 mph. A 28½ lb lump of lead was launched into the fuselage and, as Teddy explained, the whole aircraft was thrown out of trim.

The rudder control went to hell because at that time my feet were shaken out of the pedals by the vibration. The plane suddenly veered off like a wind-blown leaf, and went screaming over Bognor. Everything happened so quickly I don't recall much about it except thinking to myself as I looked at those roof tops and thought, this is a hell of a place to try and land a plane. Let's get the hell out of it.

It was only through brute force that he managed to put the aircraft back onto its true course. Teddy being Teddy, he decided that since he had already completed two runs, he ought to complete his other two before landing. It was later reported that the rudder also sustained slight damage, while a piece of metal came off one of the jet pipes in the starboard engine nacelle.

On 25 September the team pilots made another record attempt but the final average times for this day were: Duke 613 mph, Waterton 610 mph and Donaldson 614 mph.

Later that day, a call was received from Sir James Robb informing Teddy that further record attempts were to be called off: I forbid any more attempts for the record. The engines and the planes have had it. They must be returned to the works for refurbishing before any further use.

Two days later, on 27 September, the press announced that the High Speed Flight had 'closed' and that the five Gloster Meteors had already been flown back to Moreton Valence, Gloucestershire, by Teddy and his team.

The pilots had known from the very beginning that the Meteor was flying at speeds close to the limits of the airframe. It was later revealed that the leading edge of the intakes had also begun to crumble under the pressure.

Those who witnessed the record attempts reported seeing amazing effects, due to the near 100 per cent humidity caused by the high degree of condensation around the wings and fuselage. From the ground the jets appeared to be engulfed in a huge ball of spray. Waterton's aircraft, in particular, was almost completely hidden in its own cloud of vapour on one run.

Neville Duke had some of his runs disqualified for diving into the measured straight in an effort to gain additional speed. So, after all the High Speed Flight's additional endeavours, Teddy's record remained.

Of the team *The Times* wrote:

All the world loves a record breaker and Group Captain Donaldson's gallant failure to surpass himself cannot detract from the awe and terror and profound admiration already commanded by a brilliant exploit. Yet most of us would love him even better if we could come within measurable distance of grasping what he has done.

Teddy actually achieved an accurately measured speed of 623.45 mph (1003.31 Kmph) on one of his runs on 7 September and it was this that was accepted as the first time the 1,000 Kmph barrier had been broken. This achievement was recognised by the FAI, who later presented Teddy with a certificate recording this significant landmark in aviation history. A similar presentation was made by the Royal Aero Club, which reads:

> This is to certify that Group Captain E. M. Donaldson DSO, AFC, flew a Gloster Meteor IV aircraft over a 3 kilometre course on the 7th September 1946 at a timed speed of 1001.9 kilometres per hour. This flight was officially timed and observed in accordance with the regulations of the Fédération Aéronautique Internationale. It is believed that this was the first occasion that a pilot had achieved a timed speed in excess of 1,000 kilometres per hour.

The aviation magazine *Flight* wrote in its review of the year 1946: 'The aeronautical highlight of the year past. It was the setting of the World's Air Speed Record at a fraction over 616 mph by Group Captain E. M. Donaldson in the Gloster Meteor IV, EE549, on September 7th'. In fact, Teddy's record was officially ratified by the FAI as achieving an aggregate speed of 615.78 mph (990.79 Kmph).

Teddy's Star Meteor, EE549, was flown at the Paris Air Show in the autumn of 1946, after which Waterton flew it back from Le Bourget to Croydon, achieving an average speed of 618.4 mph. This did not exceed the existing record by more than the 1 per cent margin required to establish a new record and so Teddy's record remained for a further ten months.

Then on 19 June 1947, it eventually fell to the Americans when Colonel Albert Boyd flew a Lockheed P-80R Shooting Star at an average speed over four passes of 623.74 mph (1,003.60 Kmph) over a course at California's Muroc Dry Lake.

Neville Duke had his own chance to make history when, on 7 September 1953, exactly seven years to the day after Teddy's record-setting flight, he set a new absolute speed record of 727.63 mph (1,170.76 Kmph) in a Hawker Hunter 3, stealing the record away from the Americans.

Some months after Teddy's record was set, the *Daily Express* wrote of his growing fame abroad, especially in America:

> Who is Group Captain Donaldson? Does his name mean anything to you? He is being hailed in America. They call him Mr Mercury. They wish he had been born on that side of the Atlantic.
>
> Donaldson has held the world's air speed record unchallenged for Britain for nine months. When the Americans praise him they praise the qualities of our race, which produces so many fine men and so many fine machines.

Teddy was the guest flier at the Blackpool Air Pageant in the autumn of 1946. Each day, he flew the record-breaking Meteor IV along the Blackpool sea front at over 600 mph in front of a crowd of over 30,000.

It seems ironic that, during the whole of the period that Teddy was in command of the High Speed Flight, he was only a substantive squadron leader, but held the acting rank of group captain. Someone must have spotted this anomaly as he was promoted substantive wing commander on 1 October 1946, whilst thankfully retaining his higher acting rank!

Each year the Royal Aero Club makes a number of awards, including the Britannia Trophy 'for the British aviator or aviators accomplishing the most meritorious performance in aviation during the previous year'. In the years since its creation in 1913, the award had been presented only twenty-three times before. In 1947, the trophy for the previous year was awarded to Teddy Donaldson in recognition of his setting the new world air speed record. The presentation ceremony took place in the Royal Aero Club on 19 March and many of the previous winners were in attendance to see in the new era of aviation.

Also in 1947, Teddy Donaldson and Bill Waterton were both awarded a Bar to their AFCs. Teddy's award was promulgated in the *London Gazette* of Thursday 12 June 1947 under the heading:

The KING has been graciously pleased to approve the following awards:

Bar to Air Force Cross.
Group Captain.
Edward Mortlock Donaldson DSO, AFC, RAF.

The award was well deserved. During the three and a half months prior to setting the new record, Teddy had flown a total of sixty-five hours at speeds around 600 mph, each minute providing additional data to determine the behaviour of the Meteor and its airframe at its limits of durability. With each flight lasting around fifteen minutes, this made a total of some 200 High Speed Flights.

Air Marshal Sir James Robb wrote:

Dear Teddy,
    Many congratulations on the award of a Bar to your AFC I am particularly glad that the Service has recognized in the only way it can the very fine show you put up with the High Speed Flight last autumn. You will be glad to know that Waterton also has been awarded a Bar to his AFC.

Reflecting later on what he had achieved, Teddy remembered that when the two Stars had arrived at Tangmere, he was dismayed to see that they were the long-winged version. It was explained that the short-winged version was measurably slower. Teddy thought: They seem to have forgotten all that business about the reduced safety factor of the long-winged Meteor.

He knew that the break-up safety factor was reduced to 6 G at 600 mph. Even flying at low speeds in the Star he registered over 4 G and minus 9 G. There were too many people relying on the team to succeed for Teddy even to consider pulling out; they would get every second out of the Derwent Vs. As for the stated life of each engine and operational perimeters Teddy said, 'We exceeded both'.

Furthermore, he went on to explain that he partly understood the dangers but that no one yet knew exactly how every component of the jet engines would perform, not even the designers and engineers. Aware of the possibility of the loss of strength of the blades under such forces Teddy took appropriate steps to spot the dangers so they could be weighed up against possible failure.

> What we never appreciated at the time was that at this engine speed and heat the turbine lost its strength and grew with centrifugal force, and when the blades touched the rim they filed themselves. I always sent a man up the pipe when the thing cooled off to measure the gap between the blade and the rim.
>
> What I failed to appreciate was that this was always almost normal because after the blades had 'grown', when the engines cooled off they showed normal clearance.

With the High Speed Flight disbanded, the shorter-winged Meteor IV entered service with the RAF, and the first aircraft were sent to the Central Fighter Establishment at West Raynham. Several met with untimely ends. One of the few men at that time to have escaped when his aircraft failed was former Battle of Britain pilot Group Captain 'Birdy' Bird-Wilson (later Air Vice-Marshal Bird-Wilson CBE DSO DFC and Bar AFC and Bar). His Meteor disintegrated, leaving him tumbling through the air. Fortunately he was able to deploy his parachute and survived the descent.

Vickers-Armstrong was, up until about 23 September, planning to put its experimental 10/44 fighter forward as a contender to set a new record. Flown by Vickers's chief fighter test pilot, former Battle of Britain pilot Jeffrey Quill, the 10/44 was powered by a Rolls-Royce Nene jet engine, a larger version of the Derwent V, with 5,000 lb of thrust. The fuselage was bullet-shaped, with air intakes on either side. The square-tipped wings had a thin section.

Teddy was impressed with the Rolls-Royce Nene. The Americans had used it in their Shooting Star P-80 but only achieved 560 mph. Teddy felt that, in the right airframe, it would easily achieve 700 mph. He acknowledged that the Meteor was not the right airframe for such speeds and so he was not surprised when Colonel Boyd pushed his P-80R to break the record the following June.

There was to have been a second British challenger. De Havilland chief test pilot Geoffrey de Havilland Jr, the son of the aviation pioneer and aircraft designer of the same name, was to use the existing course once the Meteor flights had been completed. Two of the swept wing prototypes had been shown off for the first time at the Society of British Aircraft Constructors (SBAC) air show at Radlett on 12 September 1946, having first flown only four months earlier.

Advanced test flights began at Hatfield, Hertfordshire, in late September, recording a speed of 600 mph on the 25th. Sections of the wing's skin were found to have peeled off during the flight.

Initially the de Havilland research aircraft, the experimental tailless DH 108 Swallow which resembled a flying wing, had anti-spin parachutes attached to the tips of the swept-back wings. Teddy received a telephone call from Geoffrey de Havilland who was looking to use the measured course after the RAF's High Speed Flight and wanted any advice Teddy could give him.

Teddy explained that pressure changes created a nose-down tendency in the aircraft at such high speeds. He recommended trials at very low altitude rather than at 20,000 ft where, he explained, the results would not reflect those experienced at sea level. The pressures too would be ten times greater at sea level. 'I told him that his plane had no fuselage to provide leverage. When he ran into compressibility the aircraft would turn a complete somersault. The plane would break up and he would be knocked unconscious and be found very dead. This is exactly what happened to him.

De Havilland died on 27 September when the second of the three Swallow prototype aircraft, TG306, disintegrated in mid-air over the Thames Estuary while preparing to make an attempt at Teddy's record. He had already unofficially broken the new record. Two years later, on 6 September 1948, test pilot John Derry, flying in a de Havilland DH 108, would become the first Briton to break the sound barrier, albeit in a shallow dive from 40,000 to 30,000 ft.

Exactly four years later, on 6 September 1952, Derry had just broken the sound barrier in a de Havilland DH 110 at the Farnborough Air Show when his aircraft disintegrated and fell into the crowd. Derry and his flight test observer, Anthony Richards, were both killed, as were at least twenty-seven spectators. Many more were injured by the falling debris. It was a poignant reminder of the dangers encountered by the general public as well as test pilots of the early jet age.

Sadly for Teddy, Bill Waterton was also killed in a flying accident, having earlier won the George Medal for gallantry. Before he died, Waterton had been Chief Test Pilot of Gloster Aircraft for seven post-war years, and an aviation correspondent for the *Daily Express*. In 1956, he wrote a highly critical book about the state of the British aircraft industry, aptly entitled *The Quick and the Dead*, in which he said, 'It is a miracle that there are not mass disasters at Farnborough every year.'

CHAPTER TWENTY-EIGHT

From Hero to Zero

Despite the daily risks to life and limb, Teddy was saddened that the High Speed Flight had been wound down. The officers returned to their squadrons or were found new postings, while some of the junior NCOs and other ranks were demobbed, having stayed on in the Service to help complete the job. Although Neville Duke and Bill Waterton were denied the world speed record in 1946, both were later to claim their own honours. Waterton became the Paris – London speed record holder in 1947 and Duke claimed his own world absolute speed record in 1953.

In his inimitable style Teddy threw a party for the whole of the team before saying goodbye to his men and moving on to his next appointment. There was, however, time for a brief holiday in the South of France in late October. Now, not only a national hero but also in the gaze of the world's media, Teddy and Estellee could not travel anywhere without attracting attention. Articles appeared in a number of European newspapers and magazines. While in Cannes the couple were snapped on the beaches by the paparazzi and featured in the Italian press. One national French paper even featured a front-page picture of Teddy with the unequivocal caption '*L'homme le plus vite du monde*'. Unperturbed by the attention, Teddy took time to do some pleasure diving with the aid of an aqualung. This created some speculation that he was looking to achieve a second record.

Back in the UK Teddy reported for duty as Senior Air Staff Officer to Air Vice-Marshal T. C. Traill CB OBE DFC, AOC No. 12 Group, Fighter Command, Nottinghamshire. His role was to turn the twenty-nine regular and auxiliary Meteor squadrons of No. 12 Group into fully operational combat units ready for the trials of post-war Europe.

The conversion programme onto jets was too lengthy. Teddy analysed it carefully and came back to the Air Ministry and explained that No. 12 Group would not be operational quickly enough if it was adhered to. He maintained that jets were as easy to fly as piston-engined aircraft. Eventually his case was accepted and the conversion course was shortened dramatically, allowing No. 12 Group to become fully operational ahead of schedule at a difficult time during the earliest phases of the Cold War.

Although the Meteor had entered service in 1944 as the Allies' only jet fighter, there had been no recorded instances of air-to-air combat between jet aircraft; the first such clashes would not occur until the Korean War, some eight years later.

Tom Traill was concerned that Teddy was still serving as a temporary group captain, while a number of more junior officers had been promoted over his head. He wrote to Air Marshal Sir James Robb on 6 November 1947, praising Teddy's outstanding contribution to No. 12 Group and requested that the issue be addressed.

> I feel there is a tendency among those concerned with selection of officers for promotion to look on Donaldson as a stunt flier and no more; this is very far from the case; he is an extremely determined and active staff officer of sound judgement who insists upon a high standard of behaviour and efficiency in his subordinates.

The reply was not favourable. Traill was informed that the Air Ministry were afraid of promoting people like Teddy out of the Service (ie promoting them ahead of their years, resulting in them reaching their highest potential rank prematurely and therefore resigning their commission early due to frustration caused by lack of further promotion). Teddy would have to wait another eighteen month for promotion to the substantive rank of group captain (1 July 1949).

Meanwhile, the famous staff officer got on with his job, accepting invitations to speak at conferences and conventions whenever he could. He was popular in America and was the guest feature speaker at the National Aeronautic Association's Silver Jubilee Convention held on 2–4 June 1947 at the Blackstone Hotel, Fort Worth, Texas. On 4 June Teddy took centre stage, talking of his experiences during the setting of the world speed record and on the subject of supersonic flight in his keynote speech entitled 'How fast can man expect to fly in the foreseeable future?'

His speech was followed by a salute to the pioneering aviators of the previous twenty-five years, many attending in person.

Teddy had the distinction of becoming only the second member of the RAF to be awarded the honorary title of Command Pilot, United States Air Force. The illuminated vellum citation states that the award, with its accompanying silver wings, was presented 'in recognition of outstanding personal and professional achievements in military aviation.' He was also welcomed as an honoured guest in and around Fort Worth, being made a deputy sheriff of Tarrant County. Everywhere he went he was photographed and greeted like a movie star.

He enjoyed the adulation, which was a far cry from Britain, where it seemed heroes were a forgotten species. The war had been hard on the whole country and most people just wanted to get back to 'normal' and forget about the military. Only the police seemed to have remembered him. Whilst still the fastest man in the world, he was caught speeding through a Sussex village. 'Who do you think you are travelling at that speed – Teddy Donaldson?' The joke backfired on the astonished officer, and Teddy got off with just a warning.

A new posting came in July 1949, when Teddy was put in charge of the Air Training Corps and Combined Cadet Forces, taking over from Air Marshal Sir Alan Lees KCB CBE DSO AFC, who had been in charge of all reserve forces for three years. The cadet forces consisted of no less than 47,000 boys in 800 squadrons, all of whom came under Teddy's command.

At first he was terribly disappointed at being taken away from flying duties. The command was in the middle of a complete reorganization and needed someone at the helm who could build morale and reverse the high percentage of wastage – thousands were not fulfilling their training obligations. Teddy's role was to enforce enrolment examinations and introduce proficiency tests that had to be passed.

Although he may not have agreed at the time, it was nevertheless an inspired appointment. Naturally, Teddy brought the same determination, energy and enthusiasm to this posting that he did to all his appointments, calling in favours from many of his wartime friends and post-war test pilots, who gave talks and made personal appearances to help promote the service. He requested the use of one of the last Spitfires still flying with the RAF and used this to fly around the country visiting units and, of course, performing aerobatics.

His first appointment was a visit to the ATC Squadron at Slough where he set out his stall. His speech was reported in the press:

I am mainly interested in producing the best possible 'types' for the Air Force. If we build up a highly skilled first-class RAF nucleus in combination with the excellent aircraft we can produce, he would be a damn awful fool who tackled us. He would simply be eaten up.

We must concentrate on the quality of our aircrews, but what is even more important is the quality of our ground crews. A quick 'turn-around' of fighting aircraft by a highly efficient ground team means that twice as much fighting can be done by half the number of pilots.

While this was not a front-line posting, Teddy had the vision to see the true value of the cadets as a ripe recruiting ground of air-minded young men who aspired to promote and maintain the high standards of the

Service. The job also had its advantages, in that he had the full admiration of all those under him from the very start, and he had a Spitfire to play with too!

On 8 April 1950 he travelled to Chichester, where he gave one of his signature speeches to the ATC.

> Courage and brains – two qualities which no money can buy – have made Britain the greatest nation on earth.
>
> They have put us on top on aviation and the nation that leads in aviation, leads the world. We have produced the best bombers and the best fighters, and there is no question about the best commercial aeroplanes.
>
> When we old ones fade out of the picture, we have got to have youngsters to come along and take over where we leave off, and if Britain is to exist as a first-class nation they must be of the right spirit. We find those youngsters with the right spirit in the ATC.
>
> There we teach the cadet the job of becoming a better citizen, and that there are more important things in the world than himself. We get him air-minded, interested in aviation, give him flights all over the world, teach him to glide, and other interesting aeronautical subjects.
>
> It is all entirely voluntary and it is the finest thing in the country at the moment. You have got to be jolly good to get into the ATC as it is now.

The *Essex Daily News* of Monday, 29 May featured Teddy's visit to No. 266 ATC at the Shoreham Air Display which was attended by 15,000 people. Weather conditions were poor, which limited many of the flying displays, including the aerobatics of the Gloster Meteor and later the Tiger Moths. The newspaper article noted: 'The Meteor and Chipmunks were excellent in their individual and formation flying, but the afternoon's show was without doubt stolen by Group Captain E. M. Donaldson DSO AFC in his Spitfire. He gave as polished a performance of aerobatics as one could wish to see.'

Apart from a 45-day sojourn to the USA beginning on 14 November 1950, when he to visited Westover Air Force Base, Massachusetts, and Washington 'for the purpose of obtaining data relative to Civil Air Patrol Activities from Headquarters United States Air Force', Teddy devoted his whole time to the cadets. He used his international connections to arrange an educational exchange with American cadets, and presented the exchange programme to the press in his inimitable style.

Early in 1951 the ATC celebrated its tenth anniversary. Naturally Teddy took a leading role. He sat in on a live broadcast on the BBC with ATC cadets from both Land's End and John O' Groats.

As ever, world events moved on and the RAF needed Teddy's expertise elsewhere. On his posting to take command of Royal Air Force Fassberg in Allied-controlled West Germany, the role of Air Staff Officer, Air Training Corps, at Home Command passed to Group Captain W. S. Gardner.

CHAPTER TWENTY-NINE

White Heat of the Cold War

Post-war Europe, including the former aggressor Germany, had been divided between East and West, the two separated by what Winston Churchill had christened the Iron Curtain in his 'Sinews of Peace' speech at Westminster College, Fulton, Missouri, on 5 March 1946. Although Churchill was then Leader of the Opposition, Russian historians still date the beginning of the Cold War from this speech.

Berlin, which lay well inside Communist-controlled East Germany, was itself divided into four zones, each controlled by one of the victorious Allies – Britain, France, Russia and the United States.

For nearly a year, the Soviet Union tried to force the three Western Allies out of Berlin by blockading all road and rail routes to their sectors of the city. The blockade, which lasted from 24 June 1948 to 11 May 1949, became one of the first major crises of the new Cold War, and it had its roots in 1945 and 1946 when the breakdown of the four-power Allied Control Council rendered the reunification of post-war Germany impossible. Teddy had not been involved in the Berlin Airlift, when Allied aircraft flew food and other supplies into the Western Sector's three airfields at Tempelhof, in the American Zone, Gatow in the British, and Tegel in the French. He was, however, to play an important role in its aftermath.

In early 1951 NATO decided to strengthen their forces in the most forward areas of West Germany. The British were asked to take the lead with both their land and air forces.

Air Marshal Sir Robert Forster, formerly Air Officer Commanding Home Command, was appointed as the new Commander-in-Chief, British Air Forces of Occupation. The independent command would later be changed and became integrated within NATO as the 2nd Tactical Air Force.

On Air Marshal Forster's orders, Teddy was summoned to the Air Ministry where he was given command of the front-line air base at

Fassberg which lay only 16 miles from the Russian-controlled East German border. The station operated four squadrons of obsolete Vampire FB Mk 5s, and its task was to provide close support for the 7th Armoured Division should the need arise.

Among Teddy's wing commanders at Fassberg was 'Johnnie' Johnson DSO and two Bars DFC and Bar, the RAF's highest scoring ace of the Second World War and a combat pilot in the Korean War.

Teddy was delighted to have Johnson as his Wing Commander Flying, and remembered him with great affection. 'The world lit up whenever he entered a room, joining a party or playing a game. He was a splendid pilot and I was overjoyed to have him working with me.'

With Teddy leading combat training at tree-top level, the squadrons were soon brought up to full combat readiness. Despite the age of the Vampires, Teddy felt he had the strongest team around him since those days at North Weald when, often outnumbered ten to one, his Hawker Hurricane squadron had taken on the faster aircraft of the *Luftwaffe* and won. If the Russians had challenged the West German frontier they would have faced stiff opposition.

Teddy's involvement in every aspect of station life had an immediate effect. Morale at Fassberg had gone from what had been described as an 'all-time low' to an amazing high. He pushed his squadrons relentlessly in order to achieve the highest standards. He was ordered to ensure that the base was fully operational by May. Furthermore, he was given target hours for individual pilots, each having to double their current monthly flying hours.

Drastic measures were needed if the squadrons were to meet the Air Ministry's objectives. Teddy immediately cancelled all leave and set the pace with flying instruction and combat demonstrations. Within a month every pilot was exceeding Ministry figures and the base was setting the highest standards for the whole of NATO. However, not everything went according to plan. During one NATO exercise all the squadrons' training went to pot and their rocket ground attacks were so poor that the target, a bridge, remained undamaged.

Teddy's squadrons were again put to the test during another NATO training exercise christened Ombrelle which took place between 23 and 25 May 1951.

By the evening of 24 May the Fassberg-based Vampires had already made a series of successful low-level strikes on five targets: Volkel, Eindhoven, Ijmuiden, the airfield at Beauvechain and the dump at Wittlich. The raids were made at low level, pulling up to 3,000–4,000 ft ahead of the target to verify the aiming point and determine the final approach before the strike. Teddy had given orders not to engage the air cover if it approached after the raid, but to get out as quickly as possible and without loss.

The night of the 24th saw the raid on Eindhoven involving twenty-four Vampires led by Johnnie Johnson with Teddy flying as his wingman. Johnson attacked at 1745 hours running in from the north-west, with Wing Commander Cox's squadron coming in from the west. The aircraft were in the air for one and a half hours.

Writing of Exercise Ombrelle, *Flight* magazine said:

> We were set down at a certain well-known BAFO [British Air Force of Occupation] station commanded by an even better known officer in the person of Group Captain E. M. Donaldson. If there is anyone in the Service better suited by experience and temperament to command a fighter/bomber wing his name does not readily occur to us.

Teddy always placed great importance on the wellbeing of every man under his command. In return he demanded squadron discipline both in the air and in camp. In the officers' mess, he enjoyed a pint and usually led the merriment, organizing games and gang shows or holding court as a seasoned raconteur. One of the many methods he used to raise station morale across the ranks was to create a healthy rivalry between Fassberg and the nearby RAF station at Wunsdorf, commanded by Teddy's friend Group Captain Eric Stapleton.

One morning Teddy was heard in a Vampire roaring through the skies over Wunsdorf at low altitude. As he approached the jet's belly opened and he bombed the airbase with thousands of sheets of toilet paper just hours before an expected visit by the Secretary of State for War. Stapleton had to get everyone on base rushing around picking it up in advance of the motorcade.

Wing Commander Tom Ward, Wing Commander Flying at Wunsdorf and a former Second World War fighter pilot, led the reprisals. Teddy was alerted by air traffic control and Fassberg's aircraft were scrambled to meet the 'enemy', who were rebuffed 'without loss'.

Another 'feud' was fostered with the airbase at Celle. The station commander, Group Captain Roger Porteous, was none too pleased at the loss of a decorative cannon 'stolen' during a visit by Teddy and a small number of officers from Fassberg. To Teddy's horror it was found to be in the boot of his car. He telephoned to apologize and said it would be returned. Before he had put the telephone down, however, a raiding party from Celle had recaptured the booty.

Intelligence reports then revealed that it was hidden above the officers' mess at Celle. A party of thirty pilots and officers from the RAF Regiment made their way by bus to within a mile of the perimeter fence. Blacked up, Teddy led the raid, helping to cut the barbed wire as the men made their way through the camp's defences to the mess. A German guard dog picked up their scent and began barking. The dog-handler restrained it, hitting it until it stopped barking. Meanwhile Teddy's men had to deal with an officer who stepped out for fresh air. Half the party watched the doors to the mess to stop anyone getting out, while the remainder successfully stole the cannon. They made their way back to base unscathed.

Once back at Fassberg, the cannon was mounted at the top of a flag-pole, the bottom 10 ft of which was greased to prevent anyone climbing up to rescue the trophy. But Teddy forgot the obvious – the officers from Celle simply felled the flagpole.

Not to be outdone, Teddy arranged a special welcome for the officers from Celle on a ceremonial visit to Fassberg. As the convoy drew up a dozen anti-aircraft guns, facing the mess, opened up in salute. The joke rather backfired as, apart from scaring the officers half to death, the 40 mm Bofors shattered every window in the mess as the guns fired volley after volley of blanks. Apparently there was no way of stopping them until they had emptied their magazines. Coincidentally, Fassberg was visited by the RAF's auditors later the same day, but before anyone had time to rectify the damage which was, according to Teddy, caused by a 'freak storm'! Used to the antics of fighter pilots, nothing more was ever said about the incident by the auditors, although Celle never let Teddy forget the prank.

NATO's build-up in Germany continued and the squadrons were reinforced before being replaced by de Havilland's new single-seat fighter-bomber, the Venom. Fassberg was to be reduced to two squadrons, becoming a fast-track training ground with squadrons being brought up to full operational standard under Teddy and his experi-enced wing leaders before moving on to other bases.

General Eisenhower, the first Supreme Allied Commander Europe (SACEUR), visited RAF Fassberg on 19 September 1951 and was greeted by Teddy and his staff. He gave a brief speech before privately congrat-ulating Teddy on the base's role in maintaining the efficiency and readiness in NATO's front line forces.

In mid-September 1952 Fassberg took part in Exercise Holdfast. Teddy, as station commander, might have been expected to be behind a desk somewhere directing the movement of pins on a map. That, however, was never his style. Instead, he was flying a Vampire on low-level surprise sweeps, flying at 450 mph at less than 50 ft, to test his station's defences.

On 12 March 1953, while still commanding Fassberg, Teddy became involved in the fall-out from a serious border incident, when an Avro Lincoln B2 long-range bomber (RF531) was shot down by the Russians over East Germany at a particularly difficult phase of the Cold War. It belonged to the RAF's Central Gunnery School, and had taken off from

Leconfield in Yorkshire. It was flying a fighter affiliation exercise over West Germany when it accidentally flew into the Russian Hamburg–Berlin corridor and was attacked and shot down by a MiG fighter. Five members of the crew were killed outright and the rear gunner died as a result of injuries caused by a heavy parachute landing. One wounded crewman became a Russian prisoner.

It was an international incident that created increased East-West tension and demanded an investigation. Orders came from the very top, placing Teddy in charge of gathering evidence. The RAF's initial reaction was to ban all aircraft from flying within 10 miles of the border, effectively putting Fassberg out of action. When it came to the attention of Winston Churchill, however, he immediately had the order rescinded.

Teddy was ordered to deliver a report to the Prime Minister personally within twenty-four hours. His first step was to collate copies of all the radio communications, from both the aircraft and Russian sources. He had searches made for any eyewitnesses and interviewed one of the doctors who spoke to the injured rear gunner before he died of the injuries caused by his heavy parachute decent.

There was little wreckage to be found in the Allied Sector, although the navigator's log book was discovered. It had been kept up to date as the mission had progressed and was an important piece of the jigsaw puzzle.

The evidence pointed to the aircraft having flown towards the Russian Zone, but, at the moment it was shot out of the sky it was actually still over British-controlled soil. The next morning Teddy took off in a Vampire, heading for Biggin Hill. He arrived thirty minutes ahead of schedule. The station commander, Wing Commander 'Splinters' Smallwood, was not aware of his arrival or his mission, and when Teddy requested a car to take him to the Air Ministry, the Wing Commander informed him that 'group captains were expected to make their own arrangements'. At that very moment a Rolls-Royce pulled up – it was his lift!

As soon as he arrived in London, Teddy was whisked to a high-powered conference at the Air Ministry. Those waiting for him were the Chief of the Air Staff, Air Chief Marshal Sir William Dickson, the Secretary of State for Air, Lord De L'Isle VC (the son-in-law of Lord Gort VC) and the AOC-in-C, Flying Training Command, Air Marshal Sir Lawrence Pendred.

With his presentation complete and a draft statement prepared, the meeting adjourned to reconvene at No. 10 Downing Street where they were to report to the Prime Minister, Winston Churchill, in person.

Teddy stood amongst the portraits of the great and the good, a lowly group captain, laden with charts and an array of documents, eagerly awaiting the nod to enter the Prime Minister's private rooms. Then, from further along the corridor, came a shuffling which stopped in front of him.

'And who might you be?'

'Group Captain Donaldson, sir.'

'Ah, good morning to you.' It was the Prime Minister himself.

Churchill gestured for the little gathering to proceed. All filed into the Cabinet Room behind him. He drew up his chair, the others lining up opposite before taking their seat by rank.

Teddy watched in awe as Churchill took in the presentation, correcting here, suggesting an amendment there, all the time puffing on a big fat cigar which he had selected and lit with all due ceremony. 'Pray, hand it over to me. It is not making any sense as you read it. I doubt if it will when I read it myself, but we can alter it,' he said with an air of impatience.

He took hold of the document and began to read back over the statement as it had been edited. They all sat in absolute silence like schoolboys before the headmaster as Churchill made his adjustments. Finally he had finished and announced: 'That will do.'

Teddy was signalled to scoop up his paperwork and make for the door. As he did so, Churchill said: 'Now, pray tell me what actually happened.'

The Chief of Air Staff took the lead, explaining that the bomber could not possibly have fired on the Russians as it had no breech-blocks, a statement that caused Churchill's jaw to drop with astonishment. 'What do you mean? Here we have a bomber famous for its defensive armament, two menacing fingers of destruction pointing to the heavens, and you tell me it was incapable of firing because of an order that there were to be no breech blocks. Pray, by whose order?'

Churchill wanted to know next how Teddy could be so sure that the attack took place over the British Zone. 'Donaldson picked up some 37 mm cannon shells, sir,' was the quick response.

'But everyone knows that if they fell from an aircraft they would travel a long way. Well, it was shells you picked up, Donaldson, wasn't it?' Churchill quizzed.

Teddy replied that it was the links rather than the cases themselves which, he explained; 'fall directly beneath an aircraft'.

Seeing that Teddy was a man with his finger on the pulse, Churchill turned to him, staring over his glasses directly at him. 'Perhaps you had better let the group captain answer the questions; he seems to be better informed than you.'

He gestured and Teddy, quickly came around the table to Churchill's side, where he spread the Russian messages and the navigator's log book out ready to demonstrate the facts more graphically.

The incident revolved around two bombers flying on a fighter affiliation exercise. They were blown off course by a westerly wind 70 mph stronger than predicted. The first, flying at 18,000 ft, was escorted out of Russian airspace by two MiG fighters. The jets flew wing-tip to wing-tip with the British crew and both sides exchanged a nervous wave and smile as they parted.

Unknown to the MiG pilots, a second bomber was flying below, just about accidentally to violate Russian airspace. Having resumed their patrol, they spotted the second Lincoln and mistook it for the bomber they had just warned off. They radioed to their controller believing the Lincoln pilot had deliberately changed his course into Russian airspace. A message was sent to Moscow and the MiGs' controllers awaited orders. To compound the situation, the bomber crew, apparently still unaware of their true location, mistook the MiGs for Canadian Sabre jets and the rear gunner aimed his camera gun to take a few shots. Quite naturally the MiG pilots took this as a further act of aggression.

What Teddy could not explain was how, with 1,500 hours' flying time, and with an equally experienced navigator, the pilot managed to be so far off course, despite the westerly wind. The evidence suggested that the Lincoln crew continued to fly deeper into the Russian Zone, believing they were headed for Hamburg. It was at this point that they were engaged by one of the MiG fighters and shot down at close range.

The crew members were unable to defend themselves or fire first as the Russians had maintained, because the belt-feed mechanism had been removed from the two Hispano 20 mm guns of the upper turret, while the rear gunner was not provided with ammunition.

The Prime Minister made a statement in the House of Commons:

A study of the information available indicates that the aircraft might, through a navigational error, have accidentally crossed into the Eastern Zone of Germany at some point.

But the evidence of ground observations and the spent cannon shell links from the Russian fighter picked up in our Western Zone proved that the Russian repeatedly fired on the Lincoln and mercilessly destroyed it when it was actually west of and within the Allied Zonal frontier.

Thus it was actually over our Zone when first and mortally fired on and the lives of seven British airmen were callously taken for a navigational mistake in process of correction which could have been dealt with by the usual method of protest and inquiry.

There followed a number of questions, which were later reported in the press.

Mr A. Henderson said the fact that the Lincoln could not have fired at all, because its guns were either out of action or there was no ammunition, was vital to the British case.

He asked why this evidence was not included in either of the notes handed to the Russian authorities by the High Commission last week, more especially in view of the delay which had taken place in allowing our representatives to inspect the wreckage.

Mr Churchill replied that the full facts were not known to us at the time our first reply had to be made. They had since been ascertained and proved.

When Mr Henderson asked the Prime Minister to indicate what steps were being taken to minimize the possibility of long-range aircraft from drifting, possibly owing to navigational error, near or over the East German border, Mr Churchill said: 'Yes, all precautions will be observed.'

Mr Odey asked the Government to press for adequate compensation from the Soviet Government for the widows and dependants of the murdered airmen. He asked that if compensation was not forthcoming, would our Government accept full responsibility?

Mr Odey pressed the subject further, demanding that the Government should also protest at the suffering caused by the Soviet Government refusing to allow access to the victims for forty-eight hours. In response Mr Churchill said he had 'Deep sympathy with the points raised. It would be more convenient if questions could be put on the Order Paper and careful answers could be given. Their deep sympathy went out to the families of those who had been destroyed.'

Replying to Mr Bellenger, he said: 'The bodies of the airmen who fell in the Russian Zone had been returned to the charge of our forces'.

Air Commodore Harvey asked if the Prime Minister could deny or confirm a report that at least one member of the crew was fired at by a Russian fighter after he had parachuted from his aircraft.

Mr Churchill said he: 'had no proof about that but the plane was repeatedly and mercilessly fired on until it was destroyed. He was sorry to say that that was undoubtedly true'.

Press reports stressed the fact that the Lincoln was unarmed and that: 'the Russian assertion that the Lincoln opened fire on them is utterly untrue'.

It was maintained that the flight was part of one of the normal exercises carried out by Flying Training Command over the previous eighteen months. The Lincoln's true course should have run parallel to the border and a full 40 miles within the Allied Zone. The pilot and navigator were both experienced men.

It was conceded that the Lincoln 'might' have accidentally strayed into the Soviet Zone, but that eyewitnesses from the ground and the fall of spent cannon links indicated that the first and last shots were fired over the Allied side of the border.

The fact that the wreckage of the bomber fell 'just' within the Soviet Zone was explained by the fact that it fell from such a great height and continued in its forward motion, presumably carried further by the westerly wind.

The Allies would continue to fly in the Allied Zone, taking all necessary precautions. Any Soviet aircraft that strayed into Allied airspace would continue to be warned off in the normal way 'used by nations at peace, to avoid loss of life'.

Teddy was later to write:

> In a crude propaganda effort, the Russians staged a show-piece of the wreckage and engines to 'prove' the plane was well within their Zone.
>
> They actually took one engine from the spot where the aircraft crashed and carried it by truck 100 miles into the Zone.
>
> It was laughable. This engine was supposed to have fallen from an aircraft at 18,000 ft, as it was diving to the ground, and it simply lay on top of the soil. There was not even a dent beneath it, other than one indicating it had been dropped from the back of the truck. In the wreck itself the Russians had taken breech blocks, probably from Spitfires they had had in the war and hammered them into the Lincoln's guns with a sledge hammer; and at the same time had scattered spent ammunition shells in the fuselage.

On 23 March, Air Chief Marshal Sir Robert Foster KCB CBE DFC, Commander-in-Chief of the BAFO and 2nd Tactical Air Force, wrote to Teddy at Fassberg congratulating him on his presentation saying: 'From the attached you will see that you have collected considerable kudos from your visit to London over the Lincoln investigation.'

By the early summer of 1953, Teddy was nearing the end of his highly successful time in command of RAF Fassberg. Before his next appointment, he was sent on a course at the Joint Services Staff College at Chesham. While there his award of the CBE was promulgated in the *London Gazette* of 1 June 1953. Many of his RAF friends wrote congratulating him on his award. The consensus was clearly that they felt the award was for Teddy rather than the Station, reflecting the way he had turned both Fassberg and the jet fighter training programme around.

The investiture was held at Buckingham Palace. Teddy was accompanied by his mother and his eight-year-old son, David, his wife having, as the press put it 'left for the United States for a short holiday'.

At the time of his investiture, he was still a student at the Joint Services Staff College. The commandant, Rear Admiral Kaye Edden, later wrote congratulating him on his part on the course. He praised him for his 'splendid leadership which will long be known and remembered as "Teddy Donaldson's Course". They and we owe you a lot. In your next most important job I hope you may find useful some of the things you acquired here.'

At about the same time as Teddy's CBE investiture, the Donaldson family attended the unveiling ceremony of the Runnymede Memorial. The Selsey press covered the solemn event.

Teddy and his brother, Group Captain Arthur Hay Donaldson DSO DFC and Bar AFC then Commanding Officer, RAF Station, Waterbeach, Cambridge, together with Master Anthony Donaldson, son of their third brother, the late Squadron Leader John William Donaldson DSO AFC, who went down with HMS *Glorious* in 1940, accompanied their mother for the unveiling of the RAF Memorial Chapel by The Queen.

Teddy had lost a number of pilots over the Channel during the early phases of the Battle of Britain and it was in their memory as well as Jack's that he attended the dedication ceremony.

Following his completion of 'Teddy Donaldson's Course', Teddy received a new posting. On 16 April 1954 he was given acting air commodore rank with his appointment as Director of Operational Training at the Air Ministry. He was to hold this office for the next two years.

Ever wary of change, Teddy initially gauged the posting to be a backward step despite his acting promotion. He had always dreaded a job at the Air Ministry, although Teddy quickly found a great ally in his new boss, the Assistant Chief of Air Staff (Training), Air Vice-Marshal The Earl of Bandon. However, in his new role, Teddy soon discovered that the RAF was in the process of rebuilding, ready to face the threats of a new age, those of long-range weapons and nuclear bombers.

Teddy knew all too well the practical problems of combat flying and his experience was to be passed on to a new generation of the air force. He was to produce operational training programmes for the new planes that were coming into service. These included the swept-wing fighters and the V-bombers.

One of Teddy's first achievements was the introduction of Instrument Rating Certificates, something that had been suggested many years earlier but hadn't found particular favour in the Air Ministry. Bandon ordered Teddy to arrange for a meeting of senior officers from all Commands at which Teddy was to put the proposal for the certificates.

Teddy's presentation over, the idea was adopted as none of the senior officers could come up with a convincing argument against. Bandon wanted quick and decisive action, and this was typical of his time at the Air Ministry.

Teddy was also to be responsible for the purchase of aircraft simulators. These not only allowed pilots and aircrew to fly missions without leaving the ground but also allowed them to 'fly' with nuclear payloads and make 'bombing runs' without risk to the crews or civilians.

Teddy later recalled his struggle to get dual-control Javelin simulators. Having made his request and explained the reasons for the need to buy the simulator, Teddy was given the response:

> Air Commodore, you disappoint me. Every time I've heard this case presented before, it has ended up with the statement that if I didn't grant your request, I'd be responsible for the death of your friends.

Teddy replied:

> 'By God. You've obviously been wrongly informed. I haven't got any friends left, because you've bloody well killed them all with your meanness and stupidity.' Teddy had promised himself he would remain diplomatic, but now was not the time, and so he continued in the same vein. 'Don't you realise that when a plane crashes, it doesn't necessarily mean that the pilot is killed. It just wrecks the plane, which has cost a lot of money, and your badly trained pilot is left to get into yet another plane and crash that too. Can't you see that's why we need this trainer? We need it to teach him properly and safely.'
>
> The representative from the Treasury was taken aback by Teddy's forthright speaking but could see his logic: 'Air Commodore, you have stated a case, for the first time, that makes sense. You shall have your machines'.

The RAF as a whole needed to train both to deliver 'the bomb' and to defend against lone enemy bombers flying deep into NATO territory to deliver a nuclear device. All this had to be considered against the need to maintain a conventional air force ready to deal with jet fighters and yet capable of ground support.

Once again Teddy found himself at the forefront of training a new generation on how to survive the ultimate in air combat. He had travelled a long way from the days of 250 mph biplanes and the Brooke-Popham Air Gunnery Trophy, and yet, at forty-two, he was still at the top of his game and leading rather than following. On 1 July 1955, after over a year in his acting rank, his name eventually appeared in the half-yearly promotion list of substantive air commodores.

In this new age Teddy took solace from the fact that he was dealing with the operational end of aircrew training, and that these pilots were now flying the latest generation of jet aircraft like the Gloster Javelin, Hawker Hunter and the V-bombers – the Valiant, Victor and Vulcan. Donaldson was never really cut out to be a 'Whitehall warrior', but at least he knew that he was playing a key role in the planning of Britain's future air defence.

CHAPTER THIRTY

Crises on All Fronts

Teddy's last year at the Air Ministry, 1956, was to be dramatic and life-changing – domestically, professionally and internationally.

Returning after work one spring day to his flat in Battersea, he found a note from his American wife, Estellee. She had left for the USA with their son David, now 11 and attending Eastbourne College. He would never see them again. His world seemed to have collapsed around him; he was devastated. However, he was also a fighter and sought to fill this gaping hole in his life just as soon as he could. It was difficult. His job was making additional demands on him as the situation in the Middle East seemed to be deteriorating with Colonel Gamal Abdel Nasser, the Egyptian President, making overtures about control of the Suez Canal. Teddy suddenly had extra operational training to organize as well as numerous additional emergency planning meetings to attend, many of which lasted way into the night.

The Suez Canal was of vital importance to Britain, being the ocean trade link with India, the Far East, Australia and New Zealand. The area as a whole was also strategically critical to North Africa and the Middle East. For these reasons it was considered important to keep the canal out of Egyptian control.

In 1952, officers in the Egyptian army had overthrown the monarchy of King Farouk, who had been a close ally of the British. The new government had abandoned policies friendly to the European powers, while at the same time asserting an independent and Arab nationalist identity. In 1955, President Nasser was importing arms from the Soviet bloc to build his arsenal for confrontation with Israel.

At the height of both these crises, Teddy chanced to bump into his old friend Eric Stapleton at the RAF Club in Piccadilly. The two wartime fighter pilots and former front-line station commanders in Germany, both now air commodores, talked of times past and caught up on family news. Still reeling from his loss, Teddy asked Eric what had happened to his first wife, a Norwegian called Anne Sofie, whom Teddy remembered first meeting eighteen years previously, long before Eric divorced her in 1950. Stapleton told him that she was living in North London and that, because he was still paying her maintenance, she had evidently not remarried. The two friends parted, Teddy with a telephone number in his pocket.

After the briefest of courtships, and after applying for a 'quickie' divorce from Estellee in absentia, Teddy swept Anne Sofie off her feet, promising her the world as he was confident that he still had a glittering career ahead of him. Moreover, his passion for speed, whether in the air or on the ground, quickly became apparent to the new lady his life. He had always had the fastest sports cars he could afford; in 1956, he had a gleaming white Austin Healey 100/4. However, there was a problem. Anne Sofie had an 11-year old son, Julian, and getting the three of them into his two-seater for weekend trips to the motor racing circuits at Goodwood, Brands Hatch and Silverstone was a bit of a squeeze.

Nevertheless, Teddy was thrilled to have a 'ready-made' family to replace the one he had lost so suddenly, and Julian was just the same age as his own David. Never one to compromise, Teddy simply exchanged his four-cylinder '100' for Austin Healey's brand new model, the bigger and more powerful 100/6, which had a couple of child seats in the back.

By early July, the Suez Crisis was intensifying and all leave was cancelled. One small highlight in an otherwise hectic period was the release of the film *Reach for the Sky* – the story of Douglas Bader. As Bader did not want to see the film, Teddy, a cousin of his wife Thelma, was asked to be the guest of honour at the London premier. Resplendent in his air commodore's uniform and with a chestfull of medals, he was heralded into the cinema foyer with a fanfare and honour guard, and welcomed by all the civic dignitaries that the capital could muster. It was a big night in the West End. Teddy was joined by nearly thirty other wartime colleagues and Battle of Britain veterans, including Group Captains Hugh Dundas, 'Johnnie' Johnson and Frank Carey, and Wing Commanders Bob Stanford Tuck and Billy Drake.

On 26 July 1956, President Nasser announced the nationalization of the Suez Canal Company in which British banks and business held a 44 per cent stake; French institutions were the other stakeholders.

The Prime Minister, Sir Anthony Eden, tried to persuade the British public of the need for war and he compared Nasser's nationalization of the canal with the nationalism of Benito Mussolini and Adolf Hitler twenty years earlier. He claimed that a display of force was needed to prevent him becoming another expansionist military threat. Eden had also been annoyed by Nasser's apparent role in the dismissal of British military leader Glubb Pasha in Jordan prior to the canal company nation-alization. The French in turn were hostile because of Nasser's support for insurgents in Algeria.

Between July and October 1956, unsuccessful initiatives, encouraged by the United States, were made to reduce the tensions that would ulti-mately lead to war. International conferences were organized to discuss canal operations, but no agreement was secured.

In Whitehall, there was hardly time to catch one's breath with the speed of developments. The Air Ministry was buzzing with activity and Teddy was in the thick of it. Then, just when he didn't want any more upsets, tragedy struck. His one constant companion had been a Siamese cat called Annalou which travelled with him everywhere – even to the office. One evening, Annalou jumped out of Teddy's car outside his block of flats and ran straight under a passing car. Teddy quickly put the writhing half-dead cat out of its misery, but then his thoughts swiftly turned to getting a replacement.

In the Harrods pet department during his lunch break the next day, Teddy picked out what he thought was a particularly fine Siamese kitten from the 5 guinea basket. It was a fully 'intact' male specimen. Teddy asked the sales attendant to put it on his account. Not wanting any prob-lems with his new companion, Teddy soon arranged for the cat to be neutered. About month later, Teddy received his Harrods statement, and was shocked to see that he had been charged 25 guineas. On enquiring why, and complaining that he was 'not trying to buy Harrods – just a cat', the pet department salesman said that the Siamese Teddy had chosen was unfortunately in the wrong basket, and that it had a 'royal' pedigree and a name as long as your arm. The salesman went on to say that Harrods would gladly exchange it for one at the right price. Teddy nearly choked when he realized what he'd done to the cat world. He decided to keep quiet and keep the cat, naming it Mr Smith in defi-ance of its true identity. The kitten was about to embark on a life no other feline animal could ever have imagined – a life at full throttle, in fast cars and jet planes!

On 29 October, Israel invaded the Egyptian-controlled Gaza Strip and Sinai Peninsula, and started to make rapid progress towards the Canal Zone. Britain and France offered to reoccupy the area and separate the warring armies. Nasser refused the offer, which gave the European powers a pretext for a joint invasion to regain control of the canal and topple the Nasser regime. To support the invasion, large air forces had been dispatched to Cyprus and Malta, and several aircraft carriers were also deployed. The two airbases on Cyprus were so congested that a third field, which was in dubious condition, had to be brought into use for French aircraft. The UK deployed the aircraft carriers *Eagle*, *Albion* and *Bulwark*, and France had the *Arromanches* and *Lafayette* on station.

The United Kingdom and France initiated Operation Musketeer on 31 October with a bombing campaign. Nasser responded by sinking all forty ships in the canal, closing it to further shipping until early 1957.

After failing to stop Egyptian and Israeli fighting around the canal,

RAF Canberra and Valiant bombers flying from Malta and Cyprus, in conjunction with French Air Force aircraft, attacked twelve airfields in the Canal Zone. These attacks continued until 4 November, by which time the Egyptian Air Force had been decimated. Key installations were captured by Anglo-French airborne troops on 5 November prior to a major seaborne offensive. The operations continued until the 7th, when a cease-fire was arranged. So deep was the crisis, that the United States Air Force was brought to a high state of readiness in case of Russian intervention.

In the middle of all this, Teddy received a posting notice. He later recalled that one evening in November he was sitting in his flat, watching television, when he received a telephone call from Air Vice-Marshal Maurice Heath, whom Teddy knew well. Heath said:

Teddy, you are off to Aden, to be Chief of Staff to the Commander, British Forces, Arabian Peninsula.
Stop joking; what do you really want? replied Teddy.

Teddy was soon to understand it was no laughing matter as Heath responded:

You must be away by Friday morning. There's been some serious trouble in the Command structure, and you are needed out there urgently.

Teddy later recalled that the post was something of a 'hot seat', with four holders being dismissed in rapid succession.

So, on 11 December 1956, Air Commodore Donaldson took over as Deputy Commander, HQ British Forces Arabian Peninsula, which had been formerly known as Headquarters, British Forces Aden. He was going 'out of the frying pan and into the fire'. He had hardly had time to get engaged, let alone get married again, so he promised Anne Sofie that once he had taken over his new job and got his residence sorted out, he would come back to London, marry her, and return to Aden with her. He kept his promise, but it was to take longer than expected.

CHAPTER THIRTY-ONE

Aden and
Arab Nationalism

Aden lies on the sea route between Europe and India. Its location made it a suitable launching point for pirate attacks on traders with the British East India Company. In early 1839, Royal Marines landed on its shores, establishing an outpost there. Thus the port city of Aden itself, and the Aden and Hadhramaut hinterland, became part the British Indian Empire. On 1 April 1937 Aden became a Crown Colony and the hinterland a Protectorate before emerging as the Federation of South Arabia on 18 January 1963.

In the early 1950s, the whole of the Arabian Peninsular was fraught with disagreements, usually over land and associated oil rights. One such dispute occurred when the Imam of Oman rebelled against the Sultan of Muscat. In 1955, after initial setbacks, the Sultan called for military assistance from the UK. It was not until British Special Forces were deployed that the rebels were dislodged from their territory in the Jebel Akhbar Mountains.

Teddy's new posting at the end of 1956, coming as it did in the wake of the Suez Crisis, coincided with a time of heightened tension between Aden and the Mutawakelite Kingdom of Yemen. The Imam of Yemen was spurred by Nasser's anti-British rhetoric in Egypt, encouraging his tribesmen to mount raids along the border, stirring up trouble and riots in neighbouring villages with the aid of *agents provocateurs*. At times it seemed as though stone-throwing mobs were everywhere.

Aden was an active service zone, and Teddy revelled in being back in an operational theatre. Furthermore, in addition to his primary appointment as deputy to the Commander British Forces, Air Vice-Marshal Laurence Sinclair GC CB CBE DSO and Bar, he was also the *de facto* air commander with all the units, squadrons and detached flights at RAF Khomaksar under his direct command, Venoms and Meteors included.

Sinclair's policy was not to flaunt the British presence unless the situation demanded a show of force. However, troops at Dhaler needed supplies bringing up once a month as the local airstrip was too small to get any of the available transport aircraft down safely. It was therefore necessary to force a convoy through from Aden. It was Teddy's job to ensure air cover, something that he could have done from a desk. But this was not Teddy's style and he was to be found in the back of a truck, escorted by an armoured car and the men of the Cameron Highlanders. Teddy recalled that it was quite a hairy experience as the vehicles were shot at a number of times from unseen snipers making the most of the rough terrain.

'The enemy,' Teddy recalled, 'had a nasty habit of firing at our tents. I found it quite unnerving, but the troops seemed quite used to it.' With the troops resupplied the convoy made the equally dangerous return journey, supported by Teddy's Venoms. Having spent nearly 48 hours in the sights of the enemy, Teddy decided that he preferred aerial warfare to that of the foot-soldier.

In January 1957 Teddy, on the first of many outings from Aden to Africa, led an RAF Mission to Rhodesia. Here he met with the heads of the Royal Rhodesian Air Force and the Federal Prime Minister, discussing their future contribution to the defence of the Commonwealth. He later said:

> In a country with as small a population as Rhodesia's the contribution towards Commonwealth defence must be based on quality rather than quantity and the Federation's main contribution must accordingly come in the air.
>
> The RAF mission had come here to discuss certain questions with the Royal Rhodesian Air Force on an equal footing, and I have formed only the finest impressions of the RRAF.

Secretly, Teddy had come away with the promise from Sir Roy Welensky of support from the RRAF's Vampires. This was to be no idle promise and Teddy was to take up the offer twice during the Aden campaign.

The 4,000 troops of the Aden Protectorate Levies and Government Guards had to face the Soviet-sponsored Yemeni Army, which was fully equipped with heavy field artillery, large-calibre mortars and rocket-firing Ilyushin attack aircraft. The Yemenis were further assisted by Egyptian 'instructors' who worked both sides of the divide handing out posters of Nasser and whipping the mobs almost into a frenzy. The posters were often paraded by the mobs in a show of Arab nationalism, adding impetus to the need for a quick response.

The Colonial Office and War Office decided, on the basis of their intelligence information, that 800 extra British troops and additional field equipment were required to deter further Yemeni raids. The force was largely drawn from the King's Shropshire Light Infantry (KSLI), the

13th/18th Hussars, the Life Guards, the Buffs (East Kent Regiment) and paratroopers. These troops were supported by RAF Avro Shackeltons, Vickers Valettas and de Havilland Venoms, while Teddy orchestrated the air campaign from his personal Meteor, which he used for reconnaissance sorties – his idea of commanding, as ever, meant leading from the front.

By 27 April 1957, the Yemeni tribesmen had become bolder and their hit and run raids entered a second phase. Around 300 tribesmen, armed with rifles and Bren guns, crossed the border and laid siege to the mud-brick fort of As Sarir, trapping thirty-five locally recruited Government Guards and the British political adviser to the Emir of Dhala, Mr Fitzroy Somerset. A distant cousin of the Duke of Beaufort, Somerset was able to give a radio commentary on the unfolding events, allowing the RAF to mount air strikes to keep the enemy at bay, and making free drops of ammunition and other vital supplies over the beleaguered fort.

The rebels surrounding the fort were led by a Yemeni tribesman who claimed to be the rightful Emir of Dhala, which lay 70 miles north-east of Aden. He sought to take control of the region and make it part of Yemen. He had been in exile for five years, only becoming a potential threat due to his Soviet backing, which put guns into the hands of his followers.

A few days into the crisis, on 29 April, the press reported that two companies of the KSLI had made their way through the Kariba Pass to link up with a relief force including men of the Buffs and the Aden Protectorate Levies at Dhala. During their advance the Shropshire's column came under fire from the hills south of a village named Thumier. One man was slightly wounded and evacuated by helicopter to an RAF hospital in Aden.

An official communiqué said that two Shackelton aircraft carried out bombing missions using 20-pounders against the rebels in the area south of Jimjam during which they successfully drove off the enemy.

Beyond Thumier, Venom jets maintained continual patrols overhead. Rockets and 20 lb anti-personnel bombs were used to keep the rebels clear of high ground south-west of the blockaded fort, allowing the relief column the freedom to advance.

While Somerset could call for air support during daylight hours, it was more difficult to spot the encroaching Yemeni patrols under the cover of darkness in time to summon help, which was fifteen minutes away. The defenders kept the rebels at bay with constant firing. There had been little sleep for any of them throughout the whole period of the siege, with the Yemeni tribesmen constantly testing both their defences and their resolve.

Somerset was off the air for some time when he ran out of petrol for his generator. But after an air-drop he was soon back, keeping up his commentary on the unfolding siege. Meanwhile Colonel Lister, Commander of the Aden Protectorate Levies, was helicoptered into the battle-zone, under heavy small-arms fire, taking over the direction of the operation to mop up the rebels.

As Somerset prepared to spend a second night of siege under the tropical half-moon, about 800 troops, including two companies of the Buffs with the armoured cars of the 13th/18th Hussars and the Life Guards, were moving up, ready for the planned dawn attack on 30 April.

Teddy overflew the fort at about 50 ft in his Meteor on one of his many reconnaissance missions. He was able to get in radio contact with Somerset, who asked him; 'What's all the excitement about? We're doing all right. We could stay here two years if necessary.'

Teddy, aware that there was a prize of £1,000 on Somerset's head, later explained that the rebels were within a few hundred yards of the walls when he made his passes. He reported: 'a lot of shooting was going on. Somerset is very brave.'

The army's role was not just policing. On 30 April the British went on the offensive, the action being reported in the press.

> I watched closely through glasses as the angry flames of heavy machine-guns and anti-aircraft fire spat out at our armoured cars and patrolling aircraft from the Qataba Barracks. The barracks were attacked and a huge ammunition and fuel dump continued to burn and explode for an hour afterwards.
>
> This was the blunt and unmistakable reply to persistent Yemeni attempts at infiltrating the Western Protectorate.
>
> British troops are doing their best to sort out a complicated and dangerous situation without turning a 'Kipling war' into a full-scale campaign.
>
> Aden, and we have got to face up to the fact, has been overtaken by Arab nationalism. It would require a full brigade of troops permanently manning the frontier to hold trouble at bay for long if we are to hold on to the Protectorates as a useful 'buffer' between the Yemen and the Colony.

As a public relations exercise Teddy had flown a member of the press over the fort at As Sarir during the siege, allowing him a first-hand view of the unfolding situation. He reported:

> I had the good fortune to have a front-row seat at yesterday's operations. I was flown to the Yemen frontier by Air Commodore 'Teddy' Donaldson who commands the Air Force here.
>
> We went in a Meteor, which would be thought obsolete in any

important war but which, in this theatre of the Cold War, is admirably adapted to its reconnaissance and command role.

To have visited the Dhala area by road would have taken 15 hours; we were there in 15 minutes. We were too late, despite our speed (500 mph) to see the main air strike by Venoms with anti-personnel bombs against Yemeni forces, who had penetrated six miles into the Protectorate and who were arresting the relief column of native levies coming to the aid of the besieged fort.

Though Donaldson and I were a little too late to see the major bomb (20 lb anti-personnel) strike by the Venoms, we arrived in time to see the Valettas making their drops of food and ammunition to the garrison of native Government troops cooped up inside the small stone fort.

It was a rare pleasurable excitement to fly alongside the Valettas as they dropped their necessary stores and to see the fire which the Valettas and Donaldson attracted, well responded to by the two Venoms which accompanied the Valettas.

I have never in all my varied experience of war, seen uglier or more savage country over which Her Majesty's troops have been called upon to operate.

I have never seen a better morale among all concerned or a better spirit among the High Command.

Teddy flew his passenger between the peaks of the Shangri-la hide-out of Sheikh Mohammed Idruss on a fertile plateau reached only by a steep mule track. Mohammed Idruss was the son of one of the biggest ruling families in the Protectorate. He had tried to use British power and armed forces to settle private family and tribal disputes. This having failed, he wavered and looked to the Yemenis for support in his land claim, travelling by camel to Qataba.

He was thought to be amassing more than 1,000 fighting men around his capital of Qala ready to take on the British and the Protectorate's army. Teddy's passenger wrote:

As we flew within a few feet of the heavily fortified 'Holy City', I could see machine-gun posts on the roofs and rifle-carrying guards who loosed off at us as we roared over their heads and down into the gorge beyond.

It is believed that if the Yemenis think it worth their while to pay the price in silver and rifles, an uprising in this area can be expected soon.

Despite the relief of the besieged fort, the situation was not contained. On 3 May Sir William Luce, the Governor of Aden, declared a state of emergency throughout the colony, following two terrorist bomb attacks on restaurants, resulting in twelve people being injured. The first, on 1 May, involved three British servicemen and four European civilians who were wounded by a bomb which was thrown into the Victory Bar.

As a part of the emergency measures the Governor issued an announcement in Arabic giving additional police powers to prevent acts of violence and threats to private property. The people were urged to 'join in waging war against the terrorists.'

Meanwhile, in New York, the Yemen's representative told the United Nations they would welcome the appointment of a neutral commission to investigate 'recent British attacks on Yemen soil', referring to the reprisal attack on the Qataba Barracks. The Yemeni delegate, Mr Kamil Abdul Rahim, said in a letter to the UN Secretary-General, Mr Dag Hammarskjöld, that Britain had occupied the neighbouring Sultanate of Lahej. He alleged that more than 4,000 British troops, with artillery and tanks, had concentrated on the provisional frontier between Lahej and Yemen, and he said that the occupation of Lahej was 'by far the most disquieting act of aggression by the British'.

During the campaign, Teddy ordered an attack by his fighter pilots on gun positions in Hariba. The guns had been brought to bear on our own troops and he considered that they needed to be destroyed in a show of force. Sadly, one of the fighters was shot down and the pilot killed. The Yemeni put his body on a slab of stone in a local market square. Teddy asked to be allowed to go into the village in force and retrieve the casualty and ensure that his pilot was given a decent burial. He was, however, denied permission. Undeterred, Teddy made it be known that he would personally lead an assault on the town if his pilot was not duly returned. The bluff worked and a camel train arrived pulling a wagon carrying the body of the dead pilot minutes before Teddy's deadline expired.

On 5 May the press carried the news of a further escalation of the ground war, with the Yemenis opening up a barrage on a second British frontier fort using Russian 78 mm artillery.

The Russians had supplied a number of these mortars which the Yemeni army had massed along the frontier following the Buffs' Battle of Jebel Jinaf in late April. This and the growing Yemeni concentrations in the Qataba region threatened to fuel the conflict.

The Yemenis had something in the order of one hundred 20 mm field guns situated 8 miles from the British HQ and the vital Dhala airstrip. These could be brought to bear at a moment's notice.

Despite suffering nearly fifty casualties it was feared that the Imam, who considered the whole Protectorate as part of Yemen and illegally occupied by the British, would continue his campaign to whip up support for his cause. Any signs of anti-British demonstrations might result in the guerilla army recrossing the border.

With the siege of the As Sarir fort lifted, Fitzroy Somerset spent two days in Dhala consulting with military headquarters staff. He reported to Emir Abdullah Bin Saif of Dhala, who responded to the Yemeni attack by sending his brother to the As Sarir fort to consult with Somerset on the chances of restoring law and order to the troubled area on the plateau, only 6 or 8 miles from the Yemen frontier.

According to the press, the Emir intended to send out his tax gatherers to try to levy a 'goat and bees tax' from outlying villages as soon as peace was restored. He visited the British commanders, including Lieutenant Colonel Dawnay Bancroft, personally to express his thanks for the expulsion of the guerillas. The press recorded the meeting.

> The Emir, wearing a chequered tablecloth, sat in the Officers' Mess tent sipping lemon squash.
> Through an Arabic-speaking British officer he expressed thanks for driving out the Yemenis.
> His bodyguard sat silently beside him, twiddling his long black mustachios and fiddling with the bullets in his bandolier.

Meanwhile, in London, Ali Abdul Karim, Sultan of Lahej, was discussing conditions in the Aden Protectorate with Mr Alan Lennox-Boyd, the Colonial Secretary. He wanted British troops withdrawn from Lahej because he felt that their presence was provocative and he was therefore fearful of intervention by Yemeni irregulars. 'You do not have to be in Aden very long to realize the deadly threat implicit to Britain's interests in the Arabian Peninsula in what is going on here.'

A force of Yemeni troops crossed the frontier and occupied a position on the Jebel Dhahart. They led raids on the local villages from the hills, retreating to the safety of the caves. Teddy had asked for permission to bomb the enemy but this was denied. Teddy ordered his Venom squadrons to try to dislodge the Yemeni using rockets. The targets were partly obscured and only one rocket entered the caves over the protective stone wall. With the 'top brass' away on leave, Teddy decided it was time to get tough and sent the Shackletons over to bomb by day and night. With orders to vary the time and duration of attacks, the bombing campaign worked and the rebels surrendered. It was a small victory but added to the reputation of the British forces in the command.

Because of the ongoing local emergencies and a change of Commander British Forces in September 1957, when Lawrence Sinclair handed over to Air Vice-Marshal Maurice Heath CB OBE, it was to be a full year before

Teddy could leave the colony and fly back to England to fulfill his promise to Anne Sofie. They were married in Hendon Registry Office on 2 December 1957. In the meantime, while he had been in Aden, he had indulged himself in his other passion – fast cars. Knowing that he could take a tax-free car back to England, he made the most of this opportunity and bought a brand new Mercedes Benz 190SL, finished in British Racing Green. He sold his Austin Healey to a very grateful Flight Lieutenant called Jerry Farwell, who was not only Maurice Heath's ADC but was also courting his boss's daughter. The cream and ice-blue Healey did the trick, and he got his girl.

Although a state of emergency continued in the Protectorate, with the occasional bomb going off in Aden itself as well as in adjoining Crater, life for Teddy and Anne Sofie was fairly comfortable. However, Mr Smith did not have such an easy time. In between clocking up 'jet time' in Teddy's personal Meteor, the Siamese was having continual fights with the local mountain cats, huge beasts, which invariably ended in ignominious defeat for poor 'Smithy'. Teddy soon noticed that although most of his scars were initially on his head, which meant that at least he was not running away, he was beginning to have wounds on his legs and hindquarters as well. This was not so good.

Teddy therefore started to go out on the occasional cat shoot at night. He was a superb shot and therefore 'bagged' quite a few when he could hear and then see Mr Smith in trouble. One moonlit evening, he shot what he thought, in the dark, was a mountain cat, but it turned out to be a domestic one on the same trail as Smithy's. He quickly buried it. Shortly after this incident the Chief of Police was one of a number of guests invited to a dinner party at Teddy's residence. Halfway through the evening, the imposing policeman announced that his cat had not returned home for a few days and, after describing its colour and mark-ings, asked those around the table if anyone had seen it. A stunned silence followed.

It was while in Aden that Teddy's stepson Julian got his first taste of flying in a jet fighter, Teddy taking him up in a two-seater Meteor. Julian, who was only thirteen at the time, was suitably impressed by the flight and fared considerably better than Teddy, who had suffered terrible air-sickness during his first trip thirty years earlier.

The tensions amongst the Arabs in the Protectorate died down during the early part of 1958, but in early July a Venom of No. 8 Squadron was shot down yards over the Yemeni border by anti-aircraft fire, and the pilot was killed. A second flight of Venoms from the same squadron later bombed the house at Hariba where the gun was spotted. This was an isolated incident, but Teddy was always careful not to put himself at too much unnecessary risk when flying on reconnaissance sorties or even when driving around Aden in his sports car. He had heard that the Arabs would not lob a bomb into a car with a woman in it, so he never drove with the roof down unless Anne Sofie was with him.

Although he survived his tour unscathed, he always wanted to push the limits of authority. At the end of his tour in November 1958, he booked three seats on the Transport Command Comet home – one each for Anne Sofie and himself and one for a 'Mr Smith'. Once boarded, the air steward asked where Mr Smith was. Teddy replied, 'In his seat', pointing to a hatbox with holes in the top on the allocated seat. The steward did not want to argue with his VIP passenger so Mr Smith was left to sleep through the flight back to RAF Lyneham.

The next challenge was what to do when they went through UK customs. Teddy was keen to avoid his noble cat being incarcerated in quarantine for the statutory six months. After all, poor Smithy had been through enough over the past couple of years, fighting for his life. After collecting all their luggage, Teddy prayed hard for the 'hatbox' to stay silent. Mr Smith obliged, and the Air Commodore and his wife were ushered through to the VIP lounge before being whisked away in a shiny black staff car.

Teddy's career of undetected crime was still intact, but the Siamese was immediately renamed Walter Mitty so that friends and any potentially nosey officials could be assured that this was a totally different cat from the one he took out to Aden.

CHAPTER THIRTY-TWO

Commandant and Duty Done

On 12 November 1958 Teddy took up what was to be his last appointment with the RAF, AOC and commandant of the RAF Flying College at Manby in Lincolnshire, taking over from Air Commodore Paddy H. Dunn CB CBE DFC, and immediately putting his personal stamp on the college.

Manby had a flying and a technical wing as well as operational studies, guided weapons, specialist navigation and air warfare courses. Teddy's post-war career made him an ideal choice for this important posting. He was not only knowledgeable in all areas of this specialist training but he also brought his usual drive and enthusiasm to bear on staff and students alike, encouraging his charges at every available opportunity. The senior officers, instructors and lecturers joined him in putting on gang shows for the students and locals, Teddy's infectious smile always singling him out in the cast. To the very end of his career in the Service he loved, he remained approachable to every rank and was universally admired by everyone at the college.

Among those on his staff were Group Captain R. C. Love DSO DFC, who commanded the station, and Wing Commander B. P. T. Horsley MVO AFC, the senior instructor. Both had already had distinguished but very different careers and Teddy enjoyed their company. Ray Love, known affectionately as 'Bubbles', had, like Teddy, been a wartime fighter pilot, and had arrived at Manby after a tour with the United States Air Force at Eglin Air Force Base in Florida. Peter Horsley had spent over seven years in Buckingham Palace, working for the Royal Household. He had started his royal duties in July 1949 as a squadron leader, as Equerry to the then Princess Elizabeth, Duchess of Edinburgh, and the Duke of Edinburgh. In 1952 he became a wing commander and Equerry to Her Majesty The Queen, and in 1953 he became full-time Equerry to the Duke of Edinburgh. Many an apocryphal joke was made about Peter's past, but he went on to become an Air Marshal so his royal connections did not seem to do him much harm.

The commandant's residence at Manby, a beautiful former rectory, was an ideal home for entertaining. Teddy enjoyed reciprocating invitations from local landowners and being 'the country squire' as well as the genial host at the annual church fête which was traditionally held in the rectory's wonderfully landscaped garden. Renowned as a crack shot, he was a popular guest on local shoots. When not using his 12 bore, Teddy frequently practised his shooting skills from his bedroom window, using either an air rifle or his .22 calibre rifle, which was fitted with a telescopic sight. He shot pigeons and rooks as well as the occasional ground game. One evening he saw a rabbit at the bottom of the garden. As it was over 150 yards away, it was a challenging shot, even for Teddy. Having shot it stone dead with a single bullet, he invited his next door neighbour, the station commander, Bubbles Love, and his wife around for supper. The meal was going well until Bubbles mentioned that his pet rabbit had gone missing. It was the second time Teddy had shot a neighbour's pet.

Not long after Teddy's appointment to Manby his oldest brother, Donald, returned to England with his new bride Jean, the pair having married on 25 April 1958. Donald's career had been blighted by the New Zealand Government's denial of the Prince of Wales's Scheme. He, like many other public school boys had worked as a cadet farmer with the expectancy of assistance in setting up his own farm at the end of the programme. No assistance was forthcoming and, like Teddy in Canada, he had been forced to take up a number of menial jobs. Unlike Teddy, however, he did not feel he had the option to return; there would certainly have been no passage home paid for by his grandparents. Donald later recalled that when his grandfather, Alex, died, he was completely written out of the will while even the chauffeur was given something – the Daimler. Gwendoline, only too keenly aware of the continued slight of the Donaldson clan, was to leave him the family home of Iron Latch Cottage on her own death in 1973.

Donald had eventually found a white-collar job. He volunteered for military service on the outbreak of war but was turned down owing to his foot injury. Had he been accepted, he would undoubtedly have served with the same distinction as his siblings; he was after all their role model during their formative years.

During the war he manufactured hand grenades for Mason and Porters, remaining with the firm up until the late 1950s. After years of hard work, he was finally able to put down roots, although at this time he was still single. Mutual friends set him up on a date with Jean, who was fourteen years his junior. She was private secretary to one of the directors of Mason and Porters. The next morning the other girls gathered around at tea-break to ask Jean how the date had gone. They nearly fell on the floor when she announced what a dream Donald was and that at the end of the evening he had proposed to her.

Jean and a friend had spent the early 1950s cycling around Europe and she encouraged Donald to return to England to be reunited with his remaining family. This he did, to a tearful welcome from his mother and brothers.

Arthur's wife, Gwyneth, managed to get Donald a job in the bespoke tailoring department at Harrods, whose manager was Colonel Rubithon. Teddy developed a plan to get his brother a pay rise. He decided he would take Rubithon and his wife out for a drink and win them over to the idea. The night went extremely well and Teddy was in his element. Sadly Donald never did get his pay rise as the colonel could not remember a thing after the evening.

Whilst at Manby, Teddy and Anne Sofie were incredibly generous and very good company. On one occasion Teddy staged an impromptu aerobatics display over the station for their guests' benefit. Ever the showman, he put on a brief but spectacular show before flying low over the air base, causing all the doors and windows to rattle and forcing everyone to cover their ears. The duty commander was livid and wanted to know who it was; of course it was the commandant.

In the 1960 New Year's Honours List, Teddy was appointed a Companion of the Most Honorable Order of the Bath in recognition of his exceptional leadership during his tour in Aden. He was thrilled with this honour as not only was it a rare operational CB, but also admission to the Military Division was the highest class of British military honour obtainable. He felt it went well with his Arabian Peninsula General Service Medal, the short qualifying period for which was thirty days in-theatre service between 1 January1957 and 30 June 1960. Teddy wrote immediately to thank Maurice Heath who, he found out later, had persevered hard to get Teddy this highly deserved recognition, having failed to have his strong recommendation for the honour approved at a first attempt the previous year.

Many distinguished visitors came to give lectures at the college, most of whom were old friends of Teddy's, and he would give each one a warm and hearty welcome. His loud, infectious laugh frequently resounded around the officers' mess at the many formal functions as well as the countless informal parties he hosted. Among those who came to speak were Dr Barnes Wallis, the aeronautical engineer perhaps most famous for designing the Dam Busters' bouncing bomb, wartime Bomber Command hero Air Commodore 'Hughie' Edwards VC and Hawker's Chief Test Pilot Neville Duke.

There were also frequent staff inspections to make sure that the college was maintaining its proper standards. Apart from his Commander-in-Chief, Air Marshal Sir Hugh Constantine, one of the most important staff officers to visit Manby during Teddy's command was Air Vice-Marshal A. C. Kermode CBE, the Director of Educational Services. Following his 1960 annual inspection, Kermode wrote Teddy a letter on 8 July, complimenting him on the high standards set in all aspects of the running of the college and its courses.

> It was most encouraging to find you insisting on high standards for officers who have a chance of reaching high rank – and high standards not only in flying and other practical aspects of Air Force life but also in a basic knowledge of the fundamental principles which lie behind flying and air warfare.
>   But most of all, if I may, I would like to congratulate you on the good spirit which seems to prevail at the College; this is something that one can detect even on a short visit such as my own and is something of which you have reason to be proud.

Later that summer, Teddy was going through his mail one morning when he opened a letter from Michael Berry, Editor-in-Chief of *The Daily Telegraph*. The paper wanted him to consider becoming one of their air correspondents. This came as a bit of a shock to Teddy as he was only forty-eight and had never considered leaving the Service which had already given him so much excitement and sense of achievement. It was a dilemma.

Air Commodore L. G. S. Payne CBE MC AFC had been the *Telegraph*'s senior military air correspondent since 1945 and was now approaching his sixty-sixth birthday. He had been a brave Royal Flying Corps pilot in the First World War and had worked as the RAF's Director of Intelligence (Operations) during the Second. He had told the paper of his wish to retire, and so the Editor started to put the wheels in motion to seek a suitable successor. Teddy, with his high profile and distinguished Service record, was targeted as the favoured candidate by the paper's proprietors, the Hon. Michael Berry (created Lord Hartwell in 1968) and his elder brother Seymour (the 2nd Viscount Camrose), who had become the paper's chairman on the death of his father, the 1st Viscount, in 1954.

It was a tempting offer, as the timing coincided with a planned reduction in the number of air rank officers, and 'golden bowler' inducements of five-figure sums were on offer for volunteers to retire early. Apart from talking about this unexpected opportunity with his wife, Teddy also spoke to both the Air Secretary, his old friend Air Chief Marshal Sir Theodore McEvoy, and his Commander-in-Chief, Air Marshal Sir Hugh Constantine. Neither wanted to lose him and 'Mac' McEvoy even offered him a job in the Air Ministry with promotion to Air Vice-Marshal at the end of his time at Manby.

With apparently nothing to lose, Teddy accepted 'Mister Michael's' invitation to attend an interview in London. After all, he wanted to find out what the job entailed and what was on offer. Ever the showman, he was driven down Fleet Street in his black Humber staff car with his air commodore's star plate uncovered and his commandant's pennant flying. His driver dropped him off at the imposing entrance to the *Telegraph* building. From being 'the greatest' and king of his own domain, he suddenly felt very unimportant and unprepared. It was like being a new boy at a big school – everyone else seeming to be very important and knowledgeable. This was not his familiar Whitehall, but Fleet Street with an aura of The City about it. Teddy felt vulnerable. The Chairman and Editor-in-Chief peered at their prospective candidate. Teddy, not one of the RAF's taller officers, felt smaller than ever. However, the interview went well, and Teddy decided there and then, albeit very reluctantly and with a welling of emotion, to accept the paper's terms.

When he got back to Manby, he suddenly realized the enormity of what he had done. But then, he thought, there must be plenty of advantages too. Nevertheless, the prospect of leaving the Service and shedding his wings was difficult because of all the unknowns. Service life, he realized, was cocooned, cosy and utterly safe because everything was planned. It was also exciting, even dangerous at times. He enjoyed reflecting on his thrills and spills, and to some he was even a hero. His decision made, he would retire on 21 February 1961, the day before his forty-ninth birthday.

With the name of his successor at Manby announced – Air Commodore 'Splinters' Smallwood (who, seven years earlier, was the station commander at Biggin Hill who would not give Teddy a staff car to attend a meeting with Churchill) – the college went into full swing to give their famous commandant a memorable send-off. As he was preparing to hand over his command, Teddy posed for photographers on the first-floor balcony outside his office, totally unaware that the name of his headquarters building had been temporarily changed from Tedder Block to Teddy's Block by an innovative airman with some home-made lettering.

His 'dining-out' from the service was held in the officers' mess at Manby on 10 February 1961. It was attended by many of his former commanding officers, all eager to pay testimony to his glittering military career. Also present were his fellow pre-war display team: Air Commodore 'Top' Boxer, Group Captain 'Johnnie' Walker and Group Captain Prosser Hanks. Among the other many distinguished guests were: Sir William Luce, the Governor of Aden from 1956 to 1960; Air

Chief Marshal Sir Theodore McEvoy, the Air Secretary and Teddy's CO on No. 1 Squadron in 1937, Air Marshal Sir Hugh Constantine, AOC-in-C, Flying Training Command; Lieutenant-General Sir Charles Jones, Commander of the 1st British Army Corps; Major-General 'Jimmy' Hutton, who was Teddy's army counterpart in Aden; Air Commodore J. E. 'Johnnie' Johnson (with Teddy at Fassberg); Air Commodore 'Hughie' Edwards VC (an old friend), Group Captain Peter Horsley; Captain Percy Gick RN, who commanded the aircraft carrier HMS *Bulwark* in the Aden campaign; Group Captain Derek Thirlwell, assistant commandant of Manby; Group Captain Hugh Eccles, Manby's station commander; Group Captain 'Musty' Musgrave, Group Captain (Ops) in Aden under Teddy; Group Captain 'Bubbles' Love; Mr 'Mac' McKenna, who was Managing Director of the Gloster Aircraft Company when Teddy set the world air speed record in 1946; Mr 'Pete' Peterson, Ministry of Works area chief in Aden; and Teddy's brother Group Captain Arthur Donaldson.

Arthur had retired from the Service after commanding RAF Waterbeach two years earlier. Awarded the AFC in early July 1941, he had gone on to gain the DFC two months later, receiving a Bar in early December the following year for leading a Spitfire wing based at Takali, Malta, where he had taken the fight to the enemy. His tour of operations in Malta was also to earn him a richly deserved DSO, announced in the Second Supplement to the *London Gazette* of Friday, 30 October 1942, published on 3 November (the day prior to the announcement of the Bar to his DFC), making Arthur the third of the Donaldson brothers to be made a member of the Order, each receiving the award for service as fighter commanders.

Like Jack and Teddy, Arthur's award had been for leadership against incredible odds. John Willie's Gladiator squadron had faced ten times their own numbers in combat, while Teddy had frequently recorded his squadron, or even his section, taking on over a hundred enemy aircraft. Arthur's final combat over Malta had taken place on 15 October 1942 when he had led three Spitfires against a formation of eight bombers with over sixty Messerschmitt Bf 109s as escort. Whilst destroying one Messerschmitt Bf 109, his own aircraft had fallen to the guns of another, Arthur losing two fingers on his right hand as well as receiving head and leg wounds. Despite his injuries, he made his way back to Takali where he made a perfect belly landing.

Arthur's DSO citation read: 'A large portion of the success achieved in breaking up and destroying enemy formations has been due to the magnificent offensive spirit displayed by this officer and to his outstanding and inspirational leadership.'

During the evening there was a showing of a rare ten-minute film of No. 1 Squadron's aerobatics team, taken at Tangmere in 1937. It brought nostalgic tears to the eyes of many present as they watched the four Hawker Furies performing their spectacular 'changing formation by evolutions'. Teddy, they were reminded, had pioneered the four-man team, with the fourth man 'in the box'.

It was a fitting end to the flying career of a great airman and one of the most famous pilots of his generation. The 'Fighting Services' section of the 24 February 1961 edition of *The Aeroplane* carried the following account of his career:

Air Commodore E. M. Donaldson Retires.

So the last serving member of another of the legendary RAF families has left the Service. Air Cdre E. M. 'Teddy' Donaldson, CB CBE DSO AFC and Bar, US Legion of Merit, for the past two years Commandant of the RAF Flying College, Manby, retired on Feb 21, to join *The Daily Telegraph* as assistant air correspondent.

One of the four brothers, Donald, settled in New Zealand at an early age. The other three, encouraged by their mother, joined the RAF and made her proud and delighted by each winning the DSO and AFC. John Willie lost his life with the Navy off Norway; Arthur retired about two years ago as a group captain; and now it's Teddy's turn, after 30 years' service.

He will probably be remembered chiefly for flying a Meteor IV to the limit of controllability, a few feet above the Channel, when he set up, in September, 1946, a world speed record of 616 mph and got the Britannia Trophy for it. Ever since he joined the RAF in 1931 he has got results. While with No. 3 Squadron at Kenley he won the RAF Featherweight title; and his skill with the pistol, plus his fine 'airman's hands', helped him win the Brooke-Popham Air Firing Trophy twice – the only man to do so. (Harry Broadhurst was later to win the competition three times).

No doubt this all contributed to his shooting down 10 enemy aircraft in the Battle of Britain. He was then commanding 151 Squadron and wore, briefly, a large blonde moustache which moved me to sketch him at North Weald. Later, he was shot down near the French coast and was picked up by a rescue launch which was looking for somebody else.

Before those crowded days, he'd led a new kind of aerobatics team which had in 1937 flown at the Hendon Air Display and the Zurich International Air Rally.

In 1941, after the Battle of Britain, he became chief instructor at the Air Fighting Training School at Ternhill and later he organised gunnery schools in America, spending two years there. When the jets came, he was selected for the command of the first jet base at

Colerne. After his Speed Record achievement, Air Ministry had a
flash of inspiration and appointed him Commandant of the Air
Training Corps for two years.

In 1957, he commanded RAF Fassberg, then took a Joint Services
Staff College Course, followed by a posting to Air Ministry as
deputy Director of Training (Operations). Before he went to
Manby, he was Deputy Commandant, Air Forces, Arabian
Peninsula.

Teddy Donaldson is fully qualified to give sound advice: 'Never
let burning ambition ruin your enjoyment of the best job in the
World.' – Wren.

CHAPTER THIRTY-THREE

Cub Journalist and Amateur Sailor

aving rejected the eleventh hour offer of promotion in favour of becoming Air Correspondent of *The Daily Telegraph*, Teddy quickly found a London home within easy commuting distance of Fleet Street. His 'golden bowler' redundancy payment of a little over £10,000 paid for his two-bedroomed mews house in South Kensington with enough left over to change his sports car.

However, no sooner had he exchanged his lovely, supercharged but high-mileage Mercedes for an even faster Daimler SP250, similar to what the police were currently using to catch 'speedsters' like Teddy, than Jaguar stunned the world with the launch its new E-Type at the 1961 Geneva Motor Show. It was the fastest set of wheels money could buy and Teddy just had to have one. So as soon as the first E-Types appeared in UK dealerships, he went straight to Jaguar's Piccadilly showroom and, to the amazement of the senior salesman, bought the display model off the floor – a gleaming white coupé. The fastest man's image was complete!

Life was beginning to feel much better despite having to 'downsize' from his official eight-bedroomed rural mansion in Lincolnshire, with all the staff and trimmings of a senior military commander.

Princes Gate Mews, off Exhibition Road, was a tranquil haven for the fledgeling journalist or 'cub reporter' as Teddy called himself with unusual deprecation. No. 41 was snugly situated in the middle cul-de-sac of the three 'arms' of the mews. It was like a village in the middle of London where Harrods was the local store, and other retired air force friends were nearby too – notably Bubbles Love in No. 4 and Douglas Bader in Petersham Mews, just off Queen's Gate.

No sooner had Teddy and Anne Sofie moved in than they began to receive a string of telephone calls. Male voices, some with foreign accents, would ask for 'Madeleine' or 'Nicole'. It did not take long for Teddy to work out that he had bought No. 41 from a man who had installed a couple of posh call-girls; it had been a high-class brothel!

Teddy and Anne Sofie opened their mews house to Donald and his wife. However, in 1961 Jean, a third generation New Zealander, became pregnant and was determined that their son, Mark, would be born in her homeland. And so, after three years in England, Donald left these shores once more.

Teddy's new home, like all other mews houses, had originally been stables. His had only been partly converted and the ground floor still consisted of two double garages. Knowing what a premium he could command for letting out just one of them, he was soon bringing in some extra hard cash from the owner of a couple of Rolls Royces. The money rolled in and he soon had enough to buy himself a sailing boat – a small triple-keeled Debutante yacht which he kept on a mooring at Bosham, near Chichester. Sailing, or 'yotting' as Teddy would call it, was to become a passion for the rest of his life and he rarely missed a weekend, either on the water during the summer or in the boatyard during the winter. The E-Type was the ideal mode of transport to get him and his sailing gear to the south coast as quickly as possible, in order to catch the tide out of Chichester Harbour and over the potentially treacherous bar.

The RAF Club in Piccadilly, which Teddy was to frequent on an almost daily basis for the rest of his working life, was on his direct route through the West End to his office in the City. He became a popular figure there at lunchtime, as he would use his newly acquired expense account to pay for a round of drinks before entertaining someone to a good meal while extracting the latest inside story about some aviation matter for his afternoon copy.

Back in his office, he was keen to learn his new trade. With his barking laugh resounding around the building, causing his eyeglass to dance around his stomach, he could have been a fearsome character, but he was always without pomp. The Air Commodore (the *Telegraph* liked him to use his rank) would ring the news desk and announce, 'It's young Donaldson here.' He would then be asked if he was standing to attention while the defects in his copy were listed. Teddy was as eager as any apprentice to know how his stories turned out. Fleet Street, not short of its own characters, quickly welcomed this flamboyant émigré from Whitehall. He was to continue his second career with as much panache as he had in his first, only telling his endless anecdotes in his favourite watering hole, Ye Olde Cheshire Cheese – just a few yards from the *Telegraph* building – instead of in an officers' mess.

Out and about, he soon became one of the sights of London on his newly-acquired motor scooter, the quickest way to get around in the capital. He would tear around Hyde Park Corner, Marble Arch and

Parliament Square at full throttle and at seemingly dangerous angles on his way to assignments in Whitehall, Victoria or Pall Mall. Before motorcyclists had to wear crash helmets he rode bowler-hatted, with a rolled umbrella alongside, but when compulsory head-protection legislation was introduced in the early 1970s he simply donned his old flying 'bone dome' to comply with the new law.

After a relatively short honeymoon period, 'young Donaldson' became so completely a Fleet Street man that many of his colleagues forgot his Service rank. There were many occasions, however, when his background helped get him flights in military aircraft which might have been denied to other journalists. He flew fairly regularly, but was an unnerving airline passenger. He was a classic example of a man who knew too much and was acutely aware of what could go wrong. He always thought the worst of any sudden vibration on the many inaugural commercial flights he made as 'an air correspondent,' gloomily passing on his views to those around him.

Concorde was a big story throughout the 1960s and 1970s, and Teddy was keen to keep abreast of developments. The British prototype's first test flight was on 9 April 1969 but the airframe was to be subjected to more than 5,000 hours of testing before the maiden British Airways passenger flight took place on 21 January 1976. So when Teddy was invited on an early test flight from Paris to Washington on 1 June 1971, he had mixed feelings. He survived and was presented with a certificate and a model Concorde for his 'bravery'.

Teddy was once so dismissive of the American F-104 Starfighter – an aircraft dubbed by the pilots of the new Federal German Air Force as the *Witwenmacher* ('Widowmaker') or *Fliegender Sarg* ('Flying Coffin') after 292 of their 916 aircraft had crashed, claiming the lives of 115 pilots – that the makers, Lockheed, threatened to sue him (on the grounds that he had lost them a contract) unless he flew it himself. Teddy relished the thought and immediately agreed. The Starfighter was generally considered a rewarding, if very demanding, 'sports car' of a fighter. It was also the first combat aircraft capable of sustained Mach 2 flight – not for just a brief dash. An F-104A had set a world speed record of 1,404.19 mph (2,259.82 Kmph) on 18 May 1958, and the Starfighter was the first aircraft to hold simultaneous official world records for speed, altitude, and time-to-climb.

After returning safely from the fastest flight of his life, Teddy wrote a glowing piece for *The Telegraph*, pointing out that Spain had lost none in the same period and that the *Luftwaffe*'s losses had to be attributed in part to the German military's decision to deploy their Starfighters as fighter-bombers, the increased payload of bombs increasing the aircraft's stall speed and making for a very narrow window of safe flight-speed. Lockheed were appeased. A senior executive presented the troublesome air correspondent with a much coveted Mach 2 badge which Teddy duly affixed to his 'yotting' cap.

It later emerged that, in the 1970s, Lockheed had engaged in an extensive campaign of bribery of foreign officials to obtain sales, a scandal that nearly led to the corporation's downfall. Teddy felt compelled to report on the so-called 'deal of the century' which had produced considerable income for Lockheed but considerable political controversy in Europe, particularly in Germany, where the Minister of Defence, Franz Josef Strauss, was almost forced to resign over the issue. Prince Bernhard of the Netherlands later confessed to having received more than a million US dollars in bribes.

With great pride and not a little encouragement, Teddy saw his stepson Julian win a cadetship at the RAF College at Cranwell. When he graduated in 1967, Teddy and Anne Sofie were to be joined by Douglas Bader, who had accepted Julian's invitation to be his additional guest at the parade and graduation lunch. Sadly, Thelma (Teddy's cousin) was too ill to travel. Bader flew up from White Waltham in his Shell aircraft whilst Teddy drove up the A1 from London in his E-Type in equally quick time, despite being stopped twice by the police! After the parade, everyone sat down for lunch in the college dining room, with Pilot Officer Stapleton and his guests seated below a huge portrait of the most famous Old Cranwellian of them all – Douglas Bader in his group captain's uniform. Bader, who had watched the parade in an old duffle coat tried to look equally inconspicuous at lunch. He failed miserably; such was the aura of the man.

After lunch, Douglas flew back to White Waltham, but not before he had extended an invitation to Julian and fellow graduate Brian Pegnall to dinner at his London home, saying that he would provide 'the girls'. Meanwhile, Teddy, who had been 'chatted up' by Brian Pegnall's mother, agreed to take her for 'spin' in his E-Type.

Now Brian, who had just won the Battle of Britain Aerobatic Trophy, knew of Teddy's liking for speed from first-hand experience. When he had first seen Teddy's E-Type back in 1964, he had mockingly asked, 'Is it really capable of 150 mph?' That was a huge speed in the mid-1960s. 'Of course it's bloody capable' came the reply. 'Get in,' and Teddy had driven young Pegnall off to prove his point.

He therefore tried to warn his mother of the dangers. Warnings disregarded, they sped off for a burst of over 100 mph down the main runway, after getting permission from Air Traffic Control. Forty years on, Mrs Pegnall was still talking about her 'near orgasmic experience in that phallic car'.

Later that day, whilst preparing for the Graduation Ball, Teddy was resplendent in mess kit, a 'hanging gong' around his neck and eleven medals on his left chest. A small man, he was almost bent sideways by the weight of the latter. Brian's mother, still recovering from her high-speed experience and with no knowledge of military types, exclaimed with excitement, 'My, Teddy, you have got a lot of medals!', to which he replied, looking up (Brian's mother was somewhat taller) and without any attempt at false modesty, 'Yes my dear, I've got the lot!'

Although not without his critics, Teddy's reputation at *The Daily Telegraph* had grown to such an extent that even Harold Wilson's Labour government were beginning to respect the influence he wielded through his columns and comments. Under Lord Hartwell's shrewd and innovative leadership, the *Telegraph*'s circulation had grown to nearly double that of its rival, *The Times*. Donaldson was wined and dined by politicians from both sides of the House of Commons, each trying to steer the paper towards a 'party line'. Despite being a paper of the right, Teddy knew that he could also exercise a degree of independence in what he wrote. He loved all the attention, and ministers began to see what they thought was a possible chink in his armour.

He returned home one evening and could not wait to tell his wife what had happened. 'I think I've been offered a peerage!' he told her excitedly, his monocle bobbing up and down as he spoke. At a government reception hosted by Denis Healey, the Defence Secretary, he had been approached by some Labour minion who, as the discussion progressed, reminded Teddy of what had happened to Arthur Gwynne Jones of *The Times*. Teddy had known Gwynne Jones well. He had joined *The Times* from the army in the same year that Teddy had joined *The Daily Telegraph*, and had been their hugely influential Defence Correspondent until 1964, when he was suddenly given a life peerage by Harold Wilson. Arthur Gwynne Jones was now Lord Chalfont and Minister of State at the Foreign and Commonwealth Office.

Teddy could hardly believe his ears. He thought hard about sacrificing his right-wing views. He was then at the centre of a heated political debate between the RAF and the Royal Navy about the future of aircraft carriers. Labour had cancelled the TSR-2 in the mid-1960s and the RAF were promised American F-111s instead. That never happened. In the end, he had no decision to make as the offer of a seat in the upper house never materialized. But it made him think of what might have been – 'Baron Donaldson of South Kensington'? but in all probability he would have been sacked as a traitor by the *Telegraph* and lost all his air force friends for ever.

The peerage did, however, preoccupy him on occasions, usually when sailing. There had been recent scandals about the activities of Lords Montagu and Boothby, and Teddy was always cracking jokes about their unprintable transgressions. Once, having sailed up the Beaulieu River to Bucklers Hard, he was telling his stories rather too loudly whilst enjoying a rather good dinner at the Master Builder. Unfortunately, the lord of the manor, Montagu of Beaulieu, was sitting at another table and well within earshot. That night, the boat keeled over on its mooring, waking Teddy, who thought that the irate peer was about to get his own back.

Whilst at the *Telegraph* there were plenty of opportunities to keep in touch with old fighter pilots, whether at the annual Battle of Britain Ball at some grand hotel in Park Lane or on the major anniversaries of the battle, at great civic receptions. Ex-Battle of Britain pilots were still around in plentiful numbers in 1965, the twenty-fifth anniversary, when the city fathers laid on a huge reception at London's Guildhall. However, the 'Few' were slightly fewer by the time the corporation repeated the exercise fifteen years later.

Teddy was often fêted as a record breaker, and one such occasion took place on 9 December 1970 when he was invited to a celebratory dinner at the Grosvenor House Hotel to mark the five-millionth sale of the *Guinness Book of Records*. Among those attending was an impressive list of high achievers as well as the bold and the brave, including two holders of the VC, Brigadier the Rt Hon. Sir John Smyth Bt VC, MC, and Air Commodore Freddie West VC CBE MC, two recipients of the GC, Mrs Odette Hallowes GC MBE, and Vivian Hollowday GC, as well as a couple of Teddy's top-scoring air force friends, Wing Commander Donald Kingaby, and Squadron Leader 'Ginger' Lacey.

Whilst working at the *Telegraph*, Teddy's routine rarely changed. He would read all the daily newspapers in bed before he got up, tinker with his car for the rest of the morning, take someone out to lunch at the RAF Club, or somewhere really upmarket if he thought his source was worth it, and then proceed to Fleet Street to write his copy. At weekends, he would slip off on Friday morning down to his boat and sail from one pub to another around the Solent. He normally took three weeks off in the summer to sail across the Channel to the Cherbourg peninsular and the Channel Islands.

Always one for a challenge, he was never happier than when the wind blew a good Force 7 or 8 when, he would observe with pride, all the fair-weather sailors had either sought shelter or gone home. On returning from a particularly rough crossing from Cherbourg one summer, when it had been blowing up to Storm Force 10 over the previous few days, he eventually made Yarmouth on the Isle of Wight, flying his 'yellow duster' to signify customs clearance required, only to find that all the customs officials had gone home, thinking that nobody would be mad enough to cross in such appalling conditions. Such was the make-up of the man who just loved to push his luck and defy the odds.

By the early 1970s, both his car and his boat were getting tired and requiring inordinate maintenance, so he changed both. He bought his 'new' boat, *Ariadne*, second-hand but it was much sturdier than his first. He took on a mooring at Gosport, near Portsmouth, which, unlike Bosham with its tidal Chichester Bar, had unrestricted access to the Solent. Although still under 30 ft, *Ariadne* had a heavier, deeper keel and he therefore felt he could take on the elements with even greater bravado. Around the same time, he found a replacement E-Type in Coys Garage, which sold exotic motor cars from a mews just off Queen's Gate in South Kensington. It was a very low-mileage, Irish-registered 4.2 litre coupé in pale metallic blue. Teddy could not believe his luck – his image was preserved.

Teddy always dreaded old age. An even greater fear, surprisingly for such a brave man, was to be crippled. 'Shoot me,' he would say, 'if I ever land up in a wheelchair.' He wanted to sail for ever, and that was paramount. Then it happened; he had a severe stroke whilst on his boat in 1977, which ultimately led to his second retirement. He was taken to the Royal Naval Hospital Haslar at Gosport, where he confessed under examination to owning an E-Type Jaguar. 'At what speeds do you drive?' asked the doctor, bent over his notepad. 'Well, it cruises nicely at 123 mph,' came Teddy's reply. The doctor quickly told him to get rid of it.

That might have been the end as far as most people were concerned, but Teddy, forever the fighter pilot, defied the odds yet again. This, he admitted, was due primarily to the tremendous help and encouragement from the medical staff at the RAF Rehabilitation Unit at Headley Court, near Leatherhead in Surrey. They gave him daily exercises to build up his muscles and he was eventually able to drive a car again, albeit a small-engined automatic. It was, at least, independence. All this, and his love of sailing, had sadly taken its toll on his marriage and he was divorced from his third wife in 1982, never to remarry. Teddy bought a small flat in Gosport so that he could continue to be near his boat and sail with special aids and local crew.

The Daily Telegraph was very good to its loyal and charismatic air correspondent. They kept him on their books for another couple of years and 'the Air Commodore' continued to write articles even beyond that. One of his last main 'leaders' for the paper, which appeared on 27 January 1978, was about the future of Britain's aerospace industry and aimed fairly and squarely at James Callaghan's Labour government. 'Triumphing over ignorance, prejudice and jealous obstruction,' he wrote, 'Concorde now rules the Atlantic skies. Even some critics now realise what it can do for Europe.'

Nine years earlier, in February 1969, the governments of France and West Germany had concluded an agreement that established a consortium called Airbus Industrie to manufacture a new passenger airliner, designated the A-300. The British government, then under Harold Wilson, was invited to join as a full partner, but declined when it decided the project was doomed to failure. In its opinion, there was simply too little room in the commercial airliner market, already dominated by Boeing, McDonnell Douglas and Lockheed, to support another competitor. Now, in the late 1970s, Teddy had noticed that it was a pivotal time for the fledgling state-owned British Aerospace, and for its new chairman, Lord Beswick, to complete its reorganization as quickly as possible and to align itself with a major partner if it was to survive.

Teddy pulled no punches, even suggesting, possibly rightly, that there might be a case for using North Sea oil revenue to exploit the lead gained by Concorde in aircraft development. He wrote, provocatively, 'some tough political decisions need to be made now, urgently, so that the industry can free itself from the mess and muddle that years of political chopping and changing condemned it to. Lord Beswick,' the article concluded, 'must have full support from Downing Street over leadership and financing, otherwise Britain will end up as subcontractor to the world.' What prophetic words they were.

The fortieth anniversary of the Battle of Britain was marked in September 1980 by a number of special events including a reception held at London's Guildhall in the presence of Queen Elizabeth the Queen Mother. Teddy reported on the gathering in *The Daily Telegraph*.

> It was a shattering experience for all of us, who were lined up in squadrons to meet her. This is 40 years after the victory and the 'boys' are now around 60 years of age. Her Majesty, who I swear spoke to every one of us, seemed to remember my Squadron, No. 151. In the atmosphere of the party I remember 1940 clearly, when these kids appeared out of the blue. They went straight to meet the *Luftwaffe*, many never to return. They inspired me and the Squadron with their spirit, determination and guts.

Always an accomplished raconteur, Teddy's report then went on to give an account of the day he was shot down over the English Channel. The story, told a hundred times over a pint or two of beer and always slightly more embellished with each telling from the original version submitted to the Air Ministry, was essentially the same.

There had been a certain snobbery about the Supermarine Spitfire with many *Luftwaffe* pilots swearing they were shot down by a Spitfire when in fact they had fallen to the guns of the slower Hawker Hurricane. As Teddy often said, 'You had to be bloody brave flying Hurricanes because you couldn't run away.'

After more strokes and a short illness, Teddy died aged eighty at the Royal Naval Hospital Haslar on 2 June 1992. Nine days later, at his funeral at St Andrew's Church in Tangmere village, Air Marshal Sir Kenneth Hayr, a former CO of No. 1 Squadron and, like Teddy, the holder of two AFCs, fittingly represented the Air Force Board. Edward Mortlock Donaldson was buried a hero, his gravestone now standing proudly within earshot of both his record-breaking Meteor in the Tangmere Military Aviation Museum and the runway from which he took off in 1946 for his most famous exploit.

Dramatis Personae

Bader, Douglas, Group Captain Sir Douglas Bader CBE DSO and Bar, DFC and Bar

Bandon, 'Paddy', Air Chief Marshal The Earl of Bandon GBE CB CVO DSO

Barrett, 'Ugly', Air Chief Marshal Sir Arthur Barrett KCB CMG MC

Barthropp, 'Paddy', Wing Commander P. P. C. Barthropp DFC AFC

Beamish, Victor, Group Captain F. V. Beamish DSO and Bar DFC AFC

Beurling, George or 'Screwball', Squadron Leader G. F. Beurling DSO DFC DFM and Bar

Bird-Wilson, 'Birdy', Air Vice-Marshal H. A. C. Bird-Wilson CBE DSO DFC and Bar AFC and Bar

Blair, Kenneth, Wing Commander K. H. Blair DFC and Bar

Blomeley, David, Squadron Leader D. H. Blomeley DFC AFC

Blount, Charles, Air Vice-Marshal C. H. B. Blount CB OBE MC

Boothman, John, Air Chief Marshal Sir John Boothman KCB KBE DFC AFC

Boxer, 'Rex', Air Commodore H. E. C. Boxer CB OBE

Braham, 'Bob', Group Captain J. R. D. Braham DSO and two Bars DFC and two Bars AFC CD

Broadhurst, Harry, Air Chief Marshal Sir Harry Broadhurst GCB KBE DSO and Bar DFC and Bar AFC

Brooke-Popham, Robert, Air Chief Marshal Sir Robert Brooke-Popham GCVO KCB CMG DSO AFC

Carey, Frank, Group Captain F. R. Carey CBE DFC and two Bars AFC DFM

Chalfont, Lieutenant Colonel Alun Arthur Gwynne Jones, the Rt Hon. Lord Chalfont OBE MC PC

Churchill, Winston or 'Winnie', the Rt Hon. Sir Winston Churchill KG OM CH TD FRS PC

Constantine, Hugh, Air Chief Marshal Sir Hugh Constantine KBE CB DSO

Coryton, Alec, Air Marshal Sir Alec Coryton KCB KBE MVO DFC

Courtney, 'Buck', Group Captain R. N. H. Courtney CB DFC and Bar
    AFC
Crerar, Finlay, Air Commodore F. Crerar CBE
Cross, 'Bing', Air Chief Marshal Sir Kenneth Cross KCB CBE DSO DFC
De L'Isle, Major William Philip Sidney, 1st Viscount De L'Isle VC KG
    GCMG GCVO PC
Dickson, William, Marshal of the Royal Air Force Sir William Dickson
    GCB KBE DSO AFC
Donaldson, Arthur, Group Captain A. H. Donaldson DSO DFC and Bar
    AFC
Donaldson, 'Jack', 'Baldy', or John 'Willie', Squadron Leader J. W.
    Donaldson DSO AFC
Dowding, 'Stuffy', Air Chief Marshal Lord Dowding of Bentley Priory
    GCB GCVO CMG
Drake, 'Billy' Group Captain B. Drake DSO DFC and Bar
Duke, Neville, Squadron Leader N. F. Duke DSO OBE DFC and two Bars
    AFC
Duncan Smith, 'Smithy', Group Captain W. G. G. Duncan Smith DSO
    and Bar DFC and two Bars
Dundas, 'Cocky', Group Captain Sir Hugh Dundas CBE DSO and Bar
    DFC
Dunn, 'Paddy', Air Marshal Sir Patrick Dunn KBE CB DFC
Edden, Kaye, Vice-Admiral Sir Kaye Edden KBE CB
Edwards, Hughie, Air Commodore Sir Hughie Edwards VC KCMG CB
    DSO OBE DFC
Ellacombe, John, Air Commodore J. L. W. Ellacombe CB DFC and Bar
Embry, Basil, Air Chief Marshal Sir Basil Embry GCB KBE DSO and three
    Bars DFC AFC
Forster, Anthony, Wing Commander A. D. Forster DFC
Foster, Robert, Air Chief Marshal Sir Robert M. Foster KCB CBE DFC
Freeborn, John, Wing Commander J. C. Freeborn DFC and Bar
Gick, Percy, Rear Admiral P. D. Gick CB OBE DSC and Bar
Goodwin, Edwin, Air Vice-Marshal E. S. Goodwin CB CBE AFC and Bar
Gort, John Standish Surtees Prendergast Vereker, Field Marshal (6th)
    Viscount Gort VC GCB CBE DSO and two Bars MVO MC
Hallowes, Odette, Odette Hallowes GC MBE
Hanks, Prosser, Group Captain P. P. Hanks DSO DFC AFC
Hartwell, Michael, Lieutenant Colonel the Hon. William Michael Berry,
    Lord Hartwell MBE TD
Harris, Arthur, Marshal of the Royal Air Force Sir Arthur Harris, GCB
    OBE AFC
Harvey, Arthur, Air Commodore Lord Harvey of Prestbury CBE
Hayr, 'Ken', Air Marshal Sir Kenneth Hayr KCB KBE AFC and Bar
Heath, Maurice, Air Marshal Sir Maurice Heath KBE CB CVO

Waterton, 'Bill', Squadron Leader W. A. Waterton AFC and Bar GM
West, 'Freddie', Air Commodore F. M. F. West VC CBE MC
Wilson, 'Willie', Group Captain H. J. Wilson CBE AFC
Whittle, Frank, Air Commodore Sir Frank Whittle OM KBE CB FRS

Bibliography

Balfour, Harold (Lord Balfour of Inchrye), *Wings over Westminster*, Hutchinson, 1973.

Barthropp, Wing Commander P. P. C., *Paddy, The Life and Times of Wing Commander Patrick Barthropp* DFC, AFC, Howard Baker Press, 1987.

Beamont, Roland, *Phoenix into Ashes*, William Kimber, 1968.

Bingham, Victor, *Whirlwind, The Westland Whirlwind Fighter*, Airlife Publishing Ltd., 1987.

Brown, Squadron Leader Peter, *Honour Restored: The Battle of Britain, Dowding and the Fight for Freedom*. Spellmount, 2005.

Churchill, Winston, *The Second World War, Volume II: Their Finest Hour*, Cassell, 1949.

Clarke, Basil, *Supersonic Flight*, Frederick Muller, 1965.

Collier, Richard, *Eagle Day: The Battle of Britain*, Hodder and Stoughton, 1966.

Cull, Brian, and Lander, Bruce with Weiss, Heinrich, *Twelve Days in May*, Grub Street, 1995.

Deere, Air Commodore Alan C., *Nine Lives*, Crécy Publishing, 1959.

Deighton, Len, *Battle of Britain*, Cape, 1980.

Deighton, Len, *Fighter. The True Story of the Battle of Britain*, Cape, 1977.

Derry, T.K., *The Campaign in Norway*, HMSO, 1952.

Douglas, Sholto (Marshal of the Royal Air Force Lord Douglas of Kirtleside) with Wright, Robert, *Years of Command*, Collins, 1966.

Douglas-Hamilton, Lord James, *The Air Battle for Malta, The Diaries of a Fighter Pilot*, Mainstream Publishing Company, 1981.

Duke, Neville, *Test Pilot*, Allan Wingate, 1953.

Duncan Smith, Group Captain W.G.G., *Spitfire into Battle*, Murray, 1981.

Franks, N., *Valiant Wings*, Crécy Publishing, 1994.

HMSO *The London Gazette* (various dates)

James, T.C.G., *The Battle of Britain*, Frank Cass, 2000.

Johnson, Air Vice-Marshal J.E. ('Johnnie'), *Wing Leader*, Chatto and Windus, 1956.

Johnson, Air Vice-Marshal J.E. ('Johnnie'), *Full Circle: The Story of Air Fighting*, Chatto and Windus, 1964.

Kingcome, Brian, *A Willingness to Die, Memories from Fighter Command*, Tempus Publishing, 1999.

Levine, Joshua, in association with the Imperial War Museum, *Forgotten Voices of the Blitz and the Battle for Britain*, Ebury, 2006.

Lucas, Laddie, *Flying Colours: The Epic Story of Douglas Bader*, Hutchinson, 1981.

Lucas, Laddie, *Voices in the Air, 1939–1945*, Arrow, 2003.

MacClure, Victor, *Gladiators over Norway*, W.H. Allen, 1942.

Mason, Francis K., *The Gloster Gladiator*, Macdonald Aircraft Monographs, 1964.

Richardson, Anthony, *Wingless Victory* (Related by Sir Basil Embry), Odhams Press, 1950.

Richey, Paul, *Fighter Pilot*, Cassell, 2001.

Shaw, Michael, *Twice Vertical: The History of No. 1 (Fighter) Squadron, RAF*, Macdonald, 1971.

Shores, Christopher and Williams, Clive, *Aces High*, Grub Street, 1994.

Stokes, Doug, *Wings Aflame, The Biography of Group Captain Victor Beamish*, William Kimber, 1985.

Sutton, Barry, *The Way of a Pilot,* Macmillan, 1942.

Terraine, John, *The Right of the Line*, Wordsworth Editions, 1997.

Whittle, Sir Frank, *Jet, The Story of a Pioneer*, Frederick Muller, 1953.

Wynn Kenneth G., *Men of the Battle of Britain*, Gliddon Books, 1989.

Unpublished Primary Sources

Correspondence with Air Commodore John Ellacombe CB DFC and Bar
Correspondence with Wing Commander Anthony Forster DFC
Correspondence with Squadron Leader David Blomeley DFC AFC
Correspondence with Mrs Sally Rudman
Correspondence with Mrs Kate Gregory
Correspondence with Donald Donaldson (via Mark Donaldson)
Correspondence with Mark Donaldson
Correspondence with Wing Commander Julian Stapleton MBE
Unpublished manuscript by Neil Potter and Teddy Donaldson
Air Commodore Teddy Donaldson's log books
Squadron Leader David Blomeley's log books
No. 151 (F) squadron diary and combat reports held at the Public Record Office at Kew Diary AIR 27/1018, Combat Reports AIR 50/63
Teddy Donaldson's 'Line Book'.

Index